A Practical English Grammar

very/almost { equal
similar
identical

comparing the size of A
+ B
↑ is (the size of) req'd?

The density of A is lower
than B.

A. J. Thomson and A. V. Martinet

A Practical English Grammar

Third Edition

Oxford University Press

Oxford University Press
Walton Street, Oxford OX2 6DP

London New York Toronto
Delhi Bombay Calcutta Madras Karachi
Kuala Lumpur Singapore Hong Kong Tokyo
Nairobi Dar Es Salaam Cape Town
Melbourne Auckland

and associated companies in
Beirut Berlin Ibadan Mexico City Nicosia

OXFORD is a trade mark of Oxford University Press.

ISBN 0 19 431335 2 (hardback)
ISBN 0 19 431336 0 (paperback)

First published 1960 (reprinted seven times)
Second edition 1969 (reprinted ten times)
Third edition 1980
Ninth impression 1985

Filmset by Tradespools Ltd, Frome, Somerset
and printed in Spain by Mateu Cromo Artes
Graficas S.A.

Preface to the third edition

A Practical English Grammar is intended for intermediate and advanced students, both adults and students in the higher forms of schools. Teachers may also find it useful for reference.

The book is a comprehensive survey of grammar written in simple modern English with numerous examples to illustrate each point. Areas where students have particular difficulty, such as the use of tenses and auxiliary verbs, have been treated with particular care and fullness. The difference between strict grammatical usage and conversational forms is shown where necessary, but the emphasis is on conversational forms in order to encourage students to speak the language as it is spoken by native speakers today. To further this aim many of the examples are in the form of short conversations between two people.

In the third edition the main changes are as follows:

1 Explanations have been revised or rewritten wherever necessary to make them easier to understand.

2 New material has been added to the chapters on prepositions, pronouns, infinitives, gerunds, future and conditional forms and reported speech.

3 Both explanations and examples have been brought up to date where necessary to reflect current usage.

4 The index is now fuller (and should be more useful).

5 The book has been designed afresh and reset in a larger format and typeface to make it easier to read.

As already noted in previous editions, this is not a graded course and the chapters are not presented in order of difficulty. Difficult paragraphs or sections may therefore be met with in any part of the book. Some of these are marked with a box round their serial numbers or letters, e.g. **276**, E. Students may prefer to omit these at the first reading.

To accompany this book there are two volumes of exercises two volumes of structure drills with tapes and cassettes. Both exercises and structure drills are cross-referred to the *Grammar* and the level of difficulty is indicated where appropriate. Keys are given for both exercises and drills.

Dublin, August 1979 A. J. T., A. V. M.

Preface to the third edition

A Practical English Grammar is intended for intermediate and advanced students, both adults and students in the higher forms of schools. Teachers may also find it useful for reference.

The book is a comprehensive survey of grammar written in simple modern English with numerous examples to illustrate each point. Areas where students have particular difficulty, such as the use of tenses and auxiliary verbs, have been treated with particular care and fullness. The difference between strict grammatical usage and conversational forms is shown where necessary, but the emphasis is on conversational forms in order to encourage students to speak the language as it is spoken by native speakers today. To further this aim many of the examples are in the form of short conversations between two people.

In the third edition the main changes are as follows:

1 Explanations have been revised or rewritten wherever necessary to make them easier to understand.

2 New material has been added to the chapters on prepositions, pronouns, infinitives, gerunds, future and conditional forms and reported speech.

3 Both explanations and examples have been brought up to date where necessary to reflect current usage.

4 The index is now fuller (and should be more useful).

5 The book has been designed afresh and reset in a larger format and typeface to make it easier to read.

As already noted in previous editions, this is not a graded course and the chapters are not presented in order of difficulty. Difficult paragraphs or sections may therefore be met with in any part of the book. Some of these are marked with a box round their serial numbers or letters, e.g. [276], [E]. Students may prefer to omit these at the first reading.

To accompany this book there are two volumes of exercises, two volumes of structure drills with tapes and cassettes. Both exercises and structure drills are cross-referenced to the *Grammar* and the level of difficulty is indicated where appropriate. Keys are given for both exercises and drills.

Dublin, August 1979 A. J. T. A. V. M.

Contents

1 Articles

The indefinite article

1 Form

The indefinite article is **a** or **an**.

The form **a** is used before a word beginning with a consonant, or a vowel sounded like a consonant:

a man *a table* *a university* *a useful thing*

The form **an** is used before words beginning with a vowel (**a, e, i, o, u**) or words beginning with a mute **h**:

an hour *an honourable man* *an elephant* *an apple*

It is the same for all genders:

a man *a woman* *an actor* *an actress* *a table* *an animal*

2 The indefinite article **a** or **an** is used:

A Before a singular noun which is countable (i.e. of which there is more than one) when it is mentioned for the first time and represents no particular person or thing:

I need a holiday. *They live in a bungalow.*

There is a policeman at the door.

B Before a singular countable noun which is used as an example of a class of things:

A car must be insured = All cars/Any car must be insured.

A child needs love = All children need/Any child needs love.

C With a noun complement. This includes names of professions:

He is a doctor. *She is a teacher.* *He became an actor.*

D In certain numerical expressions:

a couple	*an eighth*	*a hundred*	*a lot of*
a dozen	*a quarter*	*a thousand*	*a great many*
half a dozen	*a score* (20)	*a million*	*a great deal of*

E In expressions of price, speed, ratio etc.:

5p a kilo *£1 a metre* *sixty kilometres an hour*

10p a dozen *four times a day*

(Note that **a** and **one** are not usually interchangeable. For the difference between them see **23**.)

F With **few** and **little**:

a few = a small number, or what the speaker considers a small number.

a little = a small amount, or what the speaker considers a small amount.

few and **little** can also be used without article but then have an almost negative meaning, and can usually be replaced by **hardly any**:

We had little time for amusement implies that we were always busy.
Few people know this (it is almost unknown).
(See **29**.)

G In exclamations before singular, countable nouns:
What a hot day! *What a pretty girl!* *Such a pity!*
But *What pretty girls!* *What big dogs!*
(Plural nouns, so no article. See **3**.)

H **a** can be placed before Mr/Mrs/Miss + surname:
a Mr Smith *a Mrs Smith* *a Miss Smith*
a Mr Smith means 'a man called Smith' and implies that he is a stranger to the speaker. *Mr Smith,* without *a*, implies that the speaker knows Mr Smith or knows of his existence.
(For the difference between **a/an** and **one** see **23**.)

3 The indefinite article is not used:

A Before plural nouns.
The indefinite article has no plural form. Therefore the plural of *a dog* is *dogs*.

B Before uncountable nouns.
The following nouns are singular and uncountable in English:
advice *information* *news* *baggage* *luggage* *furniture*
They are often preceded by *some, any, a little, a lot of, a piece of* etc.:
I'll give you a piece of advice. *There isn't any news.*
You need some more furniture.
knowledge is also considered uncountable, but when used in a particular sense takes the article:
A knowledge of languages is always useful.
He has a good knowledge of mathematics.
hair ('all the hair on one's head') is considered uncountable, but if we consider each hair separately we say *a hair, two hairs* etc.:
She has black hair.
The fisherman used a hair to tie the feather to the hook.

experience meaning 'practice in doing (something)' is uncountable. But *an experience* meaning 'something which happens to someone' is countable:
He had an exciting experience (an adventure) *last night.*

Materials, *glass, wood, iron, stone, paper, cloth, wine, coffee, tea* etc., are considered uncountable. But many of these nouns can also denote one particular thing, and then take an article:
Windows are made of glass but *Have a glass of wine.*
We write on paper but *I've got a paper* (newspaper).
Iron is a metal but *I use an iron* (electric iron).

some, any, a piece of, a lot of etc. are often used here as shown above:
Would you like some coffee? *I want a piece of wood.*

C Before abstract nouns: *beauty, happiness, fear, hope, death* etc., except when they are used in a particular sense:
He was pale with fear.
Some children suffer from a fear of the dark.

D Before names of meals, except when preceded by an adjective:
We have breakfast at eight. *He gave us a good breakfast.*
The article is also used when it is a special meal given to celebrate something or in someone's honour:
I was invited to dinner (at their house, in the ordinary way)
but *I was invited to a dinner given to welcome the new ambassador.*

The definite article

The definite article is **the**. It is the same for singular and plural and for all genders:
the boy *the boys* *the girl* *the girls* *the day* *the days*

4 Use of the definite article

A The definite article is used:

1 Before nouns of which there is only one, or which are considered as one:
the earth *the sea* *the sky* *the weather* *the North Pole*

2 Before a noun which has become definite as a result of being mentioned a second time:
His car struck a tree; you can still see the mark on the tree.

3 Before a noun made definite by the addition of a phrase or clause:
the girl in blue *the man on the donkey*
the boy that I met *the place where I met him*

4 Before a noun which by reason of locality can represent only one particular thing:
Ann is in the garden (the garden of this house).
He sent for the doctor (his own doctor).
Please pass the wine (the wine on the table).

5 Before superlatives and *first, second* etc. and *only*, used as adjectives or pronouns:
Mont Blanc is the highest mountain in Europe.
Most people think that Monday is the worst day of the week.

B **the** + singular noun can represent a class of animals or things:
The whale is in danger of becoming extinct.
The deep-freeze has made life easier for housewives.
man can be used to represent the human race, but here it has no article:
If oil supplies run out, man may have to fall back on the horse.
the can, however, be used before a member of a certain group of people:
The small shopkeeper is finding life increasingly difficult.
But in spoken English a plural noun would be more usual here:
Small shopkeepers are finding life increasingly difficult.
the + singular noun as used above takes a singular verb. The pronoun is **he, she** or **it**:
The first-class traveller pays more so he expects some comfort.

C **the** + adjective represents a class of persons:
the old = old people in general
the strong = strong people in general
The verb is plural, the pronoun is **they**:
The young are impatient; they want changes. (See also **18**.)

D **the** is used before certain proper names of seas, rivers, groups of islands, chains of mountains, plural names of countries, deserts:

the Arctic	*the Antarctic* (both land and sea)	*the Atlantic*
the Alps	*the Netherlands*	*the U.S.A.*
the Sahara	*the Gobi Desert*	

the is also used before names consisting of noun + **of** + noun:

the Cape of Good Hope	*the Bay of Biscay*
the Straits of Dover	*the U.S.S.R.*
the Rann of Kutch	*the Union of South Africa*
the Gulf of Mexico	

the is used before names consisting of adjective + noun (provided the adjective is not *east, west* etc.):

the Gold Coast	*the Ivory Coast*	*the New Forest*
the Hindu Kush	*the High Street*	

the is not used before *east/west* etc. + noun, e.g. *Yucatan is in North America.* But we use **the** if *east/west* etc. is followed by *of*, e.g. *the west of Spain*; and with *east/west* etc. used alone as nouns: *The south is warmer than the north.*

Compare:

I am going to the south (noun)

with *I am going south* (adverb)

and *North of the town there is a lake*

with *To the north (of the town) there is a lake.*

Note also *the North Pole, the South Pole, the East End.*

the is also used with certain other names:

the Sudan	*the Yemen*	*the Hague*	*the Riviera*
the Camargue	*the Costa Brava*	*the Mall*	*the Strand*

E **the** is used before musical instruments:
She learnt to play the flute.

F **the** is used before the names of meals if these are qualified by a clause:
The dinners Peter used to give were really memorable.
The tea we got on the boat was rather disappointing. (See also **3** D.)

5 Omission of the definite article

A The definite article is NOT used:

1 Before names of places except as shown above, or before names of people.

Exceptions:

the + plural surname can be used to mean 'the . . . family':
The Smiths = Mr and Mrs Smith (and children).

the + singular name can be used to distinguish one person from another of the same name:
We have two Mr Smiths. Which one do you want?
I want the Mr Smith who works in the Post Office.

Note also that although **the** is not used before title + noun:
Captain Jones was talking to Doctor Black
it is used before the title alone:
The captain seemed angry with the doctor.

We also use **the** before a title containing *of*: *the Duke of York.*

Finally, it is possible to address two unmarried sisters as **The Misses** + surname: *The Misses Jones, The Misses Smith.*

2 Before abstract nouns except when they are used in a particular sense:
Men fear death

but *The death of the Prime Minister left his party without a leader.*

3 After a noun in the possessive case, or a possessive adjective:
the boy's uncle = the uncle of the boy
It is my (blue) book. = The (blue) book is mine.

4 Before names of meals (but see **3** D):
The Scots have porridge for breakfast
but *The wedding breakfast was held in her father's house.*

5 Before parts of the body and articles of clothing, as these normally prefer a possessive adjective:
Raise your right hand. *He took off his coat.*
But notice that sentences of the type:
She seized the child's collar. *I patted his shoulder.*
The brick hit John's face.
could be expressed:
She seized the child by the collar. *I patted him on the shoulder.*
The brick hit John in the face.
Similarly in the passive:
He was hit on the head. *He was cut in the hand.*

B Note that in some languages the definite article is used before indefinite plural nouns but that in English **the** is never used in this way:
Women are expected to like housework (i.e. women in general).
Big hotels all over the world are very much the same.
If we put *the* before *women* in the first example, it would mean that we were referring to a particular group of women.

C *nature*, where it means the spirit creating and motivating the world of plants and animals etc., is used without **the**:
If you interfere with nature you will suffer for it.

6 Omission of **the** before **home** and before **church, market, school, hospital,** etc.

A **home**

When **home** is used alone, i.e. is not preceded or followed by a descriptive word or phrase, **the** is omitted:
He went home. *She left home.* *They got home late.*
They hurried home. *They arrived home after dark.*
Note that the preposition *to* is omitted and *at* is not used after *arrive.*

But when **home** is preceded or followed by a descriptive word or phrase it is treated like any other noun as regards articles and prepositions:

We went to the bride's home.
For some years this was the home of your queen.
A mud hut was the only home he had ever known.

B **chapel, church, market, college, school, hospital, court, prison, work, sea, bed**

These nouns are used without **the** when they are visited or used for their primary purpose:

We go to *church* to pray — to *market* to buy or sell
to *school* to study — to *hospital* as patients
to *college* to study — to *prison* as prisoners
to *bed* to sleep — to *court* as litigants
to *sea* as sailors — to *work* as workers

Similarly we can be
in *prison/court* as prisoners
in *hospital/bed* as patients
at *church* as worshippers
at *work/sea/market* as workers etc.
We return from *work/school/market/church*.
We get out of *bed*, leave *hospital*, escape from *prison*.

When these places are visited for other reasons the article is used:
I went to the church to see the carvings.
He comes to the school sometimes to speak to the headmaster.
He returned from the prison where he had been visiting his brother.
They are at the sea (at the seaside)
but *They are at sea* (in a ship, but not necessarily as sailors).
He went to the bed (walked over to it)
but *He went to bed* (got into it and presumably went to sleep).

In contrast to the above list, the following very common nouns take **the**: *cathedral, office* (as a place of work), *cinema, theatre*:
He is at the office (but *at work*). *She is going to the theatre.*

2 Nouns

7 Kinds and function

A There are four kinds of nouns in English:
Common nouns: *dog, table, man*
Proper nouns: *Tom, France, Madrid, Mrs Smith*
Abstract nouns: *charity, beauty, fear, courage, joy*
Collective nouns: *swarm, team, crowd, flock, group*

B A noun can function as:
The subject of a verb: *Tom arrived.*
The complement of the verb **be, become, seem**: *Tom is an actor.*
The object of a verb: *I saw Tom.*
The object of a preposition: *I spoke to Tom.*
A noun can also be in the possessive case:
Plato's works = the works of Plato (see **10**).

8 Gender

Masculine: men, boys and male animals (pronoun **he/they**).
Feminine: women, girls and female animals (pronoun **she/they**).
Neuter: inanimate things, animals whose sex we don't know and sometimes babies whose sex we don't know (pronoun **it/they**).
Exceptions:
Ships are considered feminine and sometimes cars and other vehicles when regarded with affection or respect. Countries when referred to by name are also normally considered feminine.
The ship struck an iceberg, which tore a huge hole in her side.
Scotland lost many of her bravest men in two great rebellions.

Most nouns have the same form for masculine and feminine:

parent *painter* *driver* *singer* *cousin*
child *artist* *cook* *judge* *rider*

Some have different forms:

brother, sister *uncle, aunt* *nephew, niece*
lord, lady *duke, duchess* *count, countess* *prince, princess*
bull, cow *horse, mare* *cock, hen* *drake, duck*

Some form the feminine from the masculine by adding **ess**. Note that words ending in **or** or **er** often drop the **o** or **e**:

actor, actress *conductor, conductress*
but *manager, manageress*

Note also:
salesman, saleswoman *spokesman, spokeswoman*
chairman, chairwoman
Recently there has been an attempt to de-sex these words by using *-person* instead of *-man*: *salesperson, chairperson* etc. This fashion may not last.

9 Plurals

The plural of a noun is usually made by adding **s** to the singular:
dog, dogs *day, days* *house, houses*

Exceptions:

A Nouns ending in **o** or **ss, sh, ch** or **x** form their plural by adding **es**:
tomato, tomatoes *kiss, kisses* *brush, brushes*
watch, watches *box, boxes*

But words of foreign origin or abbreviated words ending in **o** add **s** only:
piano, pianos *dynamo, dynamos* *photo, photos*
kimono, kimonos *biro, biros*

B Nouns ending in **y** following a consonant form their plural by dropping the **y** and adding **ies**:
baby, babies *lady, ladies* *country, countries* *fly, flies*
Nouns ending in **y** following a vowel form their plural by adding **s** only:
donkey, donkeys *boy, boys* *day, days*

C Twelve nouns ending in **f** or **fe** drop the **f** or **fe** and add **ves**. These nouns are *wife, life, knife, wolf, self, calf, shelf, leaf, loaf, thief, sheaf, half*:
wife, wives *wolf, wolves* *loaf, loaves* etc.
The nouns *scarf, wharf* and *hoof* take either **s** or **ves** in the plural:
scarfs or *scarves* *wharfs* or *wharves* *hoofs* or *hooves*
Other words ending in **f** or **fe** add **s** in the plural in the ordinary way:
cliff, cliffs *handkerchief, handkerchiefs* *safe, safes*

D A few nouns form their plural by a vowel change:
man, men *louse, lice* *foot, feet* *mouse, mice*
woman, women *goose, geese* *tooth, teeth* *ox, oxen*
The plural of *child* is *children*.

E Names of certain creatures do not change in the plural.

The word *fish* is normally unchanged. *fishes* exists but is uncommon.

Some types of fish do not normally change in the plural: *salmon, trout, squid, pike, mackerel, cod, turbot, plaice*; but if used in a plural sense they would take a plural verb. Others, however, do change. We talk of *herrings, sardines, lobsters, crabs* and all other shellfish, *whales, dolphins, sharks, eels*.

sheep and *deer* do not change: *one sheep, two sheep*.

Sportsmen who shoot *duck, pheasant, partridge, snipe, ptarmigan, teal, woodcock, grouse* etc. use the same form for singular and plural. But other people normally add **s** to the plural form of names of birds in common use:

ducks *pheasants* *partridges*

The word *game*, used by sportsmen to mean an animal/animals hunted, is always in the singular, and takes a singular verb.

F A few other words don't change:

aircraft, craft (boat/boats)
quid (slang for £1)
counsel (barristers working in court)

Certain words are always singular:

advice	*knowledge*	*baggage*	*furniture*
information	*news*	*luggage*	*rubbish*

(See **3** B.)

Certain words are always plural: *police, clothes*; garments consisting of two parts: *pyjamas, trousers, breeches, pants* etc.; tools or instruments consisting of two parts: *binoculars, glasses, spectacles, pliers, shears, scissors, scales*; and *premises* and *quarters* (used to mean accommodation).

All the above words take a plural verb.

There are also a number of words ending in **ics**, *mathematics, physics, acoustics, politics, hysterics, ethics, athletics* etc., which have a plural form and normally take a plural verb:

Athletics are his main interest.
His mathematics are weak.

But names of sciences, e.g. *mathematics, physics, acoustics, politics, ethics*, can be considered singular in such sentences as:

Mathematics is an exact science.
Ethics is one of the subjects on the course.

Some measurements and numerals do not change either (see **322, 326**).

G Words which retain their original Greek or Latin forms make their plurals according to the rules of Greek or Latin:

erratum, errata	*memorandum, memoranda*
radius, radii	*datum, data*
crisis, crises	*phenomenon, phenomena*
(/ˈkraisis/, /ˈkraisi:z/)	*terminus, termini*
basis, bases	*oasis, oases*
(/ˈbeisis/, /ˈbeisi:z/)	(/əuˈeisis/, /əuˈeisi:z/)
axis, axes	*thesis, theses*
(/ˈæksis/, /ˈæksi:z/)	

But there is a tendency, particularly with fairly common Latin or Greek words, to make the plural according to the rules of English:
dogma, dogmas
gymnasium, gymnasiums
formula, formulas (though *formulae* is used by scientists)

Sometimes there are two plural forms with different meanings:
index, indexes (lists of contents of books)
indices (a mathematical term)
appendix, appendixes (a medical term)
appendices (used both as a medical term and also for additions to a book)
genius, geniuses (extraordinarily intelligent persons)
genii (supernatural beings)

H Compound nouns

Normally the last word is made plural:
armchair, armchairs *bookcase, bookcases*

Where *man* or *woman* is prefixed, both parts are made plural:
men students *women students*

Compound nouns formed with prepositions or adverbs make only the first word plural:
sister-in-law, sisters-in-law *looker-on, lookers-on*

Where the compound noun has an adjective as the last word, the first word is usually made plural:
court martial, courts martial (but *court martials* is also heard)

Words ending in **ful** usually make their plural in the ordinary way:
handful, handfuls *armful, armfuls*

Initials can be made plural:
VIPs (Very Important Persons)
OAPs (Old Age Pensioners)
MPs (Members of Parliament)
QCs (Queen's Counsel)
UFOs (Unidentified Flying Objects)

10 The possessive case form

A 's is used with singular nouns and plural nouns not ending in **s**:

a man's job	*a child's voice*	*the horse's mouth*
men's work	*the children's room*	*the bull's horns*
a woman's intuition	*the people's choice*	*the butcher's (shop)*
women's clothes	*the crew's quarters*	*Russia's exports*

B A simple apostrophe (') is used with plural nouns ending in **s**:

a girls' school *the students' hostel*
the eagles' nest *the Smiths' car*

C Classical names ending in **s** usually add only the apostrophe:

Pythagoras' Theorem *Archimedes' Law* *Hercules' labours*

D Other names ending in **s** can take **'s** or the apostrophe alone:

Mr Jones's house or *Mr Jones' house*
Yeats's poems or *Yeats' poems*

E With compounds, the last word takes the **'s**:

My brother-in-law's guitar

Names consisting of several words are treated similarly:

Henry the Eighth's wives *the Prince of Wales's helicopter*

's can also be used after initials:

the PM's (Prime Minister's) *secretary* *the VIP's escort*
the MP's briefcase

Note that when the possessive case is used, the article before the person or thing 'possessed' disappears:

the daughter of the politician = *the politician's daughter*
the intervention of America = *America's intervention*
the plays of Shakespeare = *Shakespeare's plays*

11 Use of the possessive case, and **of** + noun used for possession

A The possessive case is chiefly used of people, countries or animals, as shown above. But it can also be used:

1 Of ships and boats: *the ship's bell* *the yacht's mast*

2 Of planes, trains, cars and other vehicles, though here the **of** construction is safer:

a glider's wings or *the wings of a glider*
the train's heating system or *the heating system of the train*

3 In time expressions:

a week's holiday	*today's paper*	*tomorrow's weather*
ten minutes' break	*a three days' walk*	*a ten hours' delay*

(But note that *a ten-minute break, a three-day walk, a ten-hour delay* would also be possible.)

4 In expressions of money + **worth**:
£1's worth of stamps *ten dollars' worth of ice cream*

5 With **for** + noun + **sake**:
for heaven's sake *for goodness' sake*

6 In a few expressions:
a stone's throw *journey's end* *the water's edge*

7 We can say either *a winter's day* or *a winter day* and *a summer's day* or *a summer day*, but we cannot make spring or autumn possessive, except when they are personified: *Autumn's return*.

B **of** + noun is used for possession

1 When the possessor noun is followed by a phrase or clause:
The boys ran about, obeying the directions of a man with a whistle.
Taking the advice of a couple I met on the train, I booked a room at the Red Lion.

2 With inanimate 'possessors', except those listed in A above:
the walls of the town *the roof of the church*
the keys of the car
However, it is often possible to replace noun 1 + **of** + noun 2 by noun 2 + noun 1 in that order:
the town walls *the church roof* *the car keys*
The first noun becomes a sort of adjective and is not made plural:
the roofs of the churches = *the church roofs* (see **12**).
Unfortunately noun + **of** + noun combinations cannot always be replaced in this way and the student is advised to use **of** when in doubt.

12 Noun + noun and noun + gerund combinations

A Examples of these:

1 noun + noun:

ˈLondon ˈTransport *ˈFleet Street* *ˈTower ˈBridge*
ˈhall ˈdoor *ˈtravel agent* *ˈpetrol tank*
ˈhitchhiker *ˈsky-jacker* *ˈriver ˈbank*
ˈkitchen ˈtable *ˈwinter ˈclothes*

2 noun + gerund:

ˈfruit picking *ˈlorry driving* *ˈhitchhiking*
ˈweight-lifting *ˈbird-watching* *ˈsurf-riding*
ˈstamp-collecting *ˈcoal-mining*

3 gerund + noun:

ˈwaiting list *ˈdiving-board* *ˈdriving licence*
ˈlanding card *ˈdining-room* *ˈswimming pool*
ˈfishing-rod

We can also form nouns out of verb + adverb combinations:
ˈ*fly-over* ˈ*lay-by* ˈ*break-in* ˈ*break-out*
ˈ*hold-up* ˈ*take-off* ˈ*look-out*
(See **320**.)

B Use of noun + noun and noun + gerund combinations

1 They can replace noun + **of** + noun as shown above:
ˈ*table* ˈ*leg* ˈ*college* ˈ*library* ˈ*hall* ˈ*door*
ˈ*garden* ˈ*gate* ˈ*attic* ˈ*window*

2 The first noun can indicate the place of the second:
ˈ*city* ˈ*streets* (streets in/of the city)
ˈ*country* ˈ*lanes* ˈ*corner* ˈ*shop* ˈ*kitchen* ˈ*table*
ˈ*wall* ˈ*safe* ˈ*roof rack* ˈ*roof garden*
ˈ*Park* ˈ*Lane* ˈ*Kew* ˈ*Road*

3 The first noun can indicate the time of the second:
ˈ*summer* ˈ*holidays* ˈ*Sunday* ˈ*papers* ˈ*November* ˈ*fogs*

4 The first noun can express the purpose or function of the second:
ˈ*race-track* ˈ*tennis court* ˈ*tennis racquet*
ˈ*bottle-opener* ˈ*nail-scissors* ˈ*floodlight*
ˈ*tennis club* (a club for tennis players)

5 The first noun/gerund can distinguish the second noun/gerund from its other varieties:
ˈ*love story,* ˈ*murder story,* ˈ*ghost story*
ˈ*foglamp,* ˈ*parking light,* ˈ*traffic lights,* ˈ*skylight*
ˈ*lorry driver,* ˈ*car driver,* ˈ*train driver*

6 These combinations are often used to denote occupations, sports, hobbies and the people who practise them:
ˈ*school-teaching,* ˈ*school-teacher* ˈ*bookselling,* ˈ*bookseller*
ˈ*surf-riding,* ˈ*surf-rider* ˈ*stamp-collecting,* ˈ*stamp-collector*
These categories all overlap to some extent. They are not meant to be mutually exclusive, but aim to give the student some general idea of the uses of these combinations and help with the stress.

C As will be seen from the stress-marks above:

1 The first word is stressed in noun + gerund and gerund + noun combinations, when there is an idea of purpose as in B4 above, and in combinations of type B5 and B6 above.

2 Both words are usually stressed in combinations of types A1, B1, B2 and B3 above, but inevitably there are exceptions.

3 In place name combinations both words usually have equal stress:
ˈ*King's* ˈ*Road* ˈ*Waterloo* ˈ*Bridge* ˈ*Leicester* ˈ*Square*
But there is one important exception. In combinations where the last word is *Street*, the word *Street* is unstressed:
ˈ*Bond Street* ˈ*Oxford Street*

3 Adjectives

13 Kinds and agreement

A The main kinds of adjectives are:

1 of quality: *square, good, golden, fat, heavy, dry, clever*
2 demonstrative: *this, that, these, those*
3 distributive: *each, every, either, neither*
4 quantitative: *some, any, no, few, many, much, one, twenty*
5 interrogative: *which, what, whose*
6 possessive: *my, your, his, her, its, our, your, their*

B Agreement

Adjectives in English have only one form, which is used with singular and plural, masculine and feminine nouns:

a good boy, good boys *a good girl, good girls*

The only exceptions are the demonstrative adjectives **this** and **that**, which change to **these** and **those** before plural nouns:

this cat, these cats *that man, those men*

14 Position of adjectives and the use of **and**

Adjectives in English usually come before their nouns:

a big town *a blue car* *an interesting book*

When there are two or more adjectives before a noun they are not usually separated by **and** except when the last two are adjectives of colour:

a big square box *a tall young man* *six yellow roses*

but *a black and white cap* *a red, white and blue flag*

Adjectives of quality, however, can be placed after the verbs **be, seem, appear, look** (= seem, appear); **and** is then placed between the last two adjectives:

The house looked large and inconvenient.
The weather was cold, wet and windy.

15 Comparison

A There are three degrees of comparison:

1 Positive	*dark*	*tall*	*useful*
2 Comparative	*darker*	*taller*	*more useful*
3 Superlative	*the darkest*	*the tallest*	*the most useful*

B One-syllable adjectives form their comparative and superlative by adding **er** and **est** to the positive form:

bright	*brighter*	*the brightest*
new	*newer*	*the newest*

C Adjectives of three or more syllables form their comparative and superlative by putting **more** and **the most** before the positive:

interesting	*more interesting*	*the most interesting*
frightening	*more frightening*	*the most frightening*

D Adjectives of two syllables follow one or other of the above rules. Those ending in **ful** or **re** usually take **more** and **the most**:

doubtful	*more doubtful*	*the most doubtful*
careful	*more careful*	*the most careful*
obscure	*more obscure*	*the most obscure*

Those ending in **er, y** or **ly** usually add **er, est**:

pretty	*prettier*	*the prettiest* (note that the **y** becomes **i**)
holy	*holier*	*the holiest*
clever	*cleverer*	*the cleverest*

E Irregular comparisons:

good	*better*	*the best*
bad	*worse*	*the worst*
little	*less*	*the least*
many	*more*	*the most*
much	*more*	*the most*
far	*further*	*the furthest* (of distance and time)
	farther	*the farthest* (of distance only)
old	*older*	*the oldest* (of people and things)
	elder	*the eldest* (of people only)

elder and **the eldest** imply seniority rather than age. They are chiefly used for comparisons within a family:

his eldest boy/girl/nephew   *my elder brother/sister*

but **elder** cannot be placed before **than**, so **older** must be used here:

He is older than I am (**elder** would not be possible).

Superlatives (preceded by **the**) can be used as pronouns:

Tom is the cleverest (boy in the class).

The eldest was only eight years old.

Comparatives can be used similarly:

I want a strong rope. Which is the stronger of these two?

But this use of the comparative is considered rather literary. In informal English a superlative is often used here instead:

Which is the strongest?

16 Constructions with comparisons (see also **311 B**)

A With the positive form of the adjective, e.g. *good, tall, clever* (see **15 A**), we use **as . . . as** in the affirmative and **not as/not so . . . as** in the negative:
A boy of sixteen is often as tall as his father.
Manslaughter is not as/so bad as murder.
Your coffee is not as/so good as the coffee my mother makes.

B With the comparative we use **than**:
The new tower blocks are much higher than the old buildings.
He makes fewer mistakes than you (do).
(See **17**.)

C Comparison of three or more people/things is expressed by the superlative with **the . . . in/of**:
This is the oldest theatre in London.
In old folk tales the youngest of the family is always the most successful.

We can also use a relative clause. A perfect tense is especially useful:
It is the least attractive of all the houses I have seen.
It/This is the best beer (that) I have ever drunk.
It/This is the most exciting book (that) I have ever read.
It/This was the worst film (that) he had ever seen.
He is the kindest man I have ever met.
It was the most worrying day he had ever spent.

Note that **ever** is used here, not **never**. We can however express the same idea with **never** and a comparative:
I have never drunk better beer.
I have never met a kinder man.
He had never spent a more worrying day.

Notice that *You are most kind* (without **the**) merely means *You are very kind.*

D Parallel increase is expressed by **the** + comparative . . . **the** + comparative:
HOUSE AGENT: *Do you want a big house?*
WIFE: *Yes, the bigger the better.*
HUSBAND: *I don't agree. The smaller the house, the less it will cost us to heat.*

E Gradual increase or decrease is expressed by two comparatives joined by **and**:
The weather is getting colder and colder.
He became less and less interested.

F Comparison of actions is made similarly:
Riding a horse is not as easy as riding a bicycle.
It is nicer to go with someone than to go alone.

G Other examples of comparison:
You are as obstinate as a mule.
This one is the better of the two.
Chinchilla is more expensive than mink.
Helen was the most beautiful woman in Greece.
This is less suitable than the last house you showed me.

17 **than/as** + pronoun + auxiliary (see also **311 B**)

When the same verb is used before and after **than/as** we use an auxiliary for the second verb:
He knew more than I did. *I earn less than he does.*

When **than** or **as** is followed by a first or second person pronoun it is usually possible to omit the verb:
I am not as old as you. *He has more time than I/we (have).*

In very formal English we keep **I/we**, as the pronoun is still considered to be the subject of the verb, even though the verb is not expressed. In normal English, however, **me/us** is more usual:
He has more time than me. *They are richer than us.*

This rule also applies to comparisons made with adverbs (see **65**).

18 Adjectives of quality used as nouns

good/bad, poor/rich, healthy/sick, young/old, living/dead and certain other adjectives describing human character or condition can be preceded by **the** and used as nouns. These nouns represent a class of person:
the poor = poor people *the dead* = dead people
The poor are often generous to each other.
After the battle they buried the dead.

These expressions have a plural meaning: they are followed by a plural verb and the pronoun is **they**. Note that these expressions refer to a group or class of persons considered in a general sense only. If we wish to refer to a particular group it is necessary to add a noun:
The young are usually intolerant is a general statement but
The young men are fishing refers to particular young people.

19 Use with the pronoun **one/ones**

Adjectives of quality can be used without their nouns if the pronoun **one** (singular) or **ones** (plural) is placed afterwards. This form is mainly used when there is some idea of selection or comparison:

I like those pencils: I'll take a blue one.
Small bananas are often better than big ones.

But **one** is often omitted after **the** + superlative and sometimes after **the** + comparative. It is also sometimes omitted after adjectives of colour:

I took the largest (one).
I bought the more expensive (one) of the two.
Which do you like? I like the blue (one).

(For the other kinds of adjectives see the next chapter on adjectives and pronouns.)

4 Demonstrative, distributive and quantitative adjectives and pronouns

20 **this/these, that/those** (demonstrative adjectives and pronouns)

A Examples of use as adjectives:

this/that, these/those agree with their nouns in number. (They are the only adjectives to do this.)

this boy, this girl *these boys, these girls*
that actor, that actress *those actors, those actresses*
this tree, these trees *that tree, those trees*
This beach was quite empty last year.
I have to read all these books for my course.
What is that thing in the sky? Is it a flying saucer?
Those islands used to be inhabited.

Note the use of **this/these** and **that/those** + noun + **of yours/Peter's/Ann's** etc.

That car of yours is always breaking down (= Your car is always breaking down).
That brother of yours was drunk again last night (= Your brother was drunk again last night).
This diet of yours isn't having much effect (= Your diet . . .).
This phrase can be used, instead of **your** + noun, when the speaker wishes to make an emphatic comment. The comment is quite often, though not necessarily always, unfavourable.

B Examples of use as pronouns:

This is my brother; those are Tom's brothers.
This is my umbrella; that is yours.
These are the old classrooms; those are the new ones.
What is that? It's a hovercraft.

this/that can represent clauses:

Our car broke down on the way to the airport. This made us late for the plane.
He said I was not a good wife. Wasn't that a horrible thing to say?

C **this/these, that/those** used with **one/ones**

When there is some idea of comparison or selection, the pronoun **one/ones** is often placed after these demonstratives, but it is not essential except when the demonstrative is followed by an adjective:

1 *This chair is too low. I'll sit in that (one).*
2 *Which do you like? I like this (one) best.*
3 *I like this blue one/these blue ones.*

one is optional in (1) and (2); usual in (3).

21 each, every, everyone, everybody, everything (distributive adjectives and pronouns)

A **every** compared to **all**

Technically, **every** means a number of people or things considered individually while **all** means a number of people or things considered as a group. But in practice **every** and its compounds are often used when we are thinking of a group.

B **each** (adjective and pronoun) and **every** (adjective)

each means a number of persons or things considered individually. **every** can have this meaning but with **every** there is less emphasis on the individual. *Every man had a weapon* = 'All the men had weapons', and implies that the speaker counted the men and the weapons and found that he had the same number of each. *Each man had a weapon* implies that the speaker went to each man in turn and checked that he had a weapon.

each is a pronoun and adjective: *Each (man) knows what to do.*

every is an adjective only: *Every man knows . . .*

each can be used of two or more persons or things, and is normally used of small numbers. **every** is not normally used of very small numbers.

Both take a singular verb. The possessive adjective is **his/her/its.** (For the reciprocal pronoun **each other** see **27** D, **47**.)

C **everyone/everybody** and **everything** (pronouns)

everyone/everybody + singular verb is normally preferred to **all (the) people** + plural verb, i.e. we say *Everyone is ready* instead of *All the people are ready*. There is no difference between **everyone** and **everybody**.

everything is similarly preferred to **all (the) things**, i.e. we say *Everything has been wasted* instead of *All the things have been wasted.*

The expressions **all (the) people, all (the) things** are possible when followed by a phrase or clause:

I got all the things you asked for.
All the people in the room clapped.

Otherwise they are rarely used.

D **Pronouns and possessive adjectives with everyone/everybody and everything**

As **everyone/everybody** takes a singular verb, the pronoun should be **he/him, she/her** with possessive adjectives **his** and **her**. But this is only found in formal English. In ordinary conversation the plural forms **they/them** and **their** are used instead:
Has everyone got their books?
Everyone enjoys it, don't they?
Everyone likes their own way/ways of doing things.
(See also **46**.)

everything, however, has the pronoun **it**, and possessive adjective **its**.

22 both, either, neither (pronouns and adjectives)

both means 'one and the other'. It takes a plural verb:
Both banks of the river were covered in bushes.
She has two sons. Both are taller than she is.

neither means 'not one and not the other'. It takes an affirmative singular verb:
Neither of them drinks coffee.
either means 'any one of two'.
Did you like his two songs? No, I didn't like either (of them).
neither + affirmative verb = **either** + negative verb.
neither is preferred at the beginning of a sentence:
Neither book gives the answer.
either could not be used here.
neither can also be used alone as a negative answer to a question:
Which did you buy? Neither.
either would not be used.
Pronouns and possessive adjectives with **neither**, **either** (used of people):
As they take singular verbs, the pronouns should be **he/him** and **she/her** and the possessive adjectives should be **his** and **her**. But in colloquial English there is a growing tendency to use **they/them** and **their**:
Neither of them could make up his mind (formal English).
Neither of them could make up their minds (colloquial).
Neither of them knew the way, did they? (colloquial).
(See also **46**.)
(For **both . . . and, neither . . . nor, either . . . or,** see Conjunctions **94**.)

23 Numerals, **a/an** and **one**

A Numerals present little difficulty (see **321–4**.)
The same form is used for adjectives and pronouns:
Six hundred people bought tickets.
Hundreds of tourists come to this museum.
We lost the first match but won the second and third.

one/ones must be added if the numeral is followed by an adjective alone:
Have you got a big plate? No. Would two small ones do?

B **a/an** and **one**

1 **a/an** and **one** (adjective)
When counting or measuring time, distance, weight etc. we can use either **a/an** or **one** for the singular:
£1 = a/one pound *£100 = a/one hundred pounds*
It will take a/one month.
I bought a/one kilo of potatoes.
Lessons cost a/one pound an hour.
The **an** before *hour* in this last expression is not replaceable by **one**.

But in other types of statement **a/an** and **one** are not normally interchangeable, because **one** + noun normally means 'one only/not more than one' and **a/an** does not mean this:
A shotgun is no good (it is the wrong sort of thing).
One shotgun is no good (I need two or three).

Special uses of **one**:

1 **one** (adjective/pronoun) used with **another/others**:
One (boy) wanted to read, another/others wanted to watch TV.
One day he wanted his lunch early, another day he wanted it late.

2 **one** can be used before **day/week/month/year/summer/winter** etc. or before the name of the day or month to denote a particular time when something happened:
One night there was a terrible storm.
One winter the snow fell early.
One day a telegram arrived.

3 **one day** can also be used to mean 'at some future date':
One day you'll be sorry you treated him so badly. (**some day** would also be possible.)

(For **one** and **you**, see **45**.)

2 **a/an** and **one** (pronoun)
one is the pronoun equivalent of **a/an**:
Did you get a ticket? Yes, I managed to get one.

The plural of **one** used in this way is **some** (see next paragraph):
Did you buy grapes? Yes, I bought some.
Contrast with:
Did you hear the speech? Yes, I heard it.
Did you hear the speeches? Yes, I heard them.

24 **some, any, no** and **none**

A 1 **some** and **any** (pronouns/adjectives) mean 'a certain number or amount'. They are used before plural or uncountable nouns. When used with plural nouns, **some** is a possible plural form of **a/an** and **one** (see above for **one/some**):
Would you like a biscuit/some biscuits?
I took a photo/some photos.
(For **some/any** used with singular nouns see section A3.)

2 **some** and **any** compared

some is used:

With affirmative sentences:
They took some honey.

With questions when the answer 'yes' is expected:
Can I have some coffee?
TOURIST (to travel agent): *Can you give me some information about . . . ?*

In offers and requests:
Would you like some wine? *Could you do some typing for me?*

any is used:

In negative sentences:
I haven't any matches and Tom hasn't any either.

With **hardly, barely, scarcely** (which are almost negatives):
I have hardly any time.

With questions except those noted above:
Have you any money? *Did you see any eagles?*

After **if/whether**, and in expressions of doubt:
I don't think there is any petrol in the tank.
If you have any difficulty, let me know.

3 **some** or **any** used with singular (countable) nouns

some can be used to mean 'an unspecified or unknown':
Some idiot parked his car outside my garage.
He doesn't believe in conventional medicine; he has some remedy of his own.
(See **some** + singular noun + **or other** in **27** C.)

any can mean 'practically every', 'no particular (one)':
Any book about riding will tell you how to saddle a horse.
Any dictionary will give you the meaning of these words.
anybody/anyone/anything can have this meaning (but can also, of course, be used as in 1–2 above):
Ask anyone where the house is/Anyone will tell you where the house is.
What would you like to drink? Oh, anything (I don't mind what I drink).

B **no** and **none**
no (adjective) and **none** (pronoun) can be used with affirmative verbs to express a negative; they are therefore an alternative to negative verb + **any**:
I have no apples = I haven't any apples.
Tom has none = Tom hasn't any.
I took no photos = I didn't take any photos.
On the whole a negative verb + **any** is more usual than an affirmative verb + **no/none**.

25 someone, somebody, something, anyone, anybody, anything, no one, nobody, nothing

A Compounds formed with **some, any** and **no** follow the rules in **24** A1 and B above:
A: *Somebody/Someone gave me a ticket for a pop concert.*
B: *No one/Nobody has ever given me a free ticket for anything.*
Does anyone know what time the concert starts?
Do you want anything from the chemist?
Would anybody like a drink?

B **someone, somebody, anyone, anybody, no one, nobody** can be possessive:
Someone's passport has been stolen.
Is this somebody's/anybody's seat?
I don't want to waste anyone's time.

C Pronouns and possessive adjectives with **someone, somebody, anyone, anybody, no one, nobody**
All these expressions have a singular meaning and take a singular verb:
Someone wants to speak to you on the phone.
The personal pronoun should logically be singular too, **he/she**, and the possessive adjective **his/her**, but to avoid the awkwardness of saying **his or her** whenever the gender is in doubt we generally use **they** and **their** instead:

No one saw Tom go out, did they?
Has anyone left their luggage on the train?

With **something, anything, nothing** there is no problem of gender, so we still use **it**:
Something went wrong, didn't it?

26 else placed after someone/anybody/nothing etc.

someone/somebody/something, anyone/anybody/anything, no one/nobody/nothing, everyone/everybody/everything and the adverbs **somewhere, anywhere, everywhere, nowhere** can be followed by **else**.

someone else = some other person	Also **somebody/something/somewhere else**
anyone else = any other person	Also **anybody/anything/anywhere else**
no one else = no other person	Also **nobody/nothing/nowhere else**
everyone else = every other person	Also **everybody/everything/everywhere else**

Examples:
I'm afraid I can't help you. You'll have to ask someone else.
There isn't anyone else/There's no one else to ask.

Note also:
somewhere else = in/at/to some other place
anywhere else = in/at/to any other place
nowhere else = in/at/to no other place
Are you going anywhere else?

someone/somebody, anyone/anybody, no one/nobody + else can be possessive:
I took someone else's coat.
Was anyone else's luggage opened?
No one else's luggage was opened.

27 other, another, others with one and some

A **other** forms:

	Adjective	Pronoun
Singular	*another*	*another*
Plural	*other*	*others*

A: *Have you met Bill's sisters?*
B: *I've met one. I didn't know he had another (sister).*
A: *Oh, he has two others/two other sisters.*

B **one . . . another/other(s), some . . . other/other(s)**

One student suggested a play, another (student)/other students/others wanted a concert.

Some tourists/Some of the tourists went on the beach; others explored the town.

C **some** + singular noun + **or other**

As already mentioned, **some** can mean 'an unspecified or unknown', i.e. **some** here shows that the speaker doesn't know anything about the person or thing. **or other** can be added to emphasize that the speaker isn't very interested:

He is taking some exam or other. (The speaker probably thinks exams are foolish.)

Who does that enormous yellow Rolls Royce belong to? Oh, I expect it belongs to some film star or other.

What's that noise in the streets? It's probably some demonstration or other.

D **one another** and **each other**

Tom and Ann looked at each other = Tom looked at Ann and Ann looked at Tom.

Both **one another** and **each other** can be used of two or more, but **one another** is frequently preferred when there are more than two.

28 **many** and **much** (adjectives and pronouns)

A As an adjective, **many** is used before plural countable nouns; **much** before uncountable nouns:

He didn't make many mistakes. *We haven't much milk.*

Both can be used as pronouns:

Tom gets lots of letters but Ann doesn't get many.

You have plenty of petrol but I haven't much.

many and **much** are used mainly in the negative and interrogative.

In the affirmative **many** is usually replaced by **a lot (of)**.

a lot (of) can also be used in the interrogative.

much is usually replaced by **a lot (of)** or **a great deal (of)**.

a lot (of)/a great deal (of) can also be used in the interrogative. But both these expressions expect an affirmative answer.

B **many** and **a lot (of)**

Interrogative:

Did you take many/a lot of photos?

Negative:

No, I didn't take many (photos).

Affirmative (object):
Yes, I took a lot (of photos).
many, however, is possible (1) in formal English and (2) in ordinary conversation if preceded by **a great/a good/so/too**:
1 *I have met many people who share your views* (formal).
2 *I took a great/a good many photos.*
I took so many photos the first day that I had no film left.
I took too many photos the first day.
Affirmative (subject):
Either **many** or **a lot (of)** can be used as the subject or as part of the subject of a verb:
many people think/a lot of people think/many think

C **much** and **a lot (of)/a great deal (of)**
Interrogative:
Did you have much/a lot of/a great deal of trouble getting visas?
Negative:
No, I didn't have much trouble.
Affirmative (object):
Yes, I had a lot of/a great deal of trouble.
But **much** is possible when qualified by **so**:
He ate so much at lunch that he was sleepy afterwards.
Affirmative (subject):
much is possible in formal English as the subject of a sentence.
Much will depend on what he says.
Much time has been wasted.
But *A lot of time has been wasted* would be more usual in ordinary conversation.
(For **not many/much** replacing **little/few** see **29** B.)

29 **a little/a few** and **little/few** (adjectives and pronouns)

a little/little are used before uncountable nouns:
a little time/little time
a few/few are used before plural countable nouns:
a few friends/few friends

A **a little, a few**

a little is a small amount, or what the speaker considers a small amount. **a few** is a small number, or what the speaker considers a small number.

only placed before **a little/a few** emphasizes that the number really is small in the speaker's opinion.

But **quite** placed before **a few** increases the number considerably:
I have a few books on mathematics (two or three books, or more)
but *I have quite a few books on mathematics* (a lot of books).

a little can also be an adverb of degree used with comparative adjectives or adverbs:
The paper should be a little thicker than this.
Couldn't you work a little faster?

B **little** and **few**

little and **few** denote scarcity or lack and have almost the force of a negative:
There is little danger of an earthquake = There isn't much/There is hardly any danger etc.
Few towns have such splendid trees = Not many/Hardly any towns have etc.

This use of **little** and **few** is mainly confined to written English (probably because in ordinary conversation **little** and **few** might easily be mistaken for **a little/a few**). In ordinary conversation, therefore, **little** and **few** are normally replaced by **hardly any** or **not + much/many**:
We saw little = We saw hardly anything/We didn't see much.
Few people know this = Hardly anyone knows/Not many people know this.

But **little** and **few** can be used more freely when they are qualified by **very, too, so, extremely, comparatively, relatively** etc.:
We have so few technicians that the machines are not serviced properly.

There is no difference in quantity between **little** and **very little** and **few** and **very few**. But the speaker who adds **very** wants to be more emphatic. **very little/few** might also be used alone in answer to a question:
Have you friends in this town? Very few.
You have saved something, surely? Very little.

30 **so** and **not** can represent a whole clause

A After **believe, expect, suppose, think** and after **it appears/seems**:
Will Tom be at the party? I expect so/suppose so/think so = I think he will.

For the negative we use:

1 A negative verb with **so**:
Will the scheme be a success? I don't believe so/expect so/suppose so/think so.
Are they making good progress? It doesn't seem so.

or 2 An affirmative verb with **not**:
It won't take long, will it?
No, I suppose not or *I don't suppose so.*
The plane didn't land in Calcutta, did it?
I believe not or *I don't believe so.*

Note that *I think not*, used in answer to a suggestion or request for permission, would mean that the suggestion is turned down or the request refused:
Shall we eat in the garden? I think not.

B **so** and **not** can be used similarly after **hope** and **be afraid** (= be sorry to say):
Is Peter coming with us? I hope so.
Will you have to pay duty on this? I'm afraid so.

The negative here is made with an affirmative verb + **not**:
Have you got a work permit? I'm afraid not.

C **so** and **not** can be used after **say** and **tell** + object:
How do you know there is going to be a demonstration?
Jack said so/Jack told me so.

For **tell** the only negative form is negative verb + **so**:
Tom didn't tell me so.

For **say** there are two negative forms, but the meaning is not the same:
Tom didn't say so = Tom didn't say that there would be a demonstration.
Tom said not = Tom said there wouldn't be a demonstration.

D **so** can be used after **do/did** but is not very common in modern English:
You should take an hour's walk every day. I'd do so if I had time.
But normally we would say:
I would if I had time.

5 Interrogative adjectives, pronouns and adverbs

31 Interrogative adjectives and pronouns:

Form:

For persons:	*subject*	who (pro.)
	object	whom, who (pro.)
	possessive	whose (pro. and adj.)
For things:	*subject*	what (pro. and adj.)
	object	what (pro. and adj.)
For persons or things when choice is restricted:		
	subject	which (pro. and adj.)
	object	which (pro. and adj.)

what (adjective) can be used for persons also (see **33** C, D). All these adjectives and pronouns have the same form for singular and plural.

Note that **who, whose** + noun, **what, which** when used as subjects are normally followed by an affirmative, not an interrogative verb:
Who pays the bills? Ann pays them/Ann does.
Whose horse won? The queen's horse won/The queen's horse did.
Which of your brothers is getting married? Tom is.
i.e. when we wish to find out who performs/performed/will perform an action, we use **who? whose? which?** with an affirmative verb.

what? can be used similarly:
What happened? *What delayed you?* *What went wrong?*
Possible answer: *A lorry overturned on the road and blocked it, so all the traffic was held up.*
(But with **who/what** etc. + **be** + noun/pronoun questions the interrogative verb is used: *What day is it?* We see that *is* here is interrogative when we put the question into reported speech and it becomes *He wants to know what day it is.*)

Examples of the use of **who, whom, whose, which** and **what** in questions:

A **who, whom, whose**

who as subject
Who keeps the keys? The caretaker keeps them.
Who took my gun? Tom took it.
Who are these boys? They are Bill's students.

who/whom as object
Who/Whom did you see? I saw the secretary.
Who/Whom did she pay? She paid Tom and me.
Who did they speak to ? (i.e. to whom did they speak?) *They spoke to Mary.*

whose
Whose books are these? (adj.) *They are Ann's.*
Whose are these? (pro.) *They are Ann's.*
Whose umbrella did you borrow? I borrowed Bill's.
Whose car broke down? George's car. (affirmative verb)

B **what**

As subject:
What delayed you? (pro.) *The storm delayed us.*

As object:
What paper do you read? (adj.) *I read 'The Daily Telegraph'.*
What did they eat? (pro.) *They ate rice.*
What did they eat it with? (pro.) *They ate it with chopsticks.*

C **which**

As subject:
Which of them arrived first? (affirmative verb)
Which of them is the eldest? (pro.) *Mary is the eldest.*

As object:
Which do you like best? (pro.) *I like Tom best.*
Which university did he go to? (adj.) *He went to Oxford.*

32 **who** and **whom** as objects of verbs and prepositions

A As direct objects

whom is the technically correct form and is used in formal written and spoken English. In ordinary conversation, however, we almost always use **who**, so that we can say:
Whom did you meet? (formal) or *Who did you meet?* (informal).
There is no difference in meaning but the second is much more usual than the first. Similarly we can say:
Whom did you help? or *Who did you help?*

B After prepositions

In formal English the preposition is immediately followed by **whom**:
With whom did you go?   *To whom were you speaking?*

But in ordinary spoken English we usually move the preposition to the end of the sentence. The **whom** then normally changes to **who**:
Who did you go with?   *Who were you speaking to?*

33 what (adjective and pronoun)

A **what** is a general interrogative used for things:
What time is it? *What street is this?*
What did you say? *What does he want?*

When **what** is used with prepositions, the preposition is normally placed at the end of the sentence, as shown above:
What did you open it with? I opened it with my knife.

B **what . . . for?** = why
What did you do that for? = Why did you do it?

C **what + be . . . like?** is a request for a description and can be used for things or people:
What was the exam like? It was very difficult.
What was the weather like? It was terrible.
What's the food like in your hostel?

Used of people it may concern either appearance or character:
What is he like? He's a friendly sort of man or *He's a tall man with a grey beard.*
What are your students like? They're very talkative.

what does he/it look like? concerns appearance only, and can also mean 'What does he/it resemble?':
What does he look like? He is tall and thin and very badly dressed. He looks like a scarecrow.
What does it look like? It's black and shiny. It looks like coal.

D **what is he?** = What is his profession?
What is his father? He is a tailor.

what (adjective) used for persons is possible but not common:
What men are you talking about? is possible, but
Who are you talking about? would be much more usual.

E **what** (adjective) is very common in questions about measurements. It is used in this way chiefly with the nouns: age, size, weight, length, breadth, width, height, depth:
What height is your room? or *What is the height of your room?*
What age is he? *What size is the parcel?*
What is the depth of the lake?

Note that the verb **to be** is always used here.

(Such questions can also be expressed by **how** with an adjective: *How high is your room?* See **35** D.)

34 which compared with who and what

who is a general interrogative pronoun for persons.

what is a general interrogative pronoun and adjective used mainly for things.
which (pronoun and adjective) is used instead of **who** and **what** when the choice is restricted.

A Examples of **which** and **what** used for things:
What will you have to drink?
We have gin, whisky and sherry: which will you have?
What does it cost to get to Scotland?
It depends on how you go. There are several ways of getting there. Which (way) is the cheapest or *Which is the cheapest (way)?*
I've seen the play and the film.
What did you think of them? Which (of them) did you like best?

B Examples of **which** and **who** used for people:
Who do you want to speak to?
I want to speak to Mr Smith.
We have two Smiths here: John and Joe. Which (of them) do you want?
which (pronoun) of people is not used alone as subject of a verb.
TEACHER (to a class): *Which of you knows the formula?* ('of you' is essential).
Who knows the formula? would also be possible.

C **which** (adjective) can be used of people when there is only a very slight idea of restriction:
Which poet (of all the poets) *do you like best?*
what would be possible here and would be more logical. But **what** (adjective) for people is normally avoided.

35 Interrogative adverbs

These are: **why, when, where, how**

A **why?** means 'for what reason?' and is usually answered by 'because':
Why was he late? Because he missed the bus.

B **when?** means 'at what time?':
When do you get up? 7 a.m.

C **where?** means 'in what place?':
Where do you live? In London.

D **how?** means 'in what way?':
How did you come? I came by plane.
How do you start the engine? You press this button.

how can also be used

1 With adjectives, as an alternative to **what** followed by a noun (see **33**):
How old is he?
How high is Mount Everest? It is over eight thousand metres high.
How wide is the river? It is fifty metres wide.
How long does it take to fly from London to Paris?

2 With **much** and **many**:
How much do you want?
How many pictures did you buy?

3 With adverbs:
How fast does he drive? Much too fast.
How often do you go abroad? I go every year.
How quickly can you say 'Tottenham Court Road'? I can say it in a quarter of a second.

Note that *How is she?* is an inquiry about her health. A possible answer is *She is very well.* But *What is she like?* is a request for a description. A possible answer is *She is tall and dark with green eyes.* (See **33** C.)

Do not confuse *How are you?* with *How do you do?* When two people are introduced each says *How do you do?* It is a greeting rather than a question. (See **123**).

36 ever placed after who, what, where, why, when, how

Where ever have you been? I've been looking for you everywhere!
Who ever told you to ask me to lend you the money? I've no money at all!

ever here is not necessary in the sentence but is added to emphasize the speaker's surprise/astonishment/anger/irritation/ dismay. It has the same meaning as **on earth/in the world.**

Such sentences are always spoken emphatically and the intonation will convey the speaker's emotion:
Why ever did you wash it in boiling water? (dismay)
Who ever are you? (The other person is presumably an intruder.)
Who ever left the door open? (What stupid person left it open?)
Where ever have you put my briefcase? I can't find it anywhere.
What ever are you doing in my car? (astonishment/annoyance)
When ever did you leave home? You must have left very early to be here by nine.
How ever did he manage to escape unhurt? The car was a complete wreck.

Note also **why ever not?** and **what ever for?**:
You musn't wear anything green.
Why ever not? (I can't understand the reason for this prohibition.)
Bring a knife to class tomorrow.
What ever for? (I can't understand what I need a knife for.)
(For **whoever, whichever, whatever** etc. written as one word, see **62**.)

6 Possessive adjectives, personal and other pronouns

Possessive adjectives and pronouns

37 Form

Possessive adjectives	*Possessive pronouns*
my	mine
your	yours
his/her/its	his/hers
our	ours
your	yours
their	theirs

Note that no apostrophes are used here. Students should guard particularly against the common mistake of writing the possessive **its** with an apostrophe. **it's** (with an apostrophe) means **it is** (see **44, 109**).

The old form of the second person singular, now no longer used in current English, can be found in the Bible and poetry:
thy   *thine*

38 Agreement of possessive adjectives

Possessive adjectives in English refer to the possessor and not to the thing possessed. Everything that a man or boy possesses is **his** thing; everything that a woman or girl possesses is **her** thing:
Tom's father is his father but *Mary's father is her father.*
A boy loves his mother but *A girl loves her mother.*

Everything that an animal or thing possesses is **its** thing:
A tree drops its leaves in autumn.
A dog wags its tail when it is happy.
But if the sex of the animal is known, **his/her** would often be used.

If there is more than one possessor, human or otherwise, **their** is used:
The boys are playing with their football.
The girls are with their mothers.
Trees drop their leaves in autumn.

Note that the possessive adjective remains the same whether the thing possessed is singular or plural:
my book, my books   *his aunt, his aunts*

39 Possessive pronouns are used to replace possessive adjectives + nouns

A They follow the same rules as possessive adjectives:
This is my pen or *This is mine.* *It is our room* or *It is ours.*
This is their house or *This is theirs.*
I have my pen; have you got yours?
Are those your books? No, they are hers.

B The expression **of mine** etc. means 'one of my' etc.:
a friend of mine = one of my friends
a sister of hers = one of her sisters

Personal pronouns

40 Form

		Subject	*Object*
Singular	*first person*	I	me
	second person	you	you
	third person	he/she/it	him/her/it
Plural	*first person*	we	us
	second person	you	you
	third person	they	them

The old form of the second person singular is:
thou (subject) *thee* (object)

41 Use of subject and object forms

A **you** and **it** present no difficulty as they have the same form for subject and object:
Did you see the snake? Yes, I saw it and it saw me.
Did it frighten you?

B First and third person forms (other than **it**)

1 **I, he, she, we, they** can be subjects of a verb:
I see it. *He knows you.* *They live here.*
or complements of the verb **to be:** *It is I.*
Normally, however, we use the object forms here:
Who is it? It's me. *Where's Tom? That's him over there.*
But if the pronoun is followed by a clause, we use the subject forms:
Surely the husband has the right to make the decisions since it is he who pays the bills.

2 **me, him, her, us, them** can be direct objects of a verb:
I saw her. *Tom likes them.*

or indirect objects:
Bill found me a job. *Ann gave him a book.* (See **79**.)
or objects of a preposition:
with him *for her* *without them* *to us*

42 The position of pronouns used as direct or indirect objects

A An indirect object comes before a direct object:
I told Tom/him a story.
I made Ann/her a cake.
I sent Bill the photos.

B However, if the direct object is a personal pronoun it is more usual to place it directly after the verb and use **to** or **for**:
I told it to him. *I made it for her.* *I sent them to him.*
(See **79**.)
This position rule does not apply to **one, some, any, none** etc. We can say either:
He bought one for Ann or *He bought Ann one.*
He gave something to Jack or *He gave Jack something.*

43 The position of pronoun objects of phrasal verbs

With many phrasal verbs a noun object can be either in the middle or at the end:
Blow the bridge up/Blow up the bridge.
Hand in your papers/Hand your papers in.
Hang your coat up/Hang up your coat.
Take your shoes off/Take off your shoes.
If, however, the object is a pronoun, it must be placed in the middle:
blow it up *hand them in* *hand it up* *take them off*
Similarly:
Bring back the books/Bring the books back/Bring them back.
Turn on the light/Turn the light on/Turn it on.
(See also chapter 32.)

44 The pronoun **it**

it is the third person singular neuter pronoun.
The same form, **it**, is used for subject and object. The possessive form is **its**. (Do not confuse this with **it's**, which is a contraction of **it is**.)
The plural for **it/its** is **they/them/their**, as for people.

Use

A **it** is normally used of a thing or an animal whose sex we don't know, and sometimes of a baby or small child:
This is my dictionary. I got it cheaply as its cover was torn.
Look at that bird. It always comes to my window.

it can be used of people in sentences such as:
ANN (on phone): *Who is that/Who is it?*
BILL: *It's me.*

We can also say:
It was Peter who lent us the money.
It was George who fell into the water.
(See **54** for the meaning of this form.)

B **it** is used in expressions of time, distance, weather, temperature, tide:
It is hot/cold/quiet/noisy in this room.
What time is it? It is six. *What's the date? It's the third of March.*
How far is it to York? It is 400 kilometres.
How long does it take to get there? It depends on how you go.
It is raining/snowing/freezing. *It's frosty.* *It's a fine night.*
It's high tide/low tide. *It's full moon tonight.*
In winter it's/it is dark at six o'clock.

Note also:
It's/It is three years since I saw him = I haven't seen him for three years. (See **182** E.)
(For **it is time** + subject + past tense, see also **288** B.)

C When an infinitive is subject of a sentence, we usually begin the sentence with **it** and put the infinitive later; i.e. we say:
It is easy to criticize instead of *To criticize is easy*
and *It is better to be early* instead of *To be early is better.*

Note also:
We found it easy/difficult/impossible to cross the road.
He thought it best to say nothing.
It never occurred to me to doubt him = I never thought of doubting him.

D **it** can be used similarly when the subject of a sentence is a clause.
It would be possible to say:
That he has not returned is strange.
That prices will go up is certain.
But it would be much more usual to say:
It is strange that he has not returned.
It is certain that prices will go up.

Note also:
It occurred to me that perhaps he was trying to shield someone.
It struck me that everyone was unusually silent.

E **it** also acts a subject for impersonal verbs:
it seems *it appears* *it looks* *it depends* *it happens*

45 **you** and **one** as indefinite pronouns

Either can be used:
Can one camp in the forest? *Can you camp in the forest?*
you is more common in ordinary conversation. It is a more 'friendly' pronoun and implies that the speaker can imagine himself in such a position. **one** is more impersonal and less often used, though the possessive **one's** is quite common:
It's easy to lose one's/your way in Venice.

The correct possessive form must be used:
One has to show one's pass at the door.
You have to show your pass at the door.

If instead of **one** or **you** we use **a/the**+noun, the possessive adjective will obviously be **her** or **his**:
One must be patient with one's children.
You must be patient with your children.
A parent must be patient with his children.

46 Use of **they/them/their** with **neither/either, someone/anyone/ no one** etc.

These expressions are singular and take a singular verb. Their personal pronouns therefore should be **he/she** and the possessive adjectives should be **his/her** (**he/his** for males and mixed sexes; **she/her** for females). But many native speakers find this troublesome and often use **they/their**, even when only one sex is involved:
Neither of them remembered their instructions.
Everyone has read the notice, haven't they?
Would anyone lend me their binoculars?
Everybody assembled in the hall where they were welcomed by the secretary.
Nobody objected, did they? (See also **21** D, **22**.)

Reflexive and emphasizing pronouns

47 A These are: **myself, yourself, himself, herself, itself, ourselves, yourselves, themselves.** Note the difference between the second person singular **yourself**, and the second person plural **yourselves**. The indefinite reflexive/emphasizing pronoun is **oneself**.

B Used as reflexive pronouns

myself, yourself etc. are used as objects of a verb when the action of the verb returns to the doer, i.e. when subject and object are the same person:

I cut myself. *He shaved himself.*
It is not always easy to amuse oneself on holiday.
Tom and Ann blamed themselves for the accident.

Note the change of meaning if we replace the reflexive pronoun by the reciprocal pronoun **each other**:

Tom and Ann blamed each other = Tom blamed Ann and Ann blamed Tom. (See also **27** D.)

myself, yourself etc. are used similarly after a verb + preposition:

He spoke to himself. *Did she pay for herself?*
Look after yourself. *Take care of yourselves.*
I'm annoyed with myself. *He sat by himself* (= alone).

We can also use **myself** etc. after verb + object + preposition:

She addressed the envelope to herself.

But if the preposition indicates locality, we use the ordinary, not the reflexive, pronouns:

Did you take your dog with you? *Has he any money on him?*
They put the child between them.

48 myself, himself, herself etc. used as emphasizing pronouns

myself etc. can also be used to emphasize a noun or pronoun:

The king himself gave her the medal.

When used in this way the pronoun is never essential and can be omitted without changing the sense. It usually emphasizes the subject of the sentence and is then placed after the subject:

Ann herself opened the door. *Tom himself went.*

Alternatively it can be placed after the object if there is one:

Ann opened the door herself

or after an intransitive verb:

Tom went himself.

If the intransitive verb is followed by a preposition + noun, the emphasizing pronoun can be placed after this noun:

Tom went to London himself or *Tom himself went to London.*

When it emphasizes another noun it is placed immediately after it:

I saw Tom himself. *I spoke to the President himself.*
She liked the diamond itself but not the setting.

Note the difference between:

I did it myself (it was done by me and not by someone else)
and *I did it by myself* (I did it without help).

7 Relative pronouns and relative clauses

There are three kinds of relative clauses: Defining (**49–55**), Non-defining (**56–9**) and Connective (**60–2**).

Defining relative clauses

49 These describe the preceding noun in such a way as to distinguish it from other nouns of the same class. A clause of this kind is essential to the clear understanding of the noun:
The man who told me this refused to give me his name.
'who told me this' is the relative clause. If we omit this, it is not clear what man we are talking about. Notice that there is no comma between a noun and a defining relative clause:
The noise that he made woke everybody up.

50 Relative pronouns used in defining relative clauses
These relatives vary slightly according to whether they refer to persons or things and according to whether they are subjects or objects of a verb or in the possessive case. They do not vary for singular or plural or masculine or feminine.
The forms are as follows:

	Subject	*Object*	*Possessive*
For persons	who that	who/whom that	whose
For things	which that	which that	whose/of which

It is sometimes essential to use **that** (see below).

51 Defining relative clauses: persons

A Subject: **who** or **that**

who is normally used:
The man who robbed you has been arrested.
The girls who serve in the shop are the owner's daughters.
The policeman who reported the accident thinks it was Tom's fault.
The book is about a man who deserts his wife.
The film is about a group of people who are trapped in a lift.

that is much less usual than **who** except after superlatives and after **all, nobody, no one, somebody, someone, anybody** etc., when either **who** or **that** can be used:

He was the best king who/that ever sat on the throne.
All who/that heard him were delighted. (Compare with **52** B.)

B Object of a verb: **whom** or **who** or **that**

The object form is **whom**, but this is considered very formal and seldom used in spoken English. Instead of **whom**, therefore, in spoken English we use **who** or **that** (**that** being more usual than **who**), and it is still more common to omit the object pronoun altogether:

The man whom I saw told me to come back today
or *The man who I saw . . .*
or *The man that I saw . . .*
or *The man I saw . . .* (relative pronoun omitted)
and *The girls whom he employs are always complaining about their long hours*
or *The girls that he employs . . .*
or *The girls he employs . . .* (relative pronoun omitted).

C With a preposition: **whom** or **that**

In formal English the preposition is placed before the relative pronoun, which must then be put into the form **whom**:

the man to whom I spoke

In informal speech, however, it is more usual to move the preposition to the end of the clause. **whom** then is often replaced by **that**, but it is still more common to omit the relative altogether:

the man who/whom I spoke to
or *the man that I spoke to*
or *the man I spoke to*

Similarly:

The man from whom I bought it told me to oil it
or *The man who/whom I bought it from . . .*
or *The man I bought it from . . .*
and *The friend with whom I was travelling could speak French*
or *The friend who/whom I was travelling with . . .*
or *The friend that I was travelling with . . .*
or *The friend I was travelling with . . .*

D Possessive

whose is the only possible form:

People whose rents have been raised can appeal.
The film is about a spy whose wife betrays him.

52 Defining relative clauses: things

A Subject

Either **which** or **that**; **which** is the more formal:

This is the picture which/that caused such a sensation.
The stairs which/that lead to the cellar are rather slippery.
(See also B below.)

B Object of a verb

which or **that**, or no relative at all:

The car which/that I hired broke down after five kilometres
or *The car I hired broke down after five kilometres.*

which is hardly ever used after **all, much, little, everything, none, no** and compounds of **no**, or after superlatives. Instead we use **that**, or omit the relative altogether, if it is the object of a verb:

All the apples that fall down are eaten by the pigs.
This is the best hotel (that) I know.

C Object of a preposition

The formal construction is preposition + **which**, but it is more usual to move the preposition to the end of the clause, using **which** or **that** or omitting the relative altogether:

The ladder on which I was standing began to slip
or *The ladder which/that I was standing on began to slip*
or *The ladder I was standing on began to slip.*

Note that **when** can replace **in/on which** (used of time):

the day when they arrived *the year when he was born*

where can replace **in/at which** (used of place):

the hotel where they were staying

why can replace **for which**:

The reason why he refused is . . .

when, where and **why** used in this way are called relative adverbs.

D Possessive

whose + a clause is possible but can often be replaced by **with** + a phrase:

Living in a house whose walls were made of glass would be horrible.
Living in a house with glass walls would be horrible.

53 The relative pronoun what

what = the thing that/the things that etc.:

The things that we saw astonished us
= *What we saw astonished us.*

When she sees the damage that you have done she will be furious
= *When she sees what you have done she will be furious.*
Be careful not to confuse the relative **what** with the connective relative **which**. Remember that **which** must refer to a word or group of words in the preceding sentence, while **what** does not refer back to anything. The relative **what** is also usually the object of a verb, while the connective **which** is usually the subject:
He said he had no money, which was not true.
Some of the roads were flooded, which made our journey more difficult. (See also **60**.)

54 it is/was + noun/pronoun + relative clause

It was Tom who helped us can be used instead of *Tom helped us* if we wish to emphasize that it was Tom and not someone else. Similarly, *It was in Rome that we met* emphasizes that Rome was the city, not Paris or London.
which is not normally used here, but any of the other relatives (except **what**) are possible.

55 A relative clause can sometimes be replaced by an infinitive or a participle

A After **the first/second** etc., and after **the last/only** and sometimes after superlatives:
the last man to leave the ship = the last man who left/leaves . . .
the only one to understand = the only one who understood/understands
Notice that the infinitive here replaces a subject pronoun + verb. It could not be used to replace an object pronoun + verb. For example the clause in *the first man that we saw* could not be replaced by an infinitive, for *the first man to see* would have a completely different meaning. If however **that** is the subject of a passive verb, e.g. *the first man that was seen*, we can replace the clause by a passive infinitive, e.g. *the first man to be seen.*

B When there is some idea of purpose or permission:
He has a lot of books to read = He has a lot of books that he can read/must read.
She had something to do = She had something that she could do/had to do.
a garden to play in = a garden they can/could play in
Note that here the infinitive replaces a verb + relative pronoun as object. It might be thought that these two uses of the infinitive would lead to confusion but in practice this is very rare as the meaning of the infinitive is made clear by the rest of the sentence.

By itself the phrase *the first man to see* could mean either *the first man that we must see* (*man* is the object) or *the first man who saw* (*man* is the subject), but when it is part of a sentence we can see at once which meaning is intended:

The first man to see is Tom = The first man that we must see is Tom

while *The first man to see me was Tom = The first man who saw me was Tom.*

C Relative clauses can sometimes be replaced by a present participle:

1 When the verb in the clause is in the continuous tense:

People who are/were waiting for the bus often shelter/sheltered in my doorway

= *People waiting for the bus often shelter/sheltered . . .*

2 When the verb in the clause expresses a habitual or continuous action:

Passengers who travel/travelled on this bus buy/bought their tickets in books

= *Passengers travelling . . .*

Boys who attend/attended this school have/had to wear uniform

= *Boys attending . . .*

a law which forbids/forbade the import = a law forbidding . . .

a notice which warns/warned people = a notice warning people

an advertisement which urges/urged = an advertisement urging

Similarly:

a petition asking *a letter ordering/demanding/telling*

a placard protesting *placards protesting*

3 When a verb in the clause expresses a wish, i.e. when the verb in the clause is **wish, desire, want, hope** (but not **like**):

People who wish to go on the tour must book = People wishing . . .

People who wished to go on the tour had to book

= *People wishing . . .*

fans who hope for a glimpse of the star = fans hoping . . .

fans who hoped for a glimpse of the star = fans hoping . . .

4 A non-defining clause (see next paragraph) containing one of the above verbs, or any verb of knowing or thinking, e.g. **know, think, believe, expect**, can be similarly replaced by a present participle:

Peter, who thought the journey would take at least two days, said . . .

= *Peter, thinking the journey would take at least two days, said . . .*

Tom, who expected to be paid the following week, offered . . .

= *Tom, expecting to be paid the following week, offered . . .*

Bill, who wanted to make an impression on Ann, took her to . . .

= *Bill, wanting to make an impression on Ann, took her to . . .*

Non-defining relative clauses

56 A Non-defining relative clauses are placed after nouns which are definite already. They do not therefore define the noun, but merely add something to it by giving some more information about it. Unlike defining relative clauses, they are not essential in the sentence and can be omitted without causing confusion. Also unlike defining relatives, they are separated from their noun by commas. The pronoun can never be omitted in a non-defining relative clause. The construction is fairly formal and more common in written than in spoken English.

B Relative pronouns used in non-defining relative clauses

These relatives do not vary for singular or plural, masculine or feminine:

	Subject	*Object*	*Possessive*
For persons	who	who/whom	whose
For things	which	which	whose/of which

57 Use for persons: **who, whom, whose**

A Subject: **who**

No other pronoun is possible. Note the commas.

My neighbour, who is very pessimistic, says there will be no apples this year.

Peter, who had been driving all day, suggested stopping at the next town.

Clauses such as these, which come immediately after the subject of the main verb, are found mainly in written English. In spoken English we would be more likely to say:

My neighbour is very pessimistic and says . . .

Peter had been driving all day, so/and he suggested . . .

But clauses placed later in the sentence, i.e. clauses coming after the object of the main verb, are quite common in conversation:

I've invited Ann, who lives in the next flat.

Clauses following a preposition + noun are also common:

I passed the letter to Peter, who was sitting beside me.

B Object: **whom, who**

The pronoun cannot be omitted. **whom** is the correct form, though **who** is sometimes used in conversation:

Peter, whom everyone suspected, turned out to be innocent.

As noted above, a non-defining clause in this position is unusual in spoken English. We would be more likely to say:

Everyone suspected Peter, but he turned out to be innocent.

But non-defining clauses coming later in the sentence, i.e. after the object of the main verb or after a preposition + noun, are common in conversation:

She wanted Tom, whom she liked, as a partner; but she got Jack, whom she didn't like.

She introduced me to her husband, whom I hadn't met before.

C Object of a preposition: **whom**

The pronoun cannot be omitted. The preposition is normally placed before **whom**:

Mr Jones, for whom I was working, was very generous about overtime payments.

It is however possible to move the preposition to the end of the clause. This is commonly done in conversation, and **who** then often takes the place of **whom**:

Mr Jones, who/whom I was working for, . . .

If the clause contains an expression of time or place, this will remain at the end:

Peter, with whom I played tennis on Sundays, was fitter than I was

could become

Peter, who/whom I played tennis with on Sundays, was fitter than I was.

D Possessive: **whose**

Ann, whose children are at school all day, is trying to get a job.

In conversation we would probably say:

Ann's children are at school all day, so she . . .

This is George, whose class you will be taking next week

or *This is George. You will be taking his class next week.*

I congratulated Mrs Jones, whose son had won the high jump.

58 both/some/most/all/several/few etc. + of + whom/which

This form can be used for both people and things. See examples below. Where the clause construction would sound heavy in speech a more informal equivalent is given in brackets.

Her brothers, both of whom work in Scotland, ring her up every week.

(Both her brothers work in Scotland, and/but they ring her up every week.)

I met the fruit-pickers, several of whom (or *five* etc. *of whom*) *were university students.*

(This would be quite usual in speech, but we could also say:
I met the fruit-pickers; several of them were . . .)

The house was full of boys, ten of whom were his own grandchildren.
(This could be used in speech, or *The house was full of boys; ten of them . . .*)
The buses, most of which were already full, were surrounded by an angry crowd.
(Most of the buses were full, and/but they were surrounded . . .)
I picked up the apples, some of which were badly bruised.
(This could be used in speech, or *I picked up the apples; some of them . . .*)
He went up the mountain with a group of people, few of whom were correctly equipped for such a climb.
(*He went up the mountain with a group of people; few of them were . . .*)

59 Non-defining relative clauses: **which, whose** (for things)

A Subject: **which**

that is not used here.
That tower block, which cost £5 million to build, has been empty for five years.
The 8.15 train, which is usually very punctual, was late today.
In speech we would be more likely to say:
That tower block cost £5 million to build and has been empty . . .
and *The 8.15 train is usually punctual, but it was late today.*

B Object: **which**

that is not used here, and the **which** can never be omitted:
She gave me this jumper, which she had knitted herself.
or *She gave me this jumper; she had knitted it herself.*
These books, which you can get at any bookshop, will give you all the information you need.
or *These books will give you all the information you need. You can get them at any bookshop.*

C Object of a preposition

The preposition comes before **which**, or (more informally) at the end of the clause:
Ashdown Forest, through which we'll be driving, isn't a forest any longer
or *Ashdown Forest, which we'll be driving through, isn't . . .*
His house, for which he paid £10,000 ten years ago, is now worth £30,000
or *His house, which he paid £10,000 for ten years ago, is now . . .*

D **which** with phrasal verbs

Combinations such as **look forward to, look after, put up with** (see chapter 32) should be treated as a unit, i.e. the preposition/adverb should not be separated from the verb:

This machine, which I have looked after for twenty years, is still working perfectly.

Your inefficiency, which we have put up with far too long, is beginning to annoy our customers.

E Possessive: **whose** or **of which**

whose is generally used both for animals and things. **of which**, for things, is possible but unusual except in very formal English:

His house, whose windows were all broken, was a depressing sight.

The car, whose handbrake wasn't very reliable, began to slide backwards.

Connective relative clauses

60 Pronouns **who, whom, whose, which**

These have the same form as non-defining relative clauses. They are usually placed after the object of the main verb:

I told Peter, who said it wasn't his business

or after the preposition + noun:

I threw the ball to Tom, who threw it to Ann.

Connective clauses do not describe their nouns but continue the story. They can be replaced by **and** or **but**:

I told Peter, but he said . . .

I threw the ball to Tom and he threw it . . .

As noted in **57** B non-defining relative clauses can also be placed after the object of the main verb or the object of a preposition. And sometimes it may be difficult to say whether a clause in this position is non-defining or connective. But there is no need for students to make this distinction, as there is no difference between the two forms.

More examples of connective clauses:

He ate a fungus, which made him ill = He ate a fungus and it made him ill.

We went with Peter, whose car broke down before we were halfway there.

We can use **one/two** etc., **some/several/few** etc. + **of** + **whom/which** as shown in **58**:

I bought a dozen eggs, six of which broke when I dropped the box at my door.

He introduced me to his children, one of whom offered to go with me as a guide.
The lorry crashed into a queue of people, several of whom had to have hospital treatment.

which can also stand for a whole clause:
They said they were French, which wasn't true = They said they were French, but this wasn't true.
The clock struck thirteen, which made everyone laugh.
He refused to do his share of the chores, which annoyed the others (his refusal annoyed them).
The rain rattled on the roof all night, which kept us awake.
She was much kinder to her youngest child than she was to the others, which, of course, made the others jealous.

what cannot be used as a connective relative.

61 The importance of commas in relative clauses

Remember that a defining relative clause is written without commas. Note how the meaning changes when commas are inserted:

1 *The travellers who knew about the floods took another road.*
2 *The travellers, who knew about the floods, took another road.*

In 1 we have a defining relative clause, which defines or limits the noun 'travellers'. This sentence therefore tells us that only the travellers who knew about the floods took the other road, and implies that there were other travellers who did not know and who took the flooded road. In 2 we have a non-defining clause, which does not define or limit the noun it follows. This sentence therefore implies that all the travellers knew about the floods and took the other road.

The boys who wanted to play football were disappointed when it rained.
The boys, who wanted to play football, were disappointed.

The first sentence implies that only some of the boys wanted to play football. There were presumably others who didn't mind whether it rained or not. The second sentence implies that all the boys wanted to play and all were disappointed.

The wine which was in the cellar was all ruined.
The wine, which was in the cellar, was all ruined.

The first sentence implies that only some of the wine was ruined. Presumably some was kept elsewhere and escaped damage. The second sentence states that all the wine was in the cellar and ruined.

62 whoever, whichever, whatever, whenever, wherever, however

These have a variety of meanings and can introduce relative and other clauses. The other clauses do not technically belong to this chapter but it seems best to group these **-ever** forms together.

A **whoever** (pronoun) and **whichever** (pronoun and adjective) can mean 'the one who', 'he who', 'she who':
Whoever gains the most points wins the competition.
Whichever of them gains the most points wins (**whichever** used as a pronoun).
Whichever team gains the most points wins (**whichever** used as an adjective).
Whoever gets home first starts cooking the supper.
Whichever of us gets home first starts cooking.
Whoever cleans your windows doesn't make a good job of it.

B **whatever** (pronoun and adjective), **whenever, wherever**
You can eat what/whatever you like (anything you like).
When you are older you can watch whatever programme you like.
My roof leaks when/whenever it rains (every time it rains).
You will see this product advertised everywhere/wherever you go.

C **whoever, whichever, whatever, whenever, wherever, however** can mean 'no matter who' etc.:
If I say 'heads, I win; tails, you lose', I will win whatever happens or *whichever way the coin falls.*
Whatever happens don't forget to write.
I'll find him, wherever he has gone (no matter where he has gone).

whatever you do is often placed before or after a request/command to emphasize its importance:
Whatever you do don't mention my name.

however is an adverb of degree and is used with an adjective or another adverb:
I'd rather have a room of my own, however small (it is), than share a room.
However hard I worked she was never satisfied.

D **whatever, wherever** can indicate the speaker's ignorance or indifference:
He lives in Wick, wherever that is. (I don't know where it is, and I'm not very interested.)
He says he's a phrenologist, whatever that is. (I don't know what it is and I'm not very interested.)

who ever? when ever? what ever? etc. may be written as separate words, but the meaning then changes (see **36**):

A: *I lost seven kilos in a month.*

B: *How ever did you lose so much in such a short time?*

A (suspiciously): *I know all about you!*

B (indignantly): *What ever do you mean?*

Where ever did you buy your wonderful carpets?

8 Adverbs

63 Kinds

There are eight kinds of adverbs:

1 of manner: *quickly, bravely, happily, hard, fast, well*
2 of place: *here, there, up, down, near, by* (see also **90**)
3 of time: *now, soon, yet, still, then, today*
4 of frequency: *twice, often, never, always, occasionally*
5 of certainty: *certainly, surely, definitely, obviously*
6 of degree: *very, fairly, rather, quite, too, hardly*
7 interrogative: *when? where? why?* (see **35**)
8 relative: *when, where, why* (see **52** C)

64 The formation of adverbs from adjectives

A Most adverbs of manner and some adverbs of degree are formed by adding **ly** to the corresponding adjectives:
slow, slowly *grave, gravely* *immediate, immediately*

Spelling notes:

1 A final **y** changes to **i**: *gay, gaily.*

2 A final **e** is retained: *extreme, extremely.*
Exceptions: *true, due, whole* become *truly, duly, wholly.*

3 Adjectives ending in **able/ible** drop the final **e** and add **y**:
sensible, sensibly *capable, capably*

4 Adjectives ending in a vowel + **l** follow the usual rule and add **ly**:
final, finally *beautiful, beautifully*

B Exceptions:

1 The adverb of **good** is **well**.

2 With the exception of **kindly**, adjectives ending in **ly** e.g. **friendly, likely, lonely, lovely, lowly** have no adverb form. To supply this deficiency we use a similar adverb or adverb phrase:
friendly (adj.) *in a friendly way* (adverb phrase)
likely (adj.) *probably* (adv.)

3 **high, low, deep, near, far, fast, hard, early, late, much, little, direct** (= in a straight line)**, straight, pretty, wrong, kindly, enough** can be used as adjectives or adverbs:

As adjectives	As adverbs
a high mountain	*The bird flew high.*
the near bank (the one nearest us)	*Don't come near.*

a fast train	*The train went fast.*
The work is hard (tiring or difficult).	*They worked hard* (energetically).
He took the most direct route.	*You can go direct from Victoria to Euston.*
Draw a straight line.	*He went straight home.*
She is a pretty girl.	*The problem is pretty* (very) *difficult.*
I have just enough time.	*He didn't run fast enough.*

4 The forms **highly, lowly, nearly, lately, hardly, directly, wrongly** exist, but have a narrower meaning than their corresponding adjectives.

highly is used only in an abstract sense:
He was highly placed = He had an important office.
They spoke very highly of him = They praised/recommended him.
lowly is an adjective meaning 'humble'.
deeply is used chiefly in an emotional sense:
He was deeply hurt = His feelings were very much hurt.
nearly = almost, **lately** = recently; for **hardly** see **76, 72.**
directly is chiefly used for time:
He'll be here directly (soon).
wrongly is most often used with a past participle:
You were wrongly informed (incorrectly informed).

5 **warmly, hotly, coolly, coldly, presently, shortly, scarcely** and **barely** also differ in meaning from their corresponding adjectives:

warmly, hotly, coolly and **coldly** are used mainly in an emotional sense:
She welcomed me warmly (in a friendly way).
He denied the accusation hotly (indignantly).
They behaved very coolly in a dangerous situation (calmly, courageously).
We received them coldly (in an unfriendly way).
presently = soon, **shortly** = briefly or soon; for **scarcely, barely** see **76.**

6 **surely** differs slightly from its adjective (see **69**).
just (fair, right, lawful) has the adverb **justly**. But **just** can also be an adverb of time (see **67, 180**) and degree (see **71**).

65 The comparison of adverbs

A The comparative and superlative forms

With adverbs of two or more syllables the comparative is formed by putting **more** before the adverb, and the superlative by putting **most** before the adverb:

Positive	Comparative	Superlative
quickly	*more quickly*	*most quickly*
fortunately	*more fortunately*	*most fortunately*

Single-syllable adverbs, however, and the adverb **early**, add **er, est**:

hard	*harder*	*hardest*
high	*higher*	*highest*
early	*earlier*	*earliest* (note the **y** becomes **i**)

Irregular comparisons:

well	*better*	*best*
badly	*worse*	*worst*
little	*less*	*least*
much	*more*	*most*
far	*farther*	*farthest* (of distance only)
	further	*furthest* (used of distance, time, and in an abstract sense)

B Constructions with comparisons (see also **311**)

Note that when the same verb is used in both clauses we normally express the second verb as an auxiliary.

1 With the positive form we use **as . . . as** with an affirmative verb, and **as/so . . . as** with a negative verb:
He worked as slowly as he dared.
He doesn't snore as/so loudly as you do.

2 With the comparative form we use **than**:
They arrived earlier than she did/than her (see **17**).
He eats more quickly than I do/than me.
He played better than he had ever played.
He went further than the other explorers.
They work harder than us/than we do.

the + comparative . . . **the** + comparative is also possible with adverbs:
The earlier you start the sooner you'll be back.

3 With the superlative it is possible to use **of** + noun:
He went the furthest of the explorers.
But this construction is not very common and such a sentence would normally be expressed by a comparative, as shown above (2).

A superlative adverb + **of all** is quite common:
He ran fastest of all.

But **of all** here very often refers to other actions by the same subject:
He likes swimming best of all (better than he likes anything else).
She works best of all when she is alone (better than at other times).
of all can be omitted:
He likes swimming best.

4 **most** placed before an adverb or adjective can also mean **very**:
She behaved most generously. *They were most apologetic.*

The position of adverbs

66 Adverbs of manner and place

A Manner

1 After the verb:
She danced beautifully.

2 After the object when there is one:
She worked hard. (See **76**.) *They speak English well.*
He gave her the money reluctantly.
Do not put an adverb between verb and object.

3 When we have verb + preposition + object, the adverb can be either before the preposition or after the object:
He looked at me suspiciously or *He looked suspiciously at me.*
But if the object contains a number of words we put the adverb before the preposition:
He looked suspiciously at everyone who got off the plane.

4 Similarly with verb + object sentences the length of the object affects the position of the adverb. If the object is short, we have verb + object + adverb, as shown in (2) above. But if the object is long we usually put the adverb before the verb:
She carefully picked up all the bits of broken glass.
He angrily denied that he had stolen the documents.
They secretly decided to leave the town.
Exceptions:
fast, hard, well and **badly.** See (7) below for **well** and **badly.**

5 Note that if an adverb is placed after a clause or a phrase, it is normally considered to modify the verb in that clause/phrase. If therefore we move *secretly* to the end of the last example above, we change the meaning:
They secretly decided . . . (the decision was secret).
They decided to leave the town secretly (the departure was to be secret).

6 Adverbs concerned with character and intelligence, e.g. **foolishly, kindly, generously, stupidly** etc., when placed before a verb express the idea that the action was foolish/kind/generous etc.

He kindly waited for me. *I foolishly forgot my passport.*
Would you kindly wait?

Note that we could also express this idea by:

It was kind of him to wait.
It was foolish of me to forget.
Would you be kind enough to wait? (See **249, 251**.)

The adverb can come after the verb, but the meaning changes:

He spoke kindly = His voice and words were kind.

These adverbs can also be placed after an object, but here again there is usually a difference of meaning, i.e. verb + object + adverb is not the same as adverb + verb + object:

He answered the questions foolishly (his answers were foolish).
He foolishly answered the questions (his action was foolish)
= *It was foolish of him to answer at all.*

7 **well** and **badly** can be used as adverbs of manner or adverbs of degree. As adverbs of manner they can come after the verb, after the object or before a past participle:

He reads well. *She speaks French well.*
The troops were well led. *He behaved badly.*
He treated her badly. *She was badly treated.*

well as an adverb of degree has the same position rules:

You know well that I can't drive. *He knows the town well.*
Shake the bottle well. *The children were well wrapped up.*

badly as an adverb of degree usually comes after the object or before the verb:

The door needed a coat of paint badly.
The door badly needed a coat of paint.

The meaning of both **well** and **badly** may depend on their position. Note the difference between:

You know well that I can't drive (there can be no doubt in your mind about this)
and *You know that I can't drive well* (I am not a good driver).

B Place (**here, there, near, behind, above** etc.)

Like adverbs of manner they are usually placed after the direct object if there is one, otherwise after the verb:

She painted that picture here. *I looked everywhere.*

If there is also an adverb of manner, the adverb of place comes after it:

He played well there.

somewhere, anywhere are used in the same way as **some** and **any** (see **24**):

I saw your keys somewhere. *Did you see my keys anywhere?*
I didn't see your keys anywhere.

nowhere is chiefly used in short answers:

Where are you going? Nowhere (i.e. I'm not going anywhere).

For prepositions/adverbs **near, above, below, behind, in, out, up, down** etc. see **90** and **72** B.

67 Adverbs of time

1 **afterwards, eventually, lately, recently, now, soon, then, today, tomorrow** etc.

2 **late, yet, still, just, immediately**

A Adverbs in group 1 above are normally placed at the very beginning or at the very end of a clause or sentence, the end position being the more usual:

He is coming tomorrow. *He is working now.*
Eventually it stopped raining. *Then we went home.*

B **late** and **immediately** come at the end of the clause/sentence:

He came late. *I'll go immediately.*

But when **immediately** is used as a conjunction and introduces a clause, it can be placed at the beginning of a sentence:

Immediately the rain stops we'll set out.

C **yet** and **still,** used as adverbs of time, have slightly different position rules. **yet** should be placed at the end of a sentence. **still** is usually placed before the verb, though after the verb **to be**:

He hasn't finished yet. ('He hasn't yet finished' is also possible but is a less usual order.)

She still dislikes him. *She is still in her bath.*

Note the difference in meaning:

yet means 'up to the time of speaking'. It is chiefly used with the negative or interrogative. It is not normally used with the affirmative:

He left home at six and hasn't returned yet.
The shop isn't open yet. We'll come back at nine.
Aren't you ready yet? (Used with the negative interrogative **yet** usually expresses surprise or impatience.)

still emphasizes that the action continues:

He is still in bed.

If the **still** is stressed in speech it expresses surprise or irritation. **still** is chiefly used with the affirmative but it can be used with the

negative also to emphasize the continuance of a negative action. Used in this way it is sometimes a possible alternative to **yet**:
He still doesn't understand. (The negative action of 'not understanding' continues.)
He doesn't understand yet. (The positive action of 'understanding' hasn't yet started.)
But it is on the whole safer to use **still** with the affirmative only.

Both these words can also be used as conjunctions:
You knew that the bridge was dangerous. Yet you didn't repair it.
I know that you aren't a doctor. Still (i.e. nevertheless) *you could have bandaged his cuts.*

D **just** as an adverb of time is used with perfect tenses and is placed after the auxiliary:
They have just left. (See **180**.)
I had just posted the letter when I remembered that I hadn't enclosed the cheque.
(For **just** as an adverb of degree, see **71**.)

68 Adverbs of frequency

1 **always, continually, frequently, occasionally, often, once, twice, periodically, repeatedly, usually** etc.
2 **ever, never, rarely, seldom, hardly ever**

Adverbs in both the above groups are normally placed next to verbs:

A They are placed after the simple tenses of **to be**:
He is always in time for meals

B but before the simple tenses of all other verbs:
They sometimes stay up all night.

C With tenses consisting of more than one verb, they are placed after the first auxiliary, or, with interrogative verbs, after auxiliary + subject:
Have you ever ridden a camel? *He can never understand.*
You have often been told not to do that.

Exceptions:

1 **used to** and **have to** prefer the adverb in front of them:
You hardly ever have to remind him; he always remembers.

2 Frequency adverbs are often placed before auxiliaries when these are used alone, in additions to remarks or in answers to questions:
Can you park your car near the shops? Yes, I usually can.
He expects me to be ready when he comes, but I very rarely am.
I know I should take exercise, but I never do.

3 When, to give emphasis to a compound verb, the auxiliary is stressed, the adverb of frequency is usually placed before the auxiliary:
I never ˈ*can remember.* *She hardly ever* ˈ*has met him.*
Similarly when **do** is added for emphasis:
But I always ˈ*do arrive in time.*
Note, however, that emphasis could also be given by stressing the frequency adverb and leaving it in its usual position after the auxiliary:
You should ˈ*always check your oil before starting.*

D Adverbs in group 1 above can also be put at the beginning or end of a sentence or clause.

Exceptions:

always, which can be placed at the end but is rarely found at the beginning of a sentence/clause.

often can be placed at the beginning, but if put at the end normally requires **very** or **quite**:
Often he walked. *He walked quite often.*

Adverbs in group 2 above, **hardly ever, never, rarely, seldom** (but not **ever** alone), can also be put at the beginning of a sentence, but inversion of the following main verb then becomes necessary:
Hardly ever did they manage to meet unobserved. (See **72**.)

Note that **hardly ever, rarely** and **seldom** are used with affirmative verbs only. **never** is normally used with the affirmative, though the interrogative is possible.

(For **hardly, never, ever** see **76**.)

69 Adverbs expressing degrees of certainty

1 **apparently, certainly, evidently, obviously, presumably, undoubtedly**
2 **clearly, definitely**
3 **surely**

Adverbs in group 1 above can either follow the rules for group 1 in **68** and be placed:

after **be:**
He is undoubtedly more intelligent than his brother

but before main verbs:
They certainly worked hard.
They have presumably sold their house.

or be placed at the beginning or end of a sentence or clause:
Apparently he knew the town well.
He knew the town well apparently.

clearly and **definitely** can be placed at the beginning or end, but the beginning position is less usual.

surely is normally placed at the beginning or end, though it can also be next to the verb:

Surely you've saved some money?
You've saved some money surely?
You've surely saved some money?

Note that though the adjectives **sure** and **certain** mean more or less the same, the adverbs differ in meaning:

certainly = definitely:

He was certainly there; there is no doubt about it.

surely indicates that the speaker is not quite sure that the statement which follows is true. He thinks it is, but wants reassurance.

Surely you know Peter? (I feel almost sure that you know him.)

70 Order of adverbs and adverb phrases of time, manner and place when they occur in the same sentence

Time expressions are normally placed at the beginning or end of sentences (see **67**):

On Monday he bought the tickets.
He bought the tickets on Monday.

Where there is an adverb of manner as well as a time expression, it will come after the verb, or after the object, if there is one:

On Monday he played well. *He played well on Monday.*
Every weekend she cleaned the house thoroughly.
She cleaned the house thoroughly every weekend.

i.e. if the time expression is at the end of the sentence, the adverb of manner will come before it.

Adverbs or adverb phrases of place normally come after adverbs of manner:

She put the bottles carefully on the doorstep.

We can add a time expression:

Every morning she put the bottles carefully on the doorstep.
She put the bottles carefully on the doorstep every morning.
He played very well at Wembley yesterday.

71 Adverbs of degree (**almost, nearly, quite, just, too, enough, extremely, absolutely, entirely, completely, really, so, well, only** etc.)

A An adverb of degree modifies an adjective or another adverb. It is placed before the adjective or adverb:

It was too hot to work.
The film was so good that I saw it twice.
He played extremely badly. *I know him quite well.*

B **enough** follows its adjective or adverb:
He didn't work quickly enough. *The box isn't big enough.*
(For **too/enough** + infinitive see **251**.)

C The following adverbs of degree can also modify verbs: **almost, nearly, quite, hardly, scarcely, barely** and **just**. They are then placed before the main verb, i.e. they obey the same rules as adverbs of frequency (see **68**):
I quite understand. *He can nearly swim.* *I am just going.*
I really enjoyed it.

D **only** can also modify verbs. It is supposed to be placed next to the word to which it applies, preceding verbs, adjectives and adverbs and preceding or following nouns and pronouns:
1 *He had only six apples* (i.e. not more than six).
2 *He only lent the car* (i.e. he didn't give it).
3 *He lent the car to me only* (i.e. not to anyone else).
4 *I believe only half of what he said.*
But in spoken English people usually put it before the verb, obtaining the required meaning by stressing the word to which the **only** applies:
He only had ˈsix apples is the same as 1 above.
He only lent the car to ˈme is the same as 3 above.
I only believed ˈhalf etc. is the same as 4.

E **just**, like **only**, should precede the word it qualifies:
I'll buy just one. *I had just enough money.*
It can also be placed next to the verb:
I'll just buy one. *I just had enough money.*
But sometimes this change of order would change the meaning:
Just sign here means *This is all you have to do.*
Sign just here means *Sign in this particular spot.*

72 Inversion of the verb after certain adverbs

A Certain adverbs and adverb phrases, mostly with a restrictive or negative sense, can for emphasis be placed first in a sentence and are then followed by the inverted (i.e. interrogative) form of the verb. The most important of these are: **never, seldom, scarcely, ever, scarcely . . . when, hardly . . . when, no sooner . . . than, nowhere, in no circumstances, on no account, only by, only then, only when, only in this way, not till, not only, so, neither, nor**:

I have never before been asked to accept a bribe.
Never before have I been asked to accept a bribe.

He had hardly left the house when the storm broke.
Hardly had he left the house when the storm broke.

He had no sooner left the house than the storm broke.
No sooner had he left the house than the storm broke.

This switch must not be touched on any account.
On no account must this switch be touched.

He was able to make himself heard only by shouting at the top of his voice.

Only by shouting at the top of his voice was he able to make himself heard.

He didn't realize that he had lost his keys till he got home.
Not till he got home did he realize that he had lost his keys.
They not only rob you, they smash everything.
Not only do they rob you, they smash everything.

A: *I'll come earlier next time.* B: *I will too/So will I.*

A: *I haven't got a ticket.* B: *I haven't either* or *Neither/Nor have I.*

He became so suspicious that . . .
So suspicious did he become that . . .

Note also:
He had no money and didn't know anyone he could borrow from.
He had no money, nor did he know anyone he could borrow from.
neither could not be used in this sentence. (See also **94** B, **108**.)

B The adverbs **in, out, up, down, round, over, back, forward** etc. when placed at the beginning of a sentence are followed by verb + subject in that order:
In came Tom. *Up jumped two large dogs.*
Down fell half a dozen apples.

But if the subject is a pronoun no inversion is necessary:
In he came. *Back he went again.*

The meaning and use of certain adverbs

73 **fairly** and **rather**

A Both can mean 'moderately', but **fairly** is chiefly used with 'favourable' adjectives and adverbs (e.g. **good, bravely, well, nice** etc.), while **rather** is chiefly used in this sense before 'unfavourable' adjectives and adverbs (e.g. **bad, stupidly, ugly** etc.):
Tom is fairly clever, but Peter is rather stupid.

He is fairly rich, but she is rather poor.
You did fairly well in your exam, but Ann did rather badly.
This case is rather heavy, but that one is fairly light.
Note that **quite** could replace **fairly** above. It would normally have more force than **fairly**.
The indefinite article can be placed before or after **rather**:
This is rather a silly book or *a rather silly book.*
With **fairly** the article must come first:
a fairly interesting lecture
With adjectives/adverbs such as **fast, slow, thin, thick, hot, cold** etc., which are not in themselves either 'favourable' or 'unfavourable', the speaker can express approval by using **fairly** and disapproval by using **rather**:
This soup is fairly hot implies that the speaker likes hot soup, while *This soup is rather hot* implies that it is a little too hot for him.

B **rather** can be used before **alike, like, similar, different** etc. and before comparatives. It then means 'a little' or 'slightly':
Siamese cats are rather like dogs in some ways.
The weather was rather worse than I had expected.
fairly cannot be used in this way.

C **rather** can be used before certain 'favourable' adjectives/adverbs such as **good, well, pretty, clever, amusing** but its meaning then changes; it becomes nearly equivalent to **very**, and the idea of disapproval vanishes:
She is rather clever is nearly the same as *She is very clever.*
rather used in this way is obviously much more complimentary than **fairly**. For example the expression *It is a fairly good play* would, if anything, discourage others from going to see it. But *It is rather a good play* is definitely a recommendation.
Occasionally **rather** used in this way conveys the idea of surprise:
ANN: *I suppose the house was filthy.*
TOM: *No, as a matter of fact it was rather clean.*

D **rather** can also be used before **enjoy, like** and sometimes before **dislike, object** and some similar verbs:
I rather like the smell of petrol.
Most people dislike driving on icy roads, but he rather enjoys it.
When he finally persuaded me to try oysters I found that I rather liked them.
rather here is chiefly used to express a liking which is a surprise to others or to the speaker himself.

It can also be used as in C above, to strengthen the verb:
I rather like Tom would normally imply greater interest than *I like Tom.*

But **rather** in this sense should be used sparingly.

For **would rather** see **230, 288, 243.**

74 quite

This is a confusing word because it has two meanings.

A It means 'completely' when it is used with a word or phrase which can express the idea of completeness: e.g. **full, empty, finished, wrong, right, all right, sure, certain, determined, ready** etc., and when it is used with a very strong adjective/adverb such as **perfect, amazing, horrible, extraordinary**:
The bottle was quite empty. *You're quite wrong.*
It's quite extraordinary; I can't understand it at all.

B When used with other adjectives/adverbs, **quite** has a slightly weakening effect, so that **quite good** is normally less complimentary than **good**. **quite** used in this way has approximately the same meaning as **fairly** but its strength can vary very much according to the way it is stressed:
quite ˈgood (weak **quite**, strong **good**) is very little less than 'good'.
ˈquite ˈgood (equal stress) means 'moderately good'.
ˈquite good (strong **quite**, weak **good**) is much less than 'good'.
The less **quite** is stressed the stronger the following adjective/adverb becomes. The more **quite** is stressed the weaker its adjective/adverb becomes.

Note the position of **a/an**:
quite a long walk *quite an old castle*

75 much

In the affirmative **much** is usually preceded by **very**:
I liked/enjoyed it very much. *Thank you very much.*

But **much** does not need **very** in the negative:
I don't like it much. *I don't much like it.*

much can also be an adverb of degree used with comparatives:
It is much better to say nothing.
The journey takes much longer when the roads are crowded.

76 hardly, barely, scarcely and never, ever

A **hardly, barely, scarcely**

These three are very similar. They are almost negative in meaning.

hardly is chiefly used with **any, ever, at all** or the verb **can**:
hardly any = very, very little/few.
hardly ever = very, very seldom.
hardly used with **can** means 'only with difficulty'.
I have hardly any money (i.e. very, very little money).
I hardly ever go out (i.e. I very, very seldom go out).
I can hardly see the mark (i.e. the mark is difficult to see, or it is dark, or I have bad sight).

hardly may also be used on its own:
He hardly limps at all.

Be careful not to confuse **hard** with **hardly**:
He looked hard at it = He stared at it.
He hardly looked at it = He almost ignored it/He gave it only a brief glance.

barely means 'no more than' and is often used with adjectives such as **enough** and **sufficient**:
He had barely enough to eat (implying that he was often hungry).
He was barely sixteen (i.e. only just sixteen, no older).
I can barely see it (i.e. I can only just see it).

scarcely means 'only just/not quite'. It is therefore a little more negative than **barely**:
There were barely (= not more than) *a hundred people there.*
There were scarcely (= probably less than) *a hundred people there.*

B **never, ever**

never is used with an affirmative verb. It normally means 'at no time':
I never saw him again. *I never saw him after that.*

never + affirmative, however, can be used instead of an ordinary negative verb:
I waited for him but he never turned up (he didn't turn up).

ever means 'at any time' and is chiefly used with the interrogative:
Have you ever marched in a demonstration?
A possible answer would be *No, I never have.*

For **ever** used after **how, where** etc. see **36** and **62.**
For **ever, never** in comparisons see **16** C.

9 Prepositions

77 Introduction

Prepositions are short words normally placed before nouns or pronouns (but see **78** about possible alternative positions).

Prepositions can also be followed by verbs, but the verb must be in the gerund form:

He is talking of emigrating. *They succeeded in escaping.*

The student has two main problems with prepositions. He has to know

1 whether in any construction a preposition is required or not, and
2 which preposition to use when one is required.

The first problem can be especially troublesome to a European student, who may find that a certain construction in his own language requires a preposition, whereas a similar one in English does not, and vice versa: e.g. in most European languages purpose is expressed by a preposition + infinitive; in English it is expressed by the infinitive only: *I came here to study.*

The student should note also that many words used mainly as prepositions can also be used as conjunctions and adverbs. Where this is the case it will be pointed out in the following paragraphs.

78 Position of prepositions

A As stated above, prepositions normally precede nouns or pronouns. In two constructions, however, it is possible to move the preposition to the end of the sentence:

1 Questions beginning with a preposition + **whom/which/what/whose**

Instead of	we can say
To whom were you talking?	*Who were you talking to?*
With what did you open it?	*What did you open it with?*
In which drawer does he keep it?	*Which drawer does he keep it in?*

It used to be thought ungrammatical to end a sentence with a preposition, but it is now accepted as a colloquial form.

2 Similarly in relative clauses, a preposition placed before **whom/which** can be moved to the end of the clause. The relative pronoun is then often omitted:

the people with whom I was travelling can become
the people I was travelling with.
the company from which I hire my TV set can become
the company I hire my TV set from.

B With verb + preposition combinations (see chapter 32) the preposition normally remains immediately after the verb:
The children I was looking after were interested in puppets.
Which flat did they break into?

In verb + adverb combinations the adverb remains in this position or is placed after the object:
They blew up the bridge/They blew it up.
Which bridge did they blow up?

79 Omission of **to** and **for** before indirect objects

A 1 A sentence such as *I gave the book to Tom* could also be expressed *I gave Tom the book*, i.e. the indirect object can be placed first and the preposition **to** omitted.

We can use this construction with the following verbs: **bring, give, hand, leave** (in a will), **lend, offer, pass** (= hand), **pay, play** (an instrument), **promise, sell, send, show, sing, take, tell** (= narrate, inform):
I showed the map to Bill = I showed Bill the map.
They sent £5 to Mr Smith = They sent Mr Smith £5.

2 Similarly *I'll find a job for Ann* could be expressed *I'll find Ann a job* (putting the indirect object first and omitting **for**). This construction is possible after **book, build, buy, cook (bake, fry, boil etc.), fetch, get, keep, knit, leave, make, order, reserve**:
I'll get a drink for you = I'll get you a drink.
I bought a book for James = I bought James a book.

B Normally either construction can be used. But:

1 The construction without preposition is preferred when the direct object is a phrase or clause:
Show me ***what you've got in your hand.*** *Tell her* ***the whole story.***

2 The construction with preposition is preferred

1 When the indirect object is a phrase or a clause:
We kept seats for ***everyone on our list****/for* ***everyone who had paid.***
I had to show my pass to ***the man at the door.***

2 When the direct object is **it** or **them.** Sentences such as:
They kept it for Mary. *She made them for Bill.*
We sent it to George.
cannot be expressed by a verb + noun + pronoun construction.

If the indirect object is also a pronoun (*I sent it to him*) it is sometimes possible to reverse the pronouns and omit **to** (*I sent him it*), but this cannot be done with **for** constructions and is better avoided.

This restriction does not apply to other pronoun objects:
I sent one to Bill = I sent Bill one.
He bought some for Mary = He bought Mary some.

C **tell, show, promise** can be used with indirect objects only, without **to**:
tell him *show him* *promise us*

read, write can be used similarly, but require **to**:
read to me *write to them*

play, sing can be used with **to** or **for**:
play to us *play for us* *sing to us* *sing for us*

80 Use and omission of **to** with verbs of communication

A Verbs of command, request, invitation and advice

advise, ask, beg, command, encourage, implore, invite, order, recommend, remind, request, tell, urge, warn can be followed directly by the person addressed (without **to**) + infinitive:
They advised him to wait. *I urged her to try again.* (See **301**.)

The person addressed (without **to**) can be used after **advise, remind, tell, warn** with other constructions also:
He reminded them that there were no trains after midnight.
They warned him that the ice was thin/They warned him about the ice.

But note that **recommend** when used with other constructions needs **to** before the person addressed:
He recommended me to buy it but *He recommended it to me.*
(*He recommended me* would mean he said I was suitable.)

With **ask** the person addressed is often optional. The preposition **to** is never used here:
He asked (me) a question. *He asked (me) if I wanted to apply.*
She asked (her employer) for a day off.

B **call** (= shout), **complain, describe, explain, grumble, murmur, mutter, say, shout, speak, suggest, talk, whisper** need **to** before the person addressed, though it is not essential to mention this person:
Peter complained (to her) about the food.
She said nothing (to her parents). *He spoke English (to them).*

shout at can be used when the subject is angry with the other person:

He shouted at me to get out of his way.
Compare with *He shouted to me* which means he raised his voice because I was at a distance.

81 Prepositions of time and date: **at, on, by, in**

A **at, on**

at a time:
at dawn   *at six*   *at midnight*   *at 4.30*

at an age:
at sixteen/at the age of sixteen   *She got married at seventeen.*

on a day/date:
on Monday   *on June 4*   *on Christmas Day*

Exceptions:
at night   *at Christmas, at Easter* (the period not the day only)

on the morning/afternoon/evening/night of a certain date:
We arrived on the morning of the sixth.

B **by** a time/date/period = at that time or before/not later than that date. It often implies 'before that time/date'.
The train starts at 6.10, so you had better be at the station by 6.00.
By May my garden will be a mass of blossom.

by is often used with a perfect tense, particularly the future perfect:
By the end of July I'll have read all those books.
By next summer he'll have taken his final exams.
By (the age of) fifteen he had mastered violin technique.

C **on time, in time, in good time**

on time = at the time arranged, not before, not after:
The 8.15 train started on time = It started at 8.15.

in time/in time for + noun = not late; **in good time (for)** = with a comfortable margin:
Passengers should be in time for their train.
I arrived at the concert hall in good time (for the concert). (Perhaps the concert began at 7.30 and I arrived at 7.15.)

D **on arrival, on arriving, on reaching, on getting to**

on arrival/on arriving, he . . . = when he arrives/arrived, he . . .

on can also be used similarly with the gerund of certain other verbs (chiefly verbs of information):
On checking, she found that some of the party didn't know the way.
On hearing that the plane had been diverted, they left the airport.
On learning that there were no late buses, they decided to go to the early performance.

E **at the beginning/end, in the beginning/end, at first/at last**

at the beginning (of)/at the end (of) = literally at the beginning/end.
At the beginning of a book there is often a table of contents.
At the end there may be an index.

in the beginning/at first = in the early stages. It implies that later on there was a change.

In the beginning/At first we used hand tools. Later we had machines.

in the end/at last = eventually/after some time.
At first he opposed the marriage, but in the end he gave his consent.

82 Time: **from, since, for, during**

A **from, since** and **for**

1 **from** is normally used with **to** or **till/until**:
Most people work from nine to/till five.

from can also be used of place: *Where do you come from?* (See **84** A.)

2 **since** is used for time, never for place, and means 'from that time to the time of speaking'. It is often used with a present perfect or past perfect tense. (See **182–3**.)
He has been here since Monday (from Monday till now).
He wondered where Ann was. He had not seen her since their quarrel.

since can also be a conjunction of time:
He has worked for us ever since he left school.
It is two years since I last saw Tom
= I last saw Tom two years ago/I haven't seen Tom for two years.

since can also introduce other types of clause:
Since you don't trust him, why do you employ him?
= Seeing that/As you don't trust him . . .

3 **for** is used of a period of time: **for six years, for two months, for ever**:
Bake it for two hours. *He travelled in the desert for six months.*

for + a period of time can be used with a present perfect tense or past perfect tense for an action which extends up to the time of speaking:
He has worked here for a year = He began working here a year ago and still works here.
for used in this way is replaceable by **since** with the point in time when the action began:
He has worked here since this time last year.

B. **during** and **for**

during is used with known periods of time, i.e. periods known by name, such as Christmas, Easter, or periods which have been already defined:

during the summer (of that year) *during 1941* *during the Middle Ages* *during my holidays* *during his childhood*

The action can either last the whole period or occur at some time within the period:

It rained all Monday but stopped raining during the night (at some point of time).

He was ill for a week, and during that week he ate nothing.

for (indicating purpose) may be used before known periods:

I went there/I hired a car/I rented a house for my holidays/for the summer.

for has various other uses:

He asked for £5. *I paid £1 for it.* *I left it for you.*
(See **79** B.)

for can also be a conjunction. (See **93**.)

83 Time: **to, till/until, after, afterwards** (adverb)

A **to** and **till/until**

to can be used of time and place (see **84**); **till/until** of time only.

We can use **from . . . to . . .** or **from . . . till/until . . .**

They played bridge from 6.00 to midnight.
They played bridge from 6.00 till midnight.

But if we have no **from** we use **till/until**, not **to**:

Let's start now and work till dark. (**to** would not be possible here.)

till is often used with a negative verb to emphasize lateness:

We didn't get home till 2 a.m.
He usually pays me on Friday but last week he didn't pay me till the following Monday.

till is very often used as a conjunction of time:

We'll stay here till it stops raining.
Go on till you see a swimming bath on your right.

B **after** and **afterwards** (adverb)

after is a preposition and must be followed by a noun, pronoun or gerund:

It is unwise to bathe immediately after a meal/after eating.
It is unwise to have a meal and bathe immediately after it.

If we do not wish to use a noun/pronoun or gerund, we cannot use **after**, but must use **afterwards** (= **after that**) or **then**:

They had a bathe and after the bathe played games on the beach

or *They had a bathe and afterwards played games/played games afterwards*

or *They had a bathe and then played games.*

afterwards can be used at either end of the clause and can be modified by **soon, immediately, not long** etc.:

Soon afterwards we got a letter. *We got a letter soon afterwards.*

84 Prepositions of travel and movement: **from, to, at, in, by, on, into, onto, off, out, out of**

A We travel **from** our starting place **to** our destination.

They flew/drove/cycled/walked from Paris to Rome.

When are you coming back to England?

We also send/post letters etc. **to** people and places. (But see note on **home** below.)

B **arrive at/in, get to, reach** (without preposition)

We **arrive in** a town or country, **at** or **in** a village, **at** any other destination:

They arrived in Spain/in Madrid.

I arrived at the hotel/at the airport/at the bridge/at the crossroads.

get to can be used with any destination, and so can **reach**:

He got to the station just in time for his train.

I want to get to Berlin before dark.

They reached the top of the mountain before sunrise.

get in (adverb) can mean 'arrive at a destination'. It is chiefly used of trains:

What time does the train get in? (reach the terminus/our station)

Note also **get there/get back** (adverbs).

C **home**

We can use **go/come/return/arrive/get** etc. + **home** without a preposition:

It took us an hour to get home. *They went home by bus.*

But if **home** is preceded or followed by a descriptive word or phrase a preposition is necessary:

She returned to her parents' home. (See **6** A.)

D Method of transport: **by, on, get in/into/on/onto/off/out of**

We can travel **by** car (but **in** the/my/Tom's car), **by** bus/train/ plane/ helicopter/hovercraft etc. and **by** sea/air. (We can also travel **by** a certain route, or **by (via)** a certain place: *We went by the M4* or *We went by Reading.*)

We can walk or go **on** foot. We can cycle or go **on** a bicycle or **by** bicycle. We can ride or go **on** horseback.

We get **into** a public or private vehicle, or get **in** (adverb).

We get **on/onto** a public vehicle, or get **on** (adverb).

But we go **on board** a boat (= embark).

We get **on/onto** a horse/camel/bicycle.

We get **out of** a public or private vehicle, or get **out** (adverb).

We get **off** a public vehicle, a horse, bicycle, etc., or get **off** (adverb).

E **get in/into/out/out of** can also be used of buildings, institutions and countries instead of **go/come/return** etc. when there is some difficulty in entering or leaving:

I've lost my keys! How are we going to get into the flat/to get in?
The house is on fire! We had better get out (of the house)!
It's difficult to get into a university nowadays.

F Giving directions: prepositions and adverbs **at, on, to, into, along** etc. and the conjunction **till**:

Turn right/left at the Post Office/at the second traffic lights etc.
Take the first/second etc. turning on/to the right/left or *on/to your right/left.*
Turn right/left into Fleet Street.
Go on (adverb) *to the end of the road.* (**till** could not be used here.)
Go along the Strand till you see the Savoy on your right.
You will find the bank on your left halfway down the street.
When you come out of the station you will find the bank opposite you/in front of you.
Get out (of the bus) at the tube station and walk on (adverb) *till you come to a pub.*
Get off (the bus) and walk back (adverb) *till you come to some traffic lights.*

Be careful not to confuse **to** and **till** (see also **83**).

85 at, in   in, into   on, onto

A **at** and **in**

(For **arrive in/at** see **84** B.)

at

We can be **at** home, **at** work, **at** the office, **at** school, **at** the university, **at** an address, **at** a certain point e.g. **at** the bridge, **at** the crossroads, **at** the bus-stop.

in

We can be **in** a country, a town, a village, a square, a street, a room, a forest, a wood, a field, a desert or any place which has boundaries or is enclosed.

But a small area such as a square, a street, a room, a field might be used with **at** when we mean 'at this point' rather than 'inside'.

We can be **in** or **at** a building. **in** means inside only. **at** could mean inside or in the grounds or just outside. If someone is 'at the station' he could be in the street outside, or in the ticket office/waiting room/restaurant or on the platform.

We can be **in** or **at** the sea, a river, lake, swimming pool etc. **in** here means actually in the water:

The children are swimming in the river.

at the sea means 'near/beside the sea'. But **at sea**, without article, means 'on a ship' (see **6** B).

B **in** and **into**

in as shown above normally indicates position.

into indicates movement, entrance:

They climbed into the lorry. *I poured the beer into a tankard.*

Thieves broke into my house/My house was broken into.

With the verb **put** however, either **in** or **into** can be used:

He put his hands in/into his pockets.

in can also be an adverb:

Come in = Enter. *Get in* (into the car).

C **on** and **onto**

on can be used for both position and movement:

He sat on his case. *Snow fell on the hills.*

He went on board ship.

onto can be used (chiefly of people and animals) when there is movement involving a change of level:

People climbed onto their roofs. *We lifted him onto the table.*

The cat jumped onto the mantelpiece.

on can also be an adverb: *Go on.* *Come on.*

86 above, over, under, below, beneath

A **above** and **over**

above (preposition and adverb) and **over** (preposition) can both mean 'higher than' and sometimes either can be used:

The helicopter hovered above/over us.

Flags waved above/over our heads.

But **over** can also mean 'touching' or 'covering', and **above** cannot have this meaning:
We put a rug over him.

over can also mean 'across', 'from one side to the other', 'more than':
He lives over the mountain.   *There is a bridge over the river.*
I paid over £5.

Both can mean higher in rank. But *He is over me* would normally mean 'He is my immediate superior', 'He supervises my work'. **above** would not have this meaning.

If we have a bridge over a river, *above the bridge* means 'upstream'.

B **below and under**

below (preposition and adverb) and **under** (preposition) can both mean 'lower than' and sometimes either can be used. But **under** can indicate contact:
She put the letter under her pillow.
The ice crackled under his feet.
With **below** there is always a space between the two surfaces:
They live below us (We live on the fourth floor and they live on the third). Similarly: *We live above them.* (See A above.)

below and **under** can mean 'junior in rank'. But *He is under me* implies that I am his immediate superior. **below** does not have this meaning.

(Both **over** and **under** can be used as adverbs, but with a change of meaning.)

C **beneath** can sometimes be used instead of **under**, but it is safer to keep it for abstract meanings:
He would think it beneath him to tell a lie.
She married beneath her (into a lower social class).

D **beside, between, behind, in front of, opposite**

Imagine a theatre with rows of seats: A, B, C etc., Row A being nearest the stage.

In Row A are	Tom	Ann	Bill
In Row B are	Mary	Bob	Jane

This means that:
Tom is beside Ann; Mary is beside Bob etc.
Ann is between Tom and Bill; Bob is between Mary and Jane.
Mary is behind Tom; Tom is in front of Mary.

But if Tom and Mary are having a meal and Tom is sitting at one side of the table and Mary at the other, we do not use **in front of**, but say *Tom is sitting opposite Mary* or *Tom is facing Mary.*

But *He stood in front of me* could mean either 'He stood with his back to me' or 'He faced me'. Note that *He stood before me* could also be used.

People living on one side of a street will talk of the houses on the other side as *the houses opposite (us)* rather than *the houses in front of us.*

With other things, however, these restrictions do not apply:
She put the plate on the table in front of him. (*before* would also be possible.)
She sat with a book in front of her. (*before* is also possible.)
Where's the bank? There it is, just in front of you!
There's a carpark in front of/at the back of the hotel.

E Don't confuse **beside** with **besides**.

beside = at the side of
besides (preposition and adverb) = in addition to
I do all the cooking and cleaning and besides that I help my husband with his bookwork.
Besides doing the cleaning I help my husband.

F **between** and **among**

between normally relates a person/thing to two other people/things, but it can be used of more when we have a definite number in mind:
Luxemburg lies between Belgium, Germany and France.

among relates a person/thing to more than two others; normally we have no definite number in mind:
a village among the hills
He was happy to be among friends again.

G **with** could also be used instead of **among** in the last sentence above. Also, of course, with a singular object: *He was with a friend.*

Examples of other uses:

He cut it with a knife.
Don't touch it with bare hands.
The mountains were covered with snow.
I have no money with me/on me.
He fought/quarrelled with everyone.
In descriptions:
The woman with red hair.
The man with his back to the camera/with his feet on his desk.
The boy with his hands in his pockets.

87 Prepositions used with adjectives and participles

Certain adjectives and past participles used as adjectives can be followed by a preposition + noun/gerund. (For verbs + prepositions see next paragraph.)

Usually particular adjectives and participles require particular prepositions. Some of these are given below; others can be found by consulting a good dictionary, which after any adjective will give the prepositions that can be used with it.

A **of, to, in, for** used with certain adjectives and participles

of can be used after *afraid, ashamed, aware, capable, composed, fond, scared, suspicious, terrified, tired*

to can be used after *according, accustomed, due, exposed, liable, owing, used*

in can be used after *absorbed, interested, involved, successful*

for can be used after *anxious, fit, inclined, ready*

Examples:
I was afraid of making him angry.
Are you aware of the risks?
They were tired of waiting.
She is suspicious of strangers.
According to Tom there are three hotels = Tom says there are three hotels.
Owing to (as a result of) *the rain the ground was not fit to play on.*
The petrol shortage was due to the drivers' strike. (due to = 'a result of' and must be preceded by a noun/pronoun.)
I'm accustomed/used to hard work.
He'll soon get used to getting up early.
If you exceed the speed limit you are liable to a heavy fine.
He was absorbed in his book. *I am interested in your idea.*
He is anxious for promotion = He wants promotion.
but *She is anxious about Peter* = She is worried about Peter.
Are you ready for your breakfast?

B Note also **good/bad at, keen on, sorry for/about, like** (= similar to, inclined to/for)

He's good at mathematics but bad at languages.
I'm sorry for being late on Monday (I apologize for being late)
or *I'm sorry about Monday.*
I'm sorry for forgetting the tickets (I apologize for forgetting them)
or *I'm sorry about the tickets.*

to be sorry for a person = to pity him

C **like** (preposition)

All the windows are barred. It's like a prison/It's like being in prison.

Do you feel like a drink?

(For **like/as**, see **92**.)

feel like + gerund = feel inclined + infinitive

I don't feel like walking ten miles = I don't feel inclined to walk ten miles.

For prepositions after finite verbs see next paragraph.

88 Verbs and prepositions

The best-known verb + preposition combinations are dealt with in chapter 32. But there are a great many other verbs which can be followed by prepositions and some of these are listed below. More can be found in any good dictionary which, after a verb, will give the prepositions that can be used after it.

of can be used after *dream, consist, think.*

We can also *remind* someone **of** something.

We can *accuse/suspect* him **of** (committing) a crime.

to can be used after *attend, conform, object, occur, refer, resort.*

We can *prefer* one thing/action **to** another.

in can be used after *believe, persist, succeed.*

for can be used after *apologize, apply, ask, beg, hope, long, prepare, wait, wish.*

We can also *blame, fine, punish* etc. someone **for** an offence.

on can be used after *depend, insist, live, rely.*

with can be used after *argue/quarrel/fight, compare, comply, deal.*

The police can *charge* someone **with** an offence.

Examples:

It never occurred to me to doubt him (I never thought of doubting him).

When arguments failed he resorted to threats.

Do you believe in ghosts? *They persisted in defying the law.*

They were fined for/charged with exceeding the speed limit.

Although he was drunk he insisted on driving.

You must comply with the regulations.

Passive verbs can of course be followed by **by** + agent; but they can also be followed by other prepositions:

The referee was booed by the crowd.

The referee was booed for his decision/for awarding a penalty.

The preposition **to**, when used after verbs as above, must not be confused with the **to** of the infinitive, which is also often placed after certain verbs (**have, ought, used**) to remind students that the full infinitive is used after these verbs. See **260**.

89 Gerunds after prepositions

It has already been stated that verbs placed immediately after prepositions must be in the gerund form:

He left without paying his bill.
He prefers drinking to dancing.
I apologize for not writing before.
She insisted on paying for herself.

Numerous other examples will be found in the preceding paragraphs. See also **259**.

A few noun + preposition + gerund combinations may also be noted:

There's no point in taking your car if you can't park it there.
What's the point of taking your car if you can't park?
Is there any chance/likelihood of his changing his mind?
Have you any objection to changing your working hours?
I am in favour of giving everyone a day off.
Did you have any difficulty in renewing your visa?
In spite of having no qualifications, he got the job.

The only exceptions to the gerund rule are **except** and **but** (preposition), which take the infinitive without **to**:

What could I do but accept his conditions?
He did nothing but complain.

But if **but** is used as a conjunction, i.e. if it introduces a clause, it can be followed directly by either (full) infinitive or gerund:

Being idle sometimes is agreeable, but being idle all the time might become monotonous.
To be idle sometimes is agreeable, but to be idle all the time etc.

90 Prepositions/adverbs

Many words can be used as either prepositions or adverbs:

*He got **off** the bus at the corner* (preposition).
*He got **off** at the corner* (adverb).

The most important of these are: **above, about, across, along, before, behind, below, by, down, in, near, off, on, over, round, through, under, up.**

*They were here **before** six* (preposition).
*He has done this sort of work **before*** (adverb).
*Peter is **behind** us* (preposition).
*He's a long way **behind*** (adverb).

She climbed ***over*** *the wall* (preposition).
You'll have to climb ***over*** *too* (adverb).
When the meeting was ***over*** *the delegates went home* (adverb; here *over* = finished).

The shop is just ***round*** *the corner* (preposition).
Come ***round*** *(to my house) any evening* (adverb).

He ran ***up*** *the stairs* (preposition).
He went ***up*** *in the lift* (adverb).

Many of these words are used to form phrasal verbs (see chapter 32):
The plane took off (left the ground).
He came round/to (recovered consciousness).
My plans fell through (came to nothing).
He gave up trying (stopped trying).

A few prepositions, **after, before, till** can also be used as conjunctions:
After he had explained the position . . .
Before we left the house . . .
I'll stay here till it begins to get cold.

10 Conjunctions

Conjunctions which introduce adverb clauses are dealt with in the paragraphs on the various types of adverb clause (see chapter 20 for conditional clauses and chapter 30 for clauses of purpose, comparison, reason, time, result and concession).

Pairs or groups of clauses which are sometimes confused with each other or with other forms are dealt with below.

91 though/although, nevertheless, yet, but, however and the phrase **in spite of**

(**in spite of** does not technically belong here but it is convenient to compare it with **although** with which it is often confused.)

These can be used to combine two opposing or contrasting statements. The difference between them is best seen by example. We could combine the following two sentences, *He was angry* and *He listened to me patiently,* in the following ways:

A With **but, yet** or **though/although**:
He was angry, but/yet he listened to me patiently.
Though/Although he was angry he listened to me patiently.
He listened to me patiently though he was angry.

B With **in spite of** + noun/pronoun/gerund:
In spite of being angry he listened to me patiently.
In spite of his anger he listened to me patiently.

C With **nevertheless**, which means **in spite of this/that**, or with **however** or **all the same**, which can also have this meaning:
He was angry, nevertheless/however he listened patiently.
(See also clauses of concession, **315**.)

92 like (preposition) and **as**

like is placed before nouns/pronouns in the simpler types of comparison:
He fought like a madman.

But if the noun/pronoun is followed immediately by a verb, i.e. if there is a clause of comparison, **as**, not **like**, should be used:
Can you pour wine straight down your throat, as they do in Spain?
When in Rome, do as the Romans do.

as can also be used with a noun alone, in the same way as **like**, but

there is some difference in meaning:
I worked as a slave = I was a slave.
I worked like a slave (I worked very hard; but I was a free man).
He used his umbrella as a weapon (he defended himself with it.)
(See also **95**.)

93 **for** and **because**

These conjunctions have nearly the same meaning and very often either can be used. It is, however, safer to use **because**, as a clause introduced by **for** (which we will call a '**for**-clause') has a more restricted use than a clause introduced by **because**:

1 A **for**-clause cannot precede the verb which it explains:
Because it was wet he took a taxi. (**for** is not possible.)

2 A **for**-clause cannot be preceded by **not**, **but** or any conjunction:
He stole, not because he wanted the money but because he liked stealing (**for** not possible).

3 A **for**-clause cannot be used in answer to a question:
Why did you do it? I did it because I was angry (**for** not possible).

4 A **for**-clause cannot be a mere repetition of what has been already stated, but always includes some new piece of information:
He spoke in French. She was angry because he had spoken in French (**for** not possible).

But *She was angry, for she didn't know French.* (Here **for** is correct; **because** is also possible.)

The reason for these restrictions is that a **for**-clause does not tell us why a certain action was performed, but merely presents a piece of additional information which helps to explain it.

Some examples of **for**-clauses:
The days were short, for it was now December.
He took the food eagerly, for he had eaten nothing since dawn.
When I saw her in the river I was frightened. For at that point the currents were dangerous.

In speech a short pause is usually made before a **for**-clause and in written English this place is usually marked by a comma, and sometimes, as in the last example above, by a full stop.

because could be used in the above sentences also, though **for** is better.

94 **both, either, neither, nor** and **so**

A We can express emphatically a combination of two things (nouns, verbs, adjectives etc.) by using **both . . . and**:
He has both the time and the money to play polo.

She both built and endowed the hospital.
It was both cold and wet.

We express two alternatives emphatically by **either . . . or** for the affirmative or interrogative:
We can have either tripe or liver.
Can you eat either tripe or liver?
and by using **either ... or** + a negative verb or **neither ... nor** + an affirmative verb for the negative:
I can't eat either tripe or liver
= *I can eat neither tripe nor liver.*

B **either, neither, nor** and **so,** in additions to remarks

We can say:
I went and he went too/also or *I went and so did he.*
Note that the verb must be inverted.
Similarly in the negative we can say:
He didn't go and she didn't go either
or we can use **neither/nor** + auxiliary verb (affirmative) + subject:
He didn't go and neither did she. (See **108**.)
Note also that a sentence such as:
I couldn't find Peter and didn't know where he had gone
could be rewritten:
I couldn't find Peter, nor did I know where he had gone.
Use **nor** only, not **neither**, here. Here **nor** + inverted verb replaces **and** + negative verb.
For **so** = therefore, see **312**.

95 as, when, while, if

A Used with simple tenses to express time

when is used:

1 When one action occurs at the same time as another or in the span of another:
When it is wet the buses are crowded.
When we lived in town we often went to the theatre.

2 When one action follows another:
When she pressed the button the lift stopped.

as is used:

3 When the second action occurs before the first is finished:
As I left the house I remembered the key.
This implies that I remembered the key before I had completed the action of leaving the house; I was probably still in the doorway. *While I was leaving* would have the same meaning here, but *When*

I left would give the impression that the act of leaving was complete and the door shut behind me.

4 For parallel actions (these are usually by the same subject, or one is the result of the other):
As the sun rose the fog dispersed. *He sang as he worked.*
As it grew darker it became colder = The darker it grew, the colder it became.
If we used **when** here we would lose all idea of simultaneous progression or development.

5 **as** can mean **while** (= during the time that):
As he stood there he saw two men enter the bar.
But there is no particular advantage in using **as** here, and **while** is safer.
as is chiefly used with verbs of **doing** and **becoming** rather than verbs of **being**. It is not therefore normally used with auxiliary verbs, or, except when there is an idea of development, with verbs of emotion or of the senses, or verbs of knowing and understanding. **as** used for time must be kept within its proper limits because otherwise there is danger of confusion with **as** meaning **because**:
As he was tired he sat down could only mean 'Because he was tired . . .'
As she loved him she let him stay could only mean 'Because she loved him . . .'
But **as** + noun could mean either **when** or **because**:
As a student he had lived on bread and water = When he was a student . . .
As a married man he has to think of the future = Because he is a married man/Being a married man . . .

B **as, when, while used to mean because/since, although, seeing that**

as can mean **because/since**, as shown above:
We had to walk all the way as we had no money for fares.
as + noun can mean **because/since**:
As an old customer I have a right to better treatment than this.
as can mean **although** but only in the combination adjective + as + subject + **to be/to seem/to appear**:
Tired as he was he offered to carry the child = Although he was tired . . .
while can mean **but** and is used to emphasize a contrast:
'At sea' means 'on a ship', while 'at the sea' means 'at the seaside'.
Some people waste food while others haven't enough.
while can also mean **although** and is then usually placed at the beginning of a sentence:

While I sympathize with your point of view I cannot accept it.

when can mean **seeing that/although**. It is therefore very similar to **while**, but is chiefly used to introduce a statement which makes another action seem unreasonable. It is often, though not necessarily, used with a question:

How can you expect your children to be truthful when you yourself tell lies?

It's not fair to expect her to do all the cooking when she has had no training or experience.

C Do not confuse **when** and **if**

When he comes . . . implies that we are sure he will come. *If he comes . . .* implies that we don't know whether he will come or not.

(For **if** in conditional sentences, see chapter 20.)

11 Introduction to verbs

96 A There are two classes of verbs in English:

1 The auxiliary verbs (auxiliaries): *to be, to have, to do, to dare, to need, to be able (can), may, must, will, shall, ought* and *used* (see **102–8** for function of auxiliaries).

2 All other verbs, which we may call ordinary verbs:
to work *to sing* *to pray*

B Note that English verbs are normally known by infinitives:
to work *to be* *to have*
but some of the auxiliaries have no infinitive and are known by the form used for their present tense:
may *must* *will* *shall* etc.
Before studying auxiliaries it may be helpful to look briefly at the form of the ordinary verbs.

Ordinary verbs

97 Principal parts of the active verb

	Affirmative	*Negative*
Present infinitive	to work	not to work
Continuous present infinitive	to be working	not to be working
Perfect infinitive	to have worked	not to have worked
Continuous perfect infinitive	to have been working	not to have been working
Present participle and gerund	working	not working
Perfect participle and gerund	having worked	not having worked
Past participle	worked	

In regular verbs the simple past and the past participle are both formed by adding **d** or **ed** to the infinitive. Sometimes the final consonant of the infinitive has to be doubled, e.g. *slip, slipped* (see spelling rules, **172, 327**). For irregular verbs see **317**.

The present participle and gerund are always regular and are formed by adding **ing** to the infinitive. The rule concerning the doubling of the final consonant of the infinitive before adding **ing** applies here also (see spelling rules **162, 327**).

98 Table of active tenses

Present	*simple*	he works
	continuous	he is working
	perfect	he has worked
	perfect continuous	he has been working
Past	*simple*	he worked
	continuous	he was working
	perfect	he had worked
	perfect continuous	he had been working
Future	*simple*	he will work
	continuous	he will be working
	perfect	he will have worked
	perfect continuous	he will have been working
Present	*conditional*	he would work
	conditional continuous	he would be working
Perfect	*conditional*	he would have worked
	conditional continuous	he would have been working

Contractions

In speech auxiliaries are normally contracted in affirmative and negative.

Note that **'s** may mean **is** or **has**:

he's going = he is going   *he's gone* = he has gone

and that **'d** may mean **had** or **would**:

he'd paid = he had paid

he'd like to come = he would like to come

Stress

Auxiliaries are normally unstressed. The stress falls on the main verb.

99 Negatives of tenses

For the simple present tense negative we use **does not** + infinitive for the third person and **do not** + infinitive for the other persons. Both are usually contracted in speech:

he doesn't work   *you don't work*

The simple past tense makes its negative with **did not (didn't)** + infinitive:

he/we/they didn't work

All other tenses are formed with auxiliaries, and the negative is formed by putting **not** after the auxiliaries. Contractions are usual in speech:

I have not seen him/I haven't seen him.
It will not be easy/It won't be easy.
I shall not be here tomorrow/I shan't be here tomorrow.
He would not drink wine/He wouldn't drink wine.
They had not applied for visas/They hadn't applied for visas.

The present continuous tense and the perfect tenses can be contracted in two ways:
He is not coming/He isn't coming/He's not coming.
I have not seen it/I haven't seen it/I've not seen it.

The future tense is normally contracted to **won't**, but **I'll not** is also possible.

In English a negative sentence can have only one negative expression in it. Two negative expressions give the sentence an affirmative meaning:
Nobody did nothing means that everyone did something.
So **never, no** (adj.), **none, nobody, no one, nothing, hardly, hardly ever** etc. are used with an affirmative verb. We can say:
He didn't eat anything or *He ate nothing.*
He doesn't ever complain or *He never complains.*
We haven't seen anyone or *We have seen no one.*
They didn't speak much or *They hardly spoke at all/They hardly ever spoke.*

100 Interrogative for questions and requests

A For the interrogative of the simple present tense we use **does he** + infinitive for the third person and **do I/you/we/they** + infinitive for the others. For the interrogative of the simple past tense we use **did** + subject + infinitive:
Did Peter enjoy the party?
Did you all go straight home afterwards?
In all other tenses we form the interrogative by putting the subject after the auxiliary:
Have you finished? *Are they coming?*

B The interrogative form is used for questions, but it is not used:

1 When the question is about the identity of the subject:
Who told you? *What happened?*

2 In indirect speech:
He said, 'Where does she live?'
= *He asked where she lived.*

3 If we place before the question a prefix such as **Do you know, Can you tell me, I want to know, I'd like to know, I wonder/was wondering, Have you any idea, Do you think**:
What time does the train start? but *Have you any idea what time the train starts?*
Where does Peter live? but *I wonder where Peter lives.*
Will I have to pay duty on this? but *Do you think I'll have to pay duty/Do you know if I'll have to pay duty?*

C Requests are usually expressed by the interrogative:
Can/Could you help me?
Will/Would you pay at the desk?
Would you like to come this way?
Would you mind moving your car?
But here again, if before the request we put a phrase such as *I wonder/was wondering* or *Do you think*, the verb in the request changes from interrogative to affirmative:
Could you give me a hand with this?
but *I wonder/was wondering/wondered if you could give me a hand*
or *Do you think you could give me a hand?*
In indirect speech the problem does not arise as indirect requests are expressed by a verb such as **ask** with object + infinitive:
He asked me to give him a hand.

D The interrogative is used in question tags after a negative verb:
You didn't see him, did you? (See **106**.)

E When, for emphasis, words/phrases such as **never, rarely, seldom, only when, only by, not only, not till** are placed first in a sentence the following main verb is put into the inverted (= interrogative) form:
Only when we landed did we see how badly the plane had been damaged. (See **72**.)

101 Negative interrogative

This is formed by putting **not** after the ordinary interrogative:
Did you not see her? *Is he not coming?*
But this form is almost always contracted:
Didn't you see her? *Isn't he coming?*
Note that **not** is now before the subject.
am I not? has an irregular contraction: *aren't I?*
The negative interrogative is used when the speaker expects or hopes for an affirmative answer:
Haven't you finished yet?
Don't you like my new dress?
CHILD: *Can't I stay up till the end of the programme?*
A: *I could wait ten minutes.* B: *Couldn't you wait a little longer?*
The negative interrogative is also used in question tags after an affirmative sentence:
You paid him, didn't you?
She would like to come, wouldn't she?
(See **106** C.)

Auxiliary verbs

102 List of auxiliary verbs with their principal parts

	Infinitive	*Present tense*	*Past tense*	*Past participle*
be	to be	am, is, are	was, were	been
have	to have	have, has	had	had
do	to do	do, does	did	done
can	(to be able)	can am/is/are able	could was/were able	been able
may	—	may	might	—
must	(to have to)	must	had to	had to
need	to need	need	needed	needed
will	—	will	would	—
shall	—	shall	should	—
ought	—	ought	ought	—
dare	to dare	dare	dared	dared
used	—	—	used	—

These are called auxiliary verbs because:

1 They help to form tenses, being combined with the present, the past participle or infinitive:
I am waiting. *They will be there.* *He would like to come.*

2 They are used with infinitives to indicate possibility, permission, ability, obligation, deduction etc., as will be seen in the following paragraphs; for example:
He may come tomorrow (possibility). *I can type* (ability).
We must stop now (obligation).

In the following pages we shall deal with each of the auxiliaries in the above list with the exception of **will** and **shall**, which will be dealt with separately in chapters 18, 20 and 21.

103 Rules applicable to all auxiliaries

A All auxiliaries except **be, have** and **do** are uninflected, i.e. all persons have the same form:
I can *you can* *he can* *we can* etc.
I must *you must* *he must* *we must* etc.

B The negative is formed by putting **not** after the auxiliary:
I must not *he has not* *they do not*

(But sometimes we use the infinitive of the auxiliary preceded by **do not**. See **116–17, 119–20, 123**.)

C The interrogative is formed by inverting subject and verb:
can he? *may we?* *must I?*

(But **do** + subject + infinitive is also sometimes used. See **116–17, 119–20, 123**.)

D Auxiliaries are not normally used in the continuous tenses except for certain uses of **be** (see **110, 114** A) and **have** (see **117, 120**).

E Auxiliaries are followed by infinitives (**be** and **have** can also be followed by other parts of the verb).

be, have, ought and **used** are followed by the infinitive with **to**:
He is to go. *I have to work.* *Tom ought to write to her.*
She used to know Greek.

do, can, may, must, will and **shall** are followed by the infinitive without to:
He doesn't read. *She can swim.* *You may go.*
I must see it. *He will help you.*

need and **dare** take the infinitive without **to** except when they are conjugated with **do**:
He need not go but *He doesn't need to go.*
How dare you borrow it without my permission!
He didn't dare to say anything.

F Auxiliaries are usually contracted in conversation:

be, have, would and **will** can be contracted in the affirmative.
I'm here. *We've seen it.* *They'll go.*

had and **would** have the same contraction **'d**:
I'd seen it = I had seen it. *I'd go* = I should or would go.

is and **has** have the same contraction: **'s.**

Affirmative contractions cannot be used at the end of a sentence:
I'm not French but he is. (*he is* here could not be contracted.)
All auxiliaries can be contracted in the negative.

Use of auxiliaries in short answers, agreements etc.

Auxiliaries are extremely important in conversation because in short answers, agreements, disagreements with remarks, additions to remarks etc., we use auxiliaries instead of repeating the original verb.

104 Auxiliaries in short answers

Questions requiring the answer **yes** or **no**, i.e. questions such as *Do you smoke?* or *Can you ride a bicycle?*, should be answered by **yes** or **no** and the auxiliary only. The original subject, if a noun, is replaced by a pronoun:

Do you smoke? *Yes, I do* (not *Yes, I smoke*).
Can he cook? *Yes, he can* or *No, he can't.*
Has Tom got a car? *Yes, he has* or *No, he hasn't.*
Did the twins go? *Yes, they did* or *No, they didn't.*

An answer with **yes** or **no** without the auxiliary is of course possible but could be less polite.

105 Agreements and disagreements with remarks

A Agreements with affirmative remarks are made with **yes/so** or **of course** + affirmative auxiliary. If there is an auxiliary in the first verb this is repeated; if there is no auxiliary **do/does** is used in the present, **did** in the past:

Tom drinks too much.	*Yes, he does.*
Ann may be at the station.	*Yes, she may.*
Living in London will be expensive.	*Yes, of course it will.*
Your petrol tank is leaking.	*Oh, so it is.*

B Disagreements with negative remarks are made with **yes** or **oh yes** + affirmative auxiliary:

Mary won't be there.	*Oh yes, she will.*
Tom doesn't earn much.	*Oh yes, he does.*
Bill didn't go to college.	*Yes, he did.*
I'm not getting fatter.	*Oh yes, you are.*

C Agreements with negative remarks are made with **no** + negative auxiliary:

It wouldn't take long.	*No, it wouldn't.*
I can't sing well.	*No, you can't.*
The twins mustn't be late.	*No, they mustn't.*
The door hadn't been locked.	*No, it hadn't.*

D Disagreements with affirmative remarks are expressed by **no** or **oh no** + negative auxiliary:

Your sister will lend you the money.	*No, she won't.*
Peter drinks too much.	*No, he doesn't.*
We have plenty of time.	*No, we haven't.*
Prices are coming down.	*Oh no, they aren't.*

but can be used when disagreeing with an assumption. The assumption may be expressed by a question:
Why did you travel first class? *But I didn't!*

106 Question tags

A These are short additions to sentences, asking for agreement or confirmation.

After negative statements we use the ordinary interrogative:
You didn't see him, did you? *Ann can't swim, can she?*

After affirmative statements we use the negative interrogative:
Peter helped you, didn't he? *Mary was there, wasn't she?*

Negative verbs in the tags are usually contracted. But see note at end of C.

Irregular: *I'm late, aren't I?*

Note that **let's** has the tag **shall**:
Let's go, shall we?

The subject of the tag is always a pronoun.

B Examples of question tags after negative statements

Peter doesn't smoke, does he?
Ann isn't studying music, is she?
Bill didn't want to go, did he?
James wasn't driving the car, was he?
You haven't ridden a horse for a long time, have you?
The twins hadn't seen a hovercraft before, had they?
They couldn't understand him, could they?
There wasn't enough time, was there?
People shouldn't drop litter on pavements, should they?
Ann hasn't got colour TV, has she?

Note that statements containing words such as **neither, no** (adj.), **none, no one, nobody, nothing, scarcely, barely, hardly, hardly ever, seldom** are treated as negative statements and followed by an ordinary interrogative tag:
None of your friends liked the film, did they?
Nothing was said, was it?
Peter hardly ever goes to parties, does he?

When the subject of the sentence is **no one, nobody, anyone, anybody, none, neither** we use the pronoun **they** as subject of the tag:
I don't suppose anyone will volunteer, will they?
None of the bottles are broken, are they?
Neither of them complained, did they?

C Question tags after affirmative statements

With the simple present tense we use **don't/doesn't?** in the tag.
With the simple past tense we use **didn't?**
Edward lives here, doesn't he?
You found your passport, didn't you?

After all other tenses we just put the auxiliary verb into the negative interrogative:

Mary's coming tomorrow, isn't she?
Peter's heard the news, hasn't he?

Be careful of the contraction **'s**, which can mean **is** or **has** (see above) and of the contraction **'d**, which can mean **had** or **would**:

Peter'd written before you phoned, hadn't he?
Mary'd come if you asked her, wouldn't she?
You'd better change your wet shoes, hadn't you?
Your parents'd rather go by air, wouldn't they?

With **everybody, everyone, somebody, someone** we use the pronoun **they**:

Everyone warned you, didn't they?
Someone had recognized him, hadn't they?

Negative interrogative tags without contractions are possible but the word order is different:

You saw him, did you not?

This is a much less usual form.

D Intonation

When question tags are used the speaker doesn't normally need information but merely expects agreement. These tags are therefore normally said with a falling intonation, as in statements.

Sometimes, however, the speaker does want information. He is not quite sure that the statement is true, and wants to be reassured. In this case the question tag is said with a rising intonation and the important word in the first sentence is stressed, normally with a rise of pitch.

(See Thomson and Martinet, *Structure Drills 1*, nos. 11–13.)

107 Comment tags

These are formed with auxiliary verbs, just like question tags, but after an affirmative statement we use an ordinary interrogative tag; after a negative statement we use a negative interrogative tag.

Comment tags can either be added to an affirmative statement:

You saw him, did you?

or used in answer to an affirmative or negative statement:

A: *I'm living in London now.* B: *Are you?*
A: *I didn't pay Paul.* B: *Didn't you?*

When spoken in answer to a statement the tag is roughly equivalent to *Really!* or *Indeed!*

When placed after a statement it indicates that the speaker notes this fact:

You've found a job, have you? = Oh, so you've found a job.

The chief use of these tags is to express the speaker's reaction to the statement. By the tone of his voice he can indicate that he is interested, not interested, surprised, pleased, delighted, angry, suspicious, disbelieving etc.

The speaker's feelings can be expressed more forcibly by adding an auxiliary as shown below:

I borrowed your car. Oh, you did, did you?

I didn't think you'd need it. Oh, you didn't, didn't you?

i.e. before an ordinary interrogative we use an affirmative auxiliary verb, before a negative interrogative we use a negative verb.

Again, the meaning depends on the tone of voice used. The speaker may be very angry, even truculent; but the form could also express admiration or amusement.

108 Additions to remarks

A Affirmative additions to affirmative remarks are made by using **so** + the auxiliary (or **do/does/did** if there is no auxiliary) + the subject, in that order. Instead of saying:

Bill likes tennis and Tom likes tennis too

we can say:

Bill likes tennis and so does Tom.

Similarly:

Men smoke in England and so do women.

I read the 'Guardian' and so does Mr Pitt.

You can come in my car and so can your dog.

Shakespeare wrote plays and so did Lope de Vega.

B Affirmative additions to negative remarks are made with **but** + subject + auxiliary:

Bill can't ride that horse but Diana can.

I didn't eat lobster but she did. *He won't go but they will.*

C Negative additions to negative remarks are made with **nor** or **neither** + auxiliary + subject:

She didn't give anything and neither did he.

The men were not well dressed. Nor were the women.

She hasn't much time and neither have I.

D Negative additions to affirmative remarks are made with **but** + subject + auxiliary (or **do/does/did**) in the negative:

He likes Picasso but I don't. *Henry can come but George can't.*

The Pitts will accept but the Browns won't.

My cat caught rats but yours didn't.

For auxiliaries used in comparisons, e.g. *He runs faster than I do* see **17, 65, 311**.

12 The auxiliaries **be, have, do**

to be

109 Form

Principal parts: **be** **was** **been**

A Present tense:

Affirmative	*Negative*	*Interrogative*
I am (I'm)	I am (I'm) not	am I?
you are (you're)	you are not (aren't)	are you?
he is (he's)	he is not (isn't)	is he?
she is (she's)	she is not (isn't)	is she?
it is (it's)	it is not (isn't)	is it?
we are (we're)	we are not (aren't)	are we?
you are (you're)	you are not (aren't)	are you?
they are (they're)	they are not (aren't)	are they?

Alternative negative contractions are *you're not, he's not* etc.
The interrogative is not contracted.

The negative interrogative form is *am I not?* (with contraction: *aren't I?*), *are you not? (aren't you?), is he not? (isn't he?)* etc.

B Past tense

Affirmative	*Negative*	*Interrogative*
I was	I was not (wasn't)	was I?
you were	you were not (weren't)	were you?
he/she/it was	he/she/it was not (wasn't)	was he/she/it?
we were	we were not (weren't)	were we?
you were	you were not (weren't)	were you?
they were	they were not (weren't)	were they?

The negative interrogative form is *was I not (wasn't I?), were you not? (weren't you?)* etc.

C Other tenses of **to be** follow the rules for ordinary verbs. But **be** is not normally used in the continuous forms except in the passive and as shown in **114** A.

to be as an auxiliary

110 In the formation of tenses

be is used in continuous active forms: *He is working/will be working* etc., and in all passive forms: *He was followed/is being followed.*

Note that **be** can be used in the continuous forms in the passive:
Active: *They are carrying him.*
Passive: *He is being carried.*
Active: *She was towing the car.*
Passive: *The car was being towed.* (See also **289**.)

111 Used with the infinitive

A The **be** + infinitive construction, e.g. *I am to go*, is extremely important and can be used in the following ways:

1 To convey orders or instructions:
No one is to leave this building without the permission of the police (no one must leave).
He is to stay here till we return (he must stay).
This is a rather impersonal way of giving instructions and is chiefly used with the third person. When used with **you** it often implies that the speaker is passing on instructions issued by someone else. The difference between (1) *Stay here, Tom* and (2) *You are to stay here, Tom* is that in (1) the speaker himself is ordering Tom to stay, while in (2) he may be merely conveying to Tom the wishes of another person.
This distinction disappears of course in indirect speech, and the **be** + infinitive construction is an extremely useful way of expressing indirect commands, particularly when the introductory verb is in the present tense:
He says, 'Wait till I come.'
= *He says that we are to wait till he comes.*
or when there is a clause in front of the imperative:
He said, 'If I fall asleep at the wheel wake me up.'
= *He said that if he fell asleep at the wheel she was to wake him up.*
It is also used in reporting requests for instructions:
'Where shall I put it, sir?' he asked
= *He asked where he was to put it.* (See also **300** A2, **302**.)

2 To convey a plan:
She is to be married next month.
The expedition is to start in a week's time.
This construction is very much used in newspapers:
The Prime Minister is to make a statement tomorrow.
In headlines the verb **be** is often omitted to save space:
Prime Minister to make statement tomorrow.
Past forms:
1 *He was to go* (present infinitive).
2 *He was to have gone* (perfect infinitive).

The first of these doesn't tell us whether the plan was carried out or not. The second is used for an unfulfilled plan, i.e. one which was not carried out:
The Lord Mayor was to have laid the foundation stone but he was taken ill last night so the Lady Mayoress is doing it instead.

B **was/were** + infinitive can express an idea of destiny.
He received a blow on the head. It didn't worry him at the time but it was to be very troublesome later (turned out to be/proved troublesome).
They said goodbye, little knowing that they were never to meet again (were never destined to meet).

C **be about** + infinitive expresses the immediate future:
They are about to start = They are just going to start/They are on the point of starting.
just can be added to make the future even more immediate:
They are just about to leave.
Similarly in the past:
He was just about to dive when he saw the shark.
be on the point of + gerund has the same meaning as **be about** + infinitive, but is a shade more immediate.

to be as an ordinary verb

112 To denote existence

A **to be** is the verb normally used to denote the existence of, or to give information about, a person or thing:

Tom is a carpenter.	*The dog is in the garden.*
Malta is an island.	*The roads were rough and narrow.*
Gold is a metal.	*Peter was tall and fair.*

B **there is, there are**
When a noun representing an indefinite person or thing is the subject of the verb **to be**, we usually put **there** before the verb and the noun after it:

It is possible to say	*A man is in the hall.*
But it is more usual to say	*There is a man in the hall.*
Similarly we can say	*There is an egg in that nest.*
	There are eggs in that nest.

Notice that, though **there** appears to be the subject, the real subject is the noun that follows the verb, and if this noun is plural the verb must be plural also:

There is a cigarette in that box.
There are cigarettes in that box.

There has been a storm.
There have been storms.

There was a queue at the station.
There were queues at the station.

Negative and interrogative examples:
There isn't any milk. *There won't be a queue for that film.*
Are there any apples? *Is there a doctor in the house?*

This construction is not used in general statements such as:
Gold is a metal. *Hurricanes are terrible things.*
A snake is a reptile. *Parachutes are useful.*
Mosquitoes are a nuisance.

113 it is and there is

A As noted in **44**, **it is** is used:

1 In expressions of time and date:
What time is it/What's the time? It's ten o'clock.
What date is it/What's the date? It's December 8.
It is six years since he left.
It will be a long time before we see him again.

2 In expressions of distance:
How far is it to York? It is sixty miles.
It is not far to the nearest village.
It is a long way to Australia. (*far* is not used in the affirmative.)

3 In expressions of weather and temperature etc.:
It is hot/cold/wet/windy.
It will be foggy tomorrow.
It was high tide/The tide was high.
It was full moon/The moon was full.

4 In questions and answers about identity:
TOM: *Ann, you're wanted on the phone.*
ANN: *Who is it?* or *Do you know who it is?*
TOM: *I think it's your brother.*

5 In sentences where an infinitive is the real subject:
It is easy to see why he left home.

6 In sentences where a clause is the real subject:
It is possible that he never intended to shoot her.

7 To give special emphasis to a word or phrase:
It was pollution that killed these fish (pollution—not any other cause).

It is the grandmother who makes the decisions (the grandmother—not any other member of the family).

B Some examples may help to prevent confusion between the two forms:

1 **it is** + adjective; **there is** + noun:
It is foggy or *There is a fog.*
It was very wet or *There was a lot of rain.*
It won't be very sunny or *There won't be much sun.*
Will it be dangerous? or *Will there be any danger?*

2 **it is, there is** of time and distance:
It is a long way to York.
There is a long way still to go (a large part of our journey still lies ahead of us).
It is time to go home (we planned to start home at six and it is six now).
There is time for us to go home and come back here again before the film starts (that amount of time exists).

3 **there is** + noun/pronoun and **it is** used for identity:
There is someone at the door. I think it's the man to read the meters.
Oh, it's Peter's coat. He must have forgotten to put it on.

114 Other uses of **be**

be is used to express:

A Physical or mental condition:
I am hot/cold. *He was excited/calm.*
They will be happy/unhappy.

With certain adjectives, e.g. *quiet/noisy, good/bad, wise/foolish*, it is possible to use the continuous form of **be**, e.g. *Tom is being foolish*, to imply that the subject is showing this quality at this time. Compare *Tom is being foolish*, which means Tom is talking or acting foolishly now, with *Tom is foolish*, which means that Tom always acts or talks foolishly. Similarly:
The children are being quiet = They are playing quietly now.

But *The children are quiet* might mean that they usually play quietly.

Other adjectives can be used with the continuous form:
clever/stupid, generous/mean, economical/extravagant, optimistic/pessimistic, helpful/unhelpful, selfish/unselfish, cautious/rash, polite, funny, difficult, annoying, irritating, formal, mysterious.

With some of these, e.g. *stupid, difficult, funny, polite,* the continuous form may imply that the subject is deliberately acting in this way:
You are being stupid may mean *You are not trying to understand.*

He is being difficult usually means *He is raising unnecessary objections.*
He is being funny usually means *He is only joking. Don't believe him.*
She is just being polite probably means *She is only pretending to admire your car/clothes/house* etc.

B Age:
How old are you? I am ten/I am ten years old (but not *I am ten years*).
How old is the tower? It is 400 years old. (*years old* must be used when giving the age of things.)

C Size and weight:
How tall are you?/What is your height? I am 1.65 metres.
PASSENGER (in a plane): *How high are we now?*
PILOT: *We're about 20,000 feet.*
What is your weight? or *What do you weigh/How much do you weigh? I am 65 kilos* or *I weigh 65 kilos.*

D Price:
How much is this melon? or *What does this melon cost? It's £1.*
The best seats are (=cost) *£5.*

to have

115 Form and use in the formation of tenses

A Form
Principal parts: **have** **had** **had**

1 Present tense:

Affirmative	*Negative*	*Interrogative*
I have (I've)	I have not (haven't)	have I?
you have (you've)	you have not (haven't)	have you?
he has (he's)	he has not (hasn't)	has he?
she has (she's)	she has not (hasn't)	has she?
it has (it's)	it has not (hasn't)	has it?
we have (we've)	we have not (haven't)	have we?
you have (you've)	you have not (haven't)	have you?
they have (they've)	they have not (haven't)	have they?

(The third person singular affirmative contractions for **be** and **have** are the same, i.e. **'s** in both cases. *he's* could be *he is* or *he has*.)
Alternative negative contractions are *I've not, you've not* etc.
The interrogative is not contracted.

The negative interrogative form is *have I not? (haven't I?), have you not? (haven't you?), has he not? (hasn't he?)* etc.

2 Past tense

Affirmative	*Negative*	*Interrogative*
I had (I'd)	I had not (hadn't)	had I?
you had (you'd)	you had not (hadn't)	had you?
he had (he'd)	he had not (hadn't)	had he?
she had (she'd)	she had not (hadn't)	had she?
it had (it'd)	it had not (hadn't)	had it?
we had (we'd)	we had not (hadn't)	had we?
you had (you'd)	you had not (hadn't)	had you?
they had (they'd)	they had not (hadn't)	had they?

Alternative negative contractions are *I'd not* etc., but these are less common. The interrogative is not contracted.
(The contraction **'d** is also used for **would**, e.g. *he'd* could mean *he would* or *he had.*)
The negative interrogative form is *had I not? (hadn't I?), had you not? (hadn't you?)* etc.

3 All other tenses follow the rules for ordinary verbs.

B Use in the formation of tenses

have is used with the past participle to form the following tenses:

Present perfect	I have worked.
Past perfect	I had worked.
Future perfect	I will/shall have worked.
Perfect conditional	I would/should have worked.

Other uses of **have** as an auxiliary verb

116 With the infinitive to express obligation (see also **135**)

have with the infinitive expresses obligation, having nearly the same meaning as **must**:
I have to go = I must go.
had with the infinitive expresses past obligation, and is considered as the past form of **must**, which has no past form of its own:
I had to buy some new shoes last week.

Note that the verb **have** is followed by the infinitive with **to**. To remind students of this, **have**, when used with an infinitive, is usually referred to as **have to**, with **had to** as its past form. **have to/had to** always express obligation, as **have** is not used with the infinitive in any other way.

In conversation it is often possible to use **have to/had to** alone, the infinitive being understood but not mentioned:

Why do you always wear dark glasses? I have to (wear them). My eyes are very sensitive.
I didn't want to stop but I had to (stop) as I needed petrol.

The negative and interrogative of **have to** can be formed in either of the two ways: according to the rule for auxiliaries or according to the rule for ordinary verbs (i.e. with **do**).

got (the past participle of **get**) is often added to **have to** in the affirmative, and in the negative and interrogative forms when these are not made with **do**. This makes no difference to the meaning. **have** when used with **got** is usually contracted.

The negative and interrogative forms are as follows:

	Affirmative	*Negative*	*Interrogative*
Present	have (got) to	haven't (got) to *or* don't have to	have I (got) to? etc. *or* do I have to? etc.
Past	had to	hadn't (got) to *or* didn't have to	had I (got) to? etc. *or* did I have to? etc.

In the present tense the form with **do** is the better one to use when we wish to express a habitual obligation:

Do you have to work on Saturdays?
He doesn't have to wear uniform.

117 The '**have** + object + past participle' construction

A This construction can be used to express more neatly sentences of the type 'I employed someone to do something for me'; i.e. instead of saying *I employed someone to clean my car* we can say *I had my car cleaned*, and instead of *I got a man to sweep my chimneys* ('got' here = paid/persuaded etc.), we can say *I had my chimneys swept.*

Note that this order of words, i.e. **have** + object + past participle, must be observed as otherwise the meaning will be changed:

He had his hair cut means he employed someone to do it, but *He had cut his hair* means he cut it himself some time before the time of speaking (past perfect tense).

When **have** is used in this way the negative and interrogative of its present and past tenses are formed with **do**:

Do you have your windows cleaned every month?
I don't have them cleaned; I clean them myself.
He was talking about having central heating put in. Did he have it put in in the end?

And it can be used in continuous tenses:

I can't ask you to dinner this week as I am having my house painted at the moment and everything is upside down.

While I was having my hair done the police towed away my car.
He says that the house is too small and that he is having a room built on.

get can be used in exactly the same way as **have** above but is more colloquial.

get is also used when we mention the person who performs the action:
She got him to dig away the snow = She paid/persuaded him to dig etc.
(**have** with infinitive without **to** can be used in the same way, e.g. *She had him dig away the snow*, but the **get** construction is much more usual here.)

B This **have** + object + past participle construction can also be used colloquially to replace a passive verb, usually one concerning some accident or misfortune:
His fruit was stolen before he had a chance to pick it
can be replaced by
He had his fruit stolen before he had etc.

and *Two of his teeth were knocked out in the fight* can be replaced by
He had two of his teeth knocked out.

It will be seen that, whereas in A above the subject is the person who orders the thing to be done, here the subject is the person who suffers as a result of the action. The subject could be a thing:
The houses had their roofs ripped off by the gale.

get can replace **have** here also:
The cat got her tail singed through sitting too near the fire = The cat's tail was singed etc.

118 had better and have + object + present participle

A **had better** + infinitive without **to**

had here is an unreal past; the meaning is present or future:
You had/You'd better start tomorrow.
I had/I'd better ring him at once.

The negative is formed with **not** after **better**:
You had better not miss the last bus (I advise you not to miss it).

had better is not normally used in the ordinary interrogative, but is sometimes used in the negative interrogative as an advice form:
Hadn't you better ask him first?

Use:
I had better go by air = It would be best for me to go by air.

He had better go by air = It would be best for him to go by air.
You had better go by air = It would be best for you to go by air, or I advise you to go by air.

you had better . . . is a very useful advice form.

In indirect speech **had better** with the first or third person remains unchanged; **had better** with the second person can remain unchanged or be reported by **advise** + object + infinitive:

He said, 'I had better hurry'
= *He said that he had better hurry.*
He said, 'Ann had better hurry'
= *He said that Ann had better hurry.*
He said, 'You had better hurry'
= *He said that I had better hurry*
or *He advised me to hurry.*

B **have** + object + present participle (first use)

I'll have you driving in three days = As a result of my efforts, you will be driving in three days.

This expression is often used as above with a period of future time, but can also be used in the past or present:
He had them all dancing = He taught/persuaded them all to dance.
I have them all talking to each other = I encourage/persuade them all to talk to each other.
It can be used in the interrogative:
Will you really have her driving in three days?
but is not normally used in the negative.

C **have** + object + present participle (second use)

If you give all-night parties you'll have the neighbours complaining (the neighbours will complain/will be complaining).
If film-stars put their numbers in telephone books they'd have everyone ringing them up (everyone would ring/would be ringing them up).
you'll have in the first example conveys the idea 'this will happen to you'. Similarly *they'd have* in the second example conveys the idea 'this would happen to them'.

This construction can be used in the interrogative and negative:
When they move that bus stop you won't have people sitting on your steps waiting for the bus any more.

Other examples:

If you don't put a fence round your garden you'll have people walking in and stealing your fruit (people will walk in and steal/will

be walking in and stealing it, i.e. this will happen to you).
This structure is chiefly used for actions which would be displeasing to the subject of **have**, as in the above example. But it can be used for an action which is not displeasing:
When he became famous he had people stopping him in the street and asking for his autograph = When he became famous, people stopped him in the street and asked for his autograph.
But **I won't have** + object + present participle normally means 'I won't/don't allow this':
I won't have him sitting down to dinner in his overalls. I make him change them = I won't/don't allow him to sit down etc.
This use is restricted to the first person.

have as an ordinary verb

119 **have** meaning possess

This is the basic meaning of **have**:
He has a black beard.
She will have £4,000 a year when she retires.
I have had this car for ten years.
The negative and interrogative can be formed in either of two ways:

	Affirmative	*Negative*	*Interrogative*
Present	have (got) *or* have	haven't (got) *or* don't have	have I (got)? etc. *or* do you have? etc.
Past	had	hadn't (got) *or* didn't have	had you (got)? etc. *or* did you have? etc.

have is conjugated with **do** for habitual actions:
CUSTOMER: *Do you ever have pineapples?*
SHOPKEEPER: *We don't have them very often.*
When there is not this idea of habit, the **have not (got)/have you (got)** forms are more usual in England, though other English-speaking countries (notably America) use the **do** forms here also. An American might say:
Can you help me now? Do you have time?
where an Englishman would probably say:
Can you help me now? Have you got time?
do forms can therefore be used safely throughout, but students living in England should practise the other forms as well.

got can be added to **have/have not/have you** etc. as shown above. It makes no difference to the sense so it is entirely optional, but it is quite a common addition. **got** however is not added in short answers or question tags:

Have you got an ice-axe? Yes, I have.

She's got a nice voice, hasn't she?

have (affirmative) followed by **got** is usually contracted:

I've got my ticket. *He's got a flat in Pimlico.*

The stress falls on **got**. The **'ve** or **'s** is often barely audible.

have (affirmative) without **got** is often not contracted. The **have** or **has** must then be audible.

120 **have** meaning 'take' (a meal), 'give' (a party) etc.

A **have** can also be used to mean:

'take' (a meal/food or drink/a bath/a lesson etc.)
'give' (a party), 'entertain' (guests)
'encounter' (difficulties/trouble)
'experience', 'enjoy', usually with an adjective, e.g. good.

We have lunch at one.
They are having a party tomorrow.
Did you have trouble with the Customs?
I hope you'll have a good holiday.

B **have** when used as above obeys the rules for ordinary verbs:

It is never followed by **got**.
Its negative and interrogative are made with **do**.
It can be used in the continuous tenses.

I usually have some coffee at eleven (habit).
We are having breakfast early tomorrow (near future).
She is having twenty people to dinner next Monday (near future).
I can't answer the telephone. I am having my bath (present).
How many English lessons do you have a week? I have six.
Do you have coffee or tea for breakfast? I have coffee.
Will you have some more wine/a cup of tea/a cigarette? (This is an invitation. We can also omit the 'Will you' and say *Have some more wine, Have a cigarette* etc.)
In Spain they don't have dinner till ten.
Did you have a good time at the theatre? (Did you enjoy yourself?)
Have a good time! (Enjoy yourself!)
I am having a wonderful holiday.
I didn't have a very good journey. I had a lot of trouble with my luggage.

to do

121 Form

Principal parts: **do did done**

Present tense:

Affirmative	*Negative*	*Interrogative*
I do	I do not (don't)	do I?
you do	you do not (don't)	do you?
he does	he does not (doesn't)	does he?
she does	she does not (doesn't)	does she?
it does	it does not (doesn't)	does it?
we do	we do not (don't)	do we?
you do	you do not (don't)	do you?
they do	they do not (don't)	do they?

The negative interrogative form is *do I not? (don't I?)* etc.

Past tense: *did* for all persons, negative *did not (didn't)*, interrogative *did I?* etc., negative interrogative *did I not (didn't I?)* etc.

do is followed by the infinitive without **to**:
I don't know. Did you see it? He doesn't like me.

122 **do** used as an auxiliary

A **do** is used to form the negative and interrogative of the present simple and past simple tenses of ordinary verbs; for example:

Affirmative	he works	he worked
Negative	he doesn't work	he didn't work
Interrogative	does he work?	did he work?

B It is possible to use **do/did** + infinitive in the affirmative also when we wish to add special emphasis. It is chiefly used when another speaker has expressed doubt about the action referred to:
'You didn't see him.' 'I ˈdid see him.' (The *did* is strongly stressed in speech. This is more emphatic than the normal *I saw him.*)
I know that you didn't expect me to go, but I ˈdid go.

C **do** is used to avoid repetition of a previous ordinary verb:

1 In short agreements:
Tom speaks a lot. Yes, he does.
She sang well. Yes, she did.
He didn't go. No, he didn't.

2 In short disagreements:
Your dog barks a lot. No, he doesn't.
You eat too much. No, I don't.

3 In additions:
He likes wine and so do we (note inversion).

He doesn't like caviare and neither do I.
He lives at home but I don't.
He doesn't drive the car but I do.

4 In question tags:
He lives here, doesn't he? *He didn't see you, did he?*
(See also **106**.)

D **do** is used in short answers to avoid repetition of the main verb:
Do you smoke? Yes, I do (not *Yes, I smoke)*/*No, I don't.*
Did you see him? Yes, I did/No, I didn't.
Does he love you? Yes, he does/No, I'm afraid he doesn't.

E Similarly in comparisons:
He drives faster than I do. (See **311**.)

F **do** is placed before the imperative to make a request or invitation more persuasive:
Do come with us (more persuasive than *Come with us*).
Do work a little harder. *Do help me, please.*

G It can similarly be used as an approving or encouraging affirmative answer to someone asking for approval of, or permission to do, some action:
Shall I write to him? Yes, do or *Do* alone.

123 do used as an ordinary verb

do, like **have**, can be used as an ordinary verb. It then forms its negative and interrogative in the simple present and simple past with **do** and **did**:

I do not do	*do you do?*	*don't you do?*
he does not do	*does he do?*	*doesn't he do?*
I did not do	*did he do?*	*didn't he do?* etc.

It can be used in the continuous forms, or simple forms:
What are you doing (now)? I'm doing my homework.
What's he doing tomorrow? (near future)
What does he do in the evenings? (habit)
How did you do it? I did it with my little axe.

How do you do? is said by both parties after an introduction:
HOSTESS: *Mrs Day, may I introduce Miss Knight? Miss Knight, Mrs Day.*
MRS DAY: *How do you do?*
MISS KNIGHT: *How do you do?*
Originally this was an inquiry about the other person's health. Now it is merely a formal greeting, used only at introductions.

13 may, can

may

124 Form

may for all persons in the present and future
might in the conditional and after verbs in a past tense (but see **125** A2).
Negative: *may not (mayn't), might not (mightn't).*
Interrogative: *may I?* etc., *might I?* etc.
Negative interrogative: *may I not (mayn't I)?* etc., *mightn't I?* etc.
may is followed by the infinitive without **to**.

125 **may** used to express permission (infinitive: **to allow/to be allowed**)

A Affirmative and negative

1 In the present or future:

First person

I/we may meaning 'I/we have permission to . . .' is possible:
I may leave the office as soon as I have finished my work.
But this is not a very common construction and it would be more usual to say:
I can leave/I am allowed to leave etc.
I/we may/might is however possible in indirect speech:
'You may leave when you have finished.'
= *He says we may leave* or *He said we might leave . . .*

Second and third persons

Here **may** is chiefly used when the speaker is giving or refusing permission: *You may park here* means 'I give you permission to park'. It does not normally mean 'You are allowed to park (by another authority) or 'You have a right to park'.
If the speaker has no authority in the matter he will probably say: *You can park here* or *You are allowed to park here.*
(Note that **can** can have both meanings: *You can park here* can mean 'I give you permission to park' or 'You have a right to park/The police will allow you to park etc.' See **128**.)
Examples of **may** used to express formal permission (for informal situations we use **can**):

Candidates may not bring reference books into the examination room.
Each voter may vote for only one candidate.
You may keep the book for a month. After that you must return it to us or send us a cheque for £5.

2 In the past we use **allow** in the active or passive:
I allowed him to park here last week.
Last term candidates were not allowed to bring books into the examination room
or *Last term they didn't allow candidates to bring books etc.*
In 1979 each voter was allowed to vote for only one candidate
or *They didn't allow any voter to vote for more than one candidate.*
might, however, can be used in indirect speech:
They said we might keep the book for a month.

3 **allow** is needed to form the passive, as shown above. It is also necessary when we want a perfect tense:
Since his accident he hasn't been allowed/they haven't allowed him to drive a car.

B Interrogative

1 Requests for permission

As shown above and in **128**, **may** is used for formal permission, and **can** is used in less formal situations. In requests, however, the difference is less marked. We can say:
Can/Could/May I use your phone?

may I? is a little more formal than **could I?** but is quite often used for fairly informal requests.

might I? (conditional) can be used with a present meaning as an alternative to **may I? might** used in this way is more diffident than **may** and indicates greater uncertainty about the answer.
In indirect speech **may I?** will be reported by **might** (past) if the introductory verb is in a past tense. **might I?** will be reported unchanged:
'May/Might I see the letter?' he said
= *He asked if he might see the letter.*

2 Questions about permission are expressed by **can** or **am/is/are allowed**:
Can he take the car out whenever he likes?
Is he allowed to take the car out whenever he likes?
In the past we use **could** or **was/were allowed**:
Could the students choose what they wanted to study?
Were the students allowed to choose?

126 **may/might** expressing possibility

A 1 **may/might** + present infinitive can express possibility in the present or future:

He may/might tell his wife = Perhaps he tells/will tell his wife.
He may/might emigrate = Perhaps he will emigrate.
Ann may/might know Tom's address = Perhaps Ann knows etc.
Similarly with the continuous infinitive:
He may/might be waiting at the station = Perhaps he is waiting at the station.
He may/might be waiting at the station when we arrive = Perhaps he will be waiting etc.

2 **may** or **might**

Normally either can be used. **might** slightly increases the doubt.

Note that in speech we can also indicate increased doubt by stressing **may/might**.

Tom ˈmay lend you the money (with a strong stress on *may*) implies that this is not very likely.

Tom ˈmight lend you the money (with a strong stress on *might*) implies 'I don't think this is at all likely/I think it is unlikely'.

might, however, must be used when the expression is introduced by a verb in the past tense:
I knew we might have to wait at the frontier.
He said he might hire a car (indirect speech).
He told me he might be passing through our town in a few weeks (indirect speech).

3 Negative and interrogative

Negative presents no problems:
He may/might not believe your story = Perhaps he won't/doesn't believe your story.

The interrogative is normally expressed by **do you think?** or a construction with **likely**.
Do you think the plane will be late?
Is it likely that the plane will be late?
Is the plane likely to be late?

may? for possibility can never introduce a sentence. It may be placed later on:
When may we expect you?
What may be the result of the new tax?
But a construction with **likely** or **think** is more usual:
When are you likely to arrive?
When do you think you'll arrive?

might? is just possible:
Might they be waiting outside the station?
Could they be waiting? Do you think they are waiting? would be more usual (see **133**).

may and **might** in the affirmative, however, can form part of a question:
Do you think he may/might not be able to pay?
(See **100** B3 for this type of question.)

B **may/might** + perfect infinitive is used in speculations about past actions:
He may/might have gone = *It is possible that he went/has gone* or *Perhaps he went/has gone.*

might must be used, as shown above, when the main verb is in a past tense:
He said/thought that she might have missed the plane.

might, not **may**, must be used when the uncertainty no longer exists:
He came home alone. You shouldn't have let him do that; he might have got lost (but he didn't get lost).
So in the sentence:
You shouldn't have drunk the wine: it may/might have been drugged
the words *it may have been drugged* would indicate that we are still uncertain whether it was drugged or not. *it might have been drugged* could have the same meaning but could also mean that we know it wasn't drugged.

might, not **may**, is also used when the matter was never put to the test, as in:
Perhaps we should have taken the other road. It might have been quicker.
It's a good thing you didn't lend him the money. You might never have got it back.

Sentences of this kind are very similar to the third type of conditional sentence:
If we had taken the other road we might have arrived earlier.

C **may/might** can be used in conditional sentences instead of **will/would** to indicate a possible instead of a certain result:
If he sees you he will stop (certain).
If he sees you he may stop (possible).
Similarly:
If you poured hot water into it it might crack
and *If you had left it there someone might have stolen it.* (See **217** B.)

127 **may/might** can also be used (in the affirmative only) in the following ways:

A In the expression **may/might as well**:

I may/might as well + infinitive is a very unemphatic way of expressing an intention. **may/might as well** can be used with other persons to suggest or recommend an action:
I may/might as well start at once.
You may/might as well come with me.
He said that I might as well apply for the job.

might just as well means 'it would be equally good to' and is used to suggest an alternative action. It usually implies disapproval of a previously suggested action:
TOM: *I'll go on Monday by train.*
ANN: *You might just as well wait till Tuesday and go by plane.*

B **you might** can express a very casual command. It indicates that the speaker is quite certain that he will be obeyed, and is roughly equivalent to an imperative + **will you**:
You might post these for me = Post these for me, will you.
This form should only be used between friends.

C **might** can also be used for persuasive requests, or requests which indicate that the speaker is annoyed that the action in question has not been performed already:
You might tell me what he said can mean 'Please tell me/do tell me what he said' or 'I am annoyed that you haven't told me already/ You should have told me etc.'

might can also be used with other persons to express this sort of irritation:
He might pay us can mean 'We are annoyed that he doesn't pay/hasn't paid us'.

might + perfect infinitive can express irritation at, or reproach for, the non-performance of an action in the past:
You might have warned us that the bull was dangerous means 'We think that you should have warned us (but you didn't)'.

Note that when **might** is used in this way, there is a strong stress on the word the speaker wishes to emphasize:
You might have told us ˈearlier (you told us too late).
You might ˈthank him (why don't you thank him?).

D **may** + infinitive can be used in expressions of faith and hope:
May heaven reward you! = I hope heaven will reward you.

For **may/might** in purpose clauses see **309**.

can

128 can used to express permission

A Form

Present and future: *can* for all persons
Past and conditional: *could* for all persons
Negative: *cannot/can't, could not/couldn't*
Interrogative: *can I? could I?* etc.
Negative interrogative: *can I not/can't I? could I not/couldn't I?* etc.

can has no participles, so all other tenses have to be supplied by **allow** or **permit**:

I've been allowed to smoke ever since I left school.

can is followed by the infinitive without **to**.

B Use

can used for permission is an informal alternative to **may**. But it has a wider use than **may** for it can be used not only for giving permission, but also to express the idea of having permission: *You can take two books home with you* can mean 'I allow it' or 'the library allows it'. Similarly *You can't eat your sandwiches here* can mean 'I don't allow it' or 'the boss/the college etc. doesn't allow it'.

1 Affirmative and negative

1 Present and future: **can, could**

can is normally used, but **could** is possible when there is an idea of condition; so we can say:

You can phone from my house

or *You could phone from my house (if you want to).*

2 Past: **could, was/were allowed to**

could (not **can**) is used when the main verb is in a past tense:

Tom said I could park outside his house. (Tom or the police allowed this. *was allowed to park* would also be possible but would imply police permission rather than Tom's.)

could can also be used as a main verb meaning 'was/were allowed to':

On weekdays we had to get up early but on Sundays we could/were allowed to stay in bed till ten.

could used in this way expresses a general permission. When a particular action was permitted and performed, **was/were allowed to** must be used:

I had the right visa so I was allowed to cross the frontier.

permit could be used instead of **allow** in the above examples. (For **could** + perfect infinitive used for permission see **132** C.)

2 Interrogative: requests for permission (see also **125** B)

Either **can** or **could** can be used for present or future:

Can I/Could I park here?

could is a little more formal than **can** here and students are recommended to use it.

can't I/couldn't I? is also possible:

Can't I/Couldn't I pay by cheque? (See **101**.)

Note that answers will normally be with **can/can't**, though **could** is possible:

Can I/Could I leave my case here? Yes, you can/No, you can't.

(For **can/could** in purpose and conditional clauses see **215–17**, **309**.)

129 **can** used to express possibility

A General possibility

you/one can can mean 'it is possible', i.e. circumstances permit (this is quite different from the kind of possibility expressed by **may**):

You can ski on the hills (there is enough snow).

You can't bathe here on account of the sharks (it isn't safe).

Can you get to the top of the mountain in one day? (is it possible?)

can cannot be used in this way in a future sense. To express a future possibility of this type we have to use **it will be possible** or **people/you/we** etc. **will be able**:

When the new tunnel is ready we'll be able to get to the town much more easily.

B **can** can also express occasional possibility:

Measles can be quite dangerous (sometimes it is possible for them to be quite dangerous/sometimes they are quite dangerous).

The Straits of Dover can be very rough (it is possible for the Straits to be rough; this sometimes happens).

could is used in the past:

He could be very unreasonable (sometimes he was unreasonable; this was a possibility).

can is used in this way in the present or past tense only, and only in the affirmative.

130 **can** expressing ability: **can** and **be able**

can here is used in conjunction with **to be able** (the verb **be** + the

adjective **able**), which supplies the missing parts of **can** and provides an alternative form for the present and past tense. We have therefore the following forms:
Infinitive: *to be able*
Past participle: *been able*

	Affirmative	*Negative*	*Interrogative*
Present	can *or* am able	cannot *or* am not able	can I? *or* am I able?
Past	could *or* was able	could not *or* was not able	could I? *or* was I able?
Future	I will/shall be able *or* he will be able	I will/shall not be able *or* he will not be able	will/shall I be able? *or* will he be able?

There is only one future form, for **can** is not used in the future except to express permission. In the conditional, however, we have two forms: *could* and *would be able.*

All other tenses are formed with **be able** according to the rules for ordinary verbs: e.g.
Present perfect: *have been able*
Past perfect: *had been able*

Negative interrogatives are formed in the usual way:
couldn't you/weren't you able? *won't you be able?* etc.

can, be, will, shall not and **have** can be contracted in the usual way:
I wasn't able *he won't be able* *I'd been able*

can is followed by the infinitive without **to**.
be able is followed by the infinitive with **to**.

131 can/am able, could/was able

A can and be able

1 **shall/will be able** is the only future form:
Our baby will be able to walk in a few weeks.

2 Either **can** or **am able** may be used in the present. **can** is the more usual:
Can you/Are you able to type?
I can't pay you today. Can you wait till tomorrow? (See also B below).

3 For the present perfect, however, we must use the **be able** form:
Since his accident he hasn't been able to leave the house.

B could

1 **could** can be used with a present meaning when there is an idea of condition:
Could you run the business by yourself? (if this was necessary)

Could he get another job? (if he left this one)
I could get you a copy (if you want one).
In the first two examples **could** is replaceable by **would be able**.

2 **could you?** is a very good way of introducing a request. It is an alternative to **would you** and a little more polite:
Could you show me the way/lend me £5/wait half an hour?
Could you please send me an application form?
couldn't you? is also useful:
HOUSEHOLDER: *Could you come round and mend a leak in my hot water tank?*
PLUMBER: *Would sometime next month suit you?*
HOUSEHOLDER: *Couldn't you come a little earlier?*

C **could** and **was able** used for past ability:

1 For ability only, either can be used:
When I was young I could/was able to climb any tree in the forest.

2 For ability + particular action, use **was able**:
Although the pilot was badly hurt he was able to explain what had happened (he could and did explain).
The boat capsized quite near the bank so the children were able to swim to safety (they could and did swim).
This rule, however, is relaxed in the negative and with verbs of the senses:
He read the message but he couldn't/wasn't able to understand it.
I could/was able to see him through the window.

D **had been able** is the past perfect form:
He said he had lost his passport and hadn't been able to leave the country.
(For **could** in reported speech see **307**.)

132 **could** + perfect infinitive is used for past ability when:

A the action was not performed:
I could have lent you the money. Why didn't you ask me?
(See also **148**.)

or B we don't know whether it was performed or not:
The money has disappeared! Who could have taken it?
Tom could have (taken it); he was here alone yesterday.
Compare:
He was able to send a message (he sent it)
with *He could have sent a message* (he didn't send it or we don't know whether he sent it or not).

C This form can also be used for permission:
You could have gone yesterday = You were free to go yesterday, but you didn't go.

133 could is sometimes a possible alternative to **may/might** (possibility)

A **could be** can be used instead of **may/might be**:
A: *I wonder where Tom is.*
B: *He may/might/could be in the library* = Perhaps he is in the library.
Similarly when **be** is part of the continuous infinitive:
A: *I wonder why Bill isn't here?*
B: *He may/might/could be still waiting for a bus* = Perhaps he is still waiting for a bus.
And when **be** is part of a passive infinitive:
A: *Do you think the plane will be on time?*
B: *I don't know. It may/might/could be delayed by fog* = Perhaps it will be delayed by fog.
In the interrogative we can use either **could** or **might**:
Might/Could he be waiting for us at the station? = Do you think he is waiting . . . ?
But in the negative there is a difference of meaning between **could** and **may/might**:
He may/might not be driving the car himself = Perhaps he isn't driving the car himself.
But *He couldn't be driving the car himself* expresses a negative deduction. It means 'This is impossible. He can't drive'. (See **134**.)

B **could** + the perfect infinitive of any verb can be used instead of **may/might** + perfect infinitive (possibility):
A: *I wonder how Tom knew about Ann's engagement.*
B: *He may/might/could have heard it from Jack* = Perhaps he heard it from Jack.
As in A above, in the interrogative we can use **might** or **could**:
Could/Might the bank have made a mistake? = Do you think it is possible that the bank (has) made a mistake?
But in the negative the meanings differ:
Ann might not have seen Tom yesterday (perhaps she didn't see him)
but *Ann couldn't have seen Tom yesterday* (negative deduction—perhaps Ann and Tom were in different towns).

134 **can't** and **couldn't** used to express negative deduction

A Negative deduction about a present event can be expressed by **can't** or **couldn't** with the present infinitive of the verb **be**:

ANN: *He says he is still reading 'The Old Man and the Sea'.*
TOM: *He can't/couldn't be still reading it. I gave it to him ages ago and it's quite a short book.*

CHILD: *Can I have some sweets? I'm hungry.*
MOTHER: *You can't/couldn't be hungry. You've just had dinner.*

ANN: *There's an aeroplane hovering over our house.*
TOM: *Then it can't/couldn't be an aeroplane. It must be a helicopter.*

B Negative deduction about a past event is expressed by **can't/ couldn't** + perfect infinitive of any verb:

ANN: *Who brought the grand piano upstairs?*
MARY: *Perhaps it was Tom.*
ANN: *He can't/couldn't have done it by himself.*

TOM: *A man answered the phone. I suppose it was her husband.*
ANN: *It couldn't have been her husband. He's been dead for ages.*

TOM: *I feel terribly ill this morning.*
ANN: *The meat you had for dinner last night can't/couldn't have been good* (the meat probably wasn't good).

couldn't must be used when the supposition or deduction forms part of a sentence whose main verb is in the past tense:
Ann said that the meat couldn't have been good.

14 must, have to, need

Obligation

135 must, have to and need in tabular form

(The **have to** forms are not given in full.)

	Obligation	*Absence of obligation*	*Negative obligation*
Future	must will have to	need not won't have to won't need to	must not
Present	must have to	need not don't have to don't need to	must not
Past	had to	didn't have to didn't need to hadn't (got) to	

136 must, must not and need not compared to the other forms

A **must, must not** and **need not** express the speaker's authority:
MOTHER (to child): *You must do your homework before you watch TV*
or *You must not turn on the TV till you have done your homework.*
But on Friday she might say:
You needn't do your homework tonight. You can leave it till tomorrow.

B The other forms **have to/will have to/had to** and **won't/don't/didn't need to** express external obligation:
TOM'S SISTER: *Tom is starting work next week. He'll have to get up early. He'll hate that.*
Sometimes **must** and **need not** can be used for external obligation also. **need not** is quite often used in this way, especially in the first person, e.g. *We needn't hurry. We've got lots of time.* The matter will be dealt with in the following paragraphs.

137 must not and need not compared

must not expresses negative obligation or the speaker's emphatic advice:
You must not tell anyone = Don't tell anyone/It would be wrong or foolish to tell anyone.
ZOO NOTICE: *Visitors must not feed the giraffes.*

RAILWAY NOTICE: *Passengers must not walk on the railway line.*
You mustn't wear pink; it doesn't suit you (advice).

need not expresses absence of obligation. The speaker gives permission for an action not to be performed, or sometimes merely states that an action is unnecessary:
EMPLOYER (to secretary): *You needn't make two copies. One will do.*
ANN (to friend who has come to visit her): *You needn't lock your car. This is a very honest area.*

Examples of **must not** and **need not**:
You must not drive fast. There is a speed limit here.
You need not drive fast; we have plenty of time.
You must not take more than two of these pills at once. Three would be harmful.
You need not take any more pills. You are well again now.

138 must and have to

A **must** has the same form for all persons of the present and future. The negative is **must not (mustn't)** and the interrogative is **must I?** etc.

must has no infinitive and no past tense. We use **had to** for the past tense.

must is followed by the infinitive without **to** and expresses obligation or emphatic advice:
EXAM REGULATIONS: *Candidates must be in their places by 9 a.m.*
You don't know enough people. You must join a club and make friends.

B **have to** (The **'to'** is part of the following infinitives. See **116**.)
Forms

	Affirmative	*Negative*	*Interrogative*
Future	will/shall have to	won't/shan't have to	shall I have to? will he have to?
Present	have (got) to* have to*	haven't (got) to* don't have to*	have I (got) to?* do you have to?*
Past	had to	didn't have to hadn't (got) to	did you have to? had you (got) to?

***have to** (without **got**) is the correct form for habitual actions, but it can be used for single actions also.
have got to is for single actions only.
In the negative, **don't have to** is the correct form for habitual action, but can be used for single actions also.
haven't (got) to is for single actions only.

139 Difference between the **must** and **have to** forms in the affirmative

Both express obligation but **must** expresses an obligation imposed by the speaker while **have to** expresses an external obligation, i.e. one imposed by external authority or circumstances:

You must clean your own boots (these are my orders).
You will have to clean your boots when you join the army (the army will oblige you to do it).
That boy has to practise the piano every day (his parents insist).
Mr Pitt has to work very hard (circumstances make this necessary).

If the speaker adds his support or approval to the existing external authority he may use **must**:

Children must obey their parents (the speaker approves).
Children have to obey their parents (the speaker merely states the fact).

In the first person this difference is less important and very often either form is possible, though **have to** should be used for habits and **must** for an important or urgent obligation:

I have to be at my office at nine every day (habit).
We have to water this cactus once a month (habit).
I must be at the station at ten. It's most important.

140 Difference between the **must** and **have to** forms in the interrogative

It is always safe to use a **have to** form here.

have to must be used for external obligations in the future:

A: *Shall I have to obey the teachers when I go to school?*
B: *Yes, they will be very angry if you don't obey them.*

A: *Will Mr Pitt have to cook his own meals when his wife is away?*
B: *Yes, I expect he will.*

A: *Will you have to read Spinoza when you go to college?*
B: *Yes, it is one of the set books.*

It should also be used in the third person for external obligations in the present:

Has that man got to carry all those parcels by himself?
Does she have to do it by hand?

Otherwise either form can be used, though **have to** is better for habits (see below):

CHILD: *Must I clean my teeth tonight?/Have I got to clean them?*
When must I do it?/When have I got to do it?
Must you go/Have you got to go now or can you wait a little longer?

have to has alternative interrogative forms (see **116**), i.e. in the present we can say *Have I got to?* or *Do I have to?* etc. There is no difference in meaning but *Do I have to?* etc. is better for habits: *Do you have to wind your watch every day?*

For the past we have *Had you (got) to?* and *Did you have to?* etc. There is no difference but *Did you have to?* etc. is more usual: *Did you have to pay customs duty on that?*

141 Some more examples (all persons and tenses)

MOTHER (to son): *You must change your socks if they get wet* (obligation imposed by speaker).

RAILWAY NOTICE: *Passengers must cross the line by the footbridge* (obligation imposed by the railway company).

NOTICE (in an art gallery): *Visitors must leave bags and umbrellas in the cloakroom* (obligation imposed by the authorities).

I will have to go/must go in a few minutes. I don't want to miss my train.

We can't afford to employ people. We have to do all our own repairs.

I must tell you something very important.

ANGRY FATHER: *If Tom comes in after midnight he must come in quietly; he woke me up last night.*

You must get your hair cut (I think it is too long).

You will have to get your hair cut when you join the army (the army will make you cut it).

You must come and have dinner with me some time (quite a usual way of expressing a casual invitation).

We must celebrate your engagement (a casual way of expressing an intention).

He must be here in time tomorrow; I can't wait for him.

He has to be at his office in time; his employer is very angry if he's late.

If there are no taxis we shall have to walk.

If your father was a poor man you would have to work.

Have you got to finish that tonight?

Did you have to clean the house yourself?

Will you have to pay tax on what I pay you?

(For **must/needn't** in reported speech see **306**.)

142 need

need can be treated as an auxiliary or as an ordinary verb. As an auxiliary, it is used mainly in the negative and interrogative. It has no past tense and the same form, **need**, is used for present and future.

Present/future:
Affirmative: *need* for all persons*
Negative: *need not/needn't* for all persons
Interrogative: *need I? need you? need he? need we?* etc.

***need** as an auxiliary is used in the affirmative only when a negative or interrogative sentence is prefixed by an expression, which changes the negative or interrogative verb into an affirmative:

I needn't wear a coat but *I don't suppose I need wear a coat.*
Need I tell Tom? but *Do you think I need tell Tom?*

need not, as already explained in **137**, expresses absence of obligation, and must not be confused with **must not**, which expresses negative obligation.

need I? etc. however is very similar to **must I?** etc. (See **145**.)

143 Other forms of **need**

need can also be conjugated as an ordinary verb. It then follows the normal pattern for regular verbs (see **149**).

The negative and interrogative forms are:

	Negative	*Interrogative*
Future	won't/shan't need	shall I/we need? will you/he etc. need?
Present	I/we/you/they don't need he/she doesn't need	do I/we/you etc. need? does he/she need?
Past	didn't need	did I etc. need?

These forms, followed by the infinitive with **to**, are possible alternatives to the negative and interrogative **have to** forms, i.e.

won't/shan't need to = won't/shan't have to
don't/doesn't need to = don't/doesn't have to (for habits or single actions)
didn't need to = didn't have to

(**to need** in the affirmative is not normally used for obligation.)

144 Absence of obligation: **need not** contrasted with other forms

A Present and future

1 As already stated, **need not** expresses the speaker's authority or advice:

TOM (lending money to Bill): *You needn't pay me back till next month.*
TEACHER: *You needn't bring your textbooks tomorrow.*
JULIA (to friend who is coming to stay with her): *You needn't bring warm clothes. It's very hot here.*

2 The other forms are used when we are concerned with external authority or external circumstances:
Ann hasn't got to go to the lecture. Attendance is optional.
Peter doesn't have to pay for his lunch. He gets his meals free.

3 Sometimes, however, **need not** can be used for external authority also, as an alternative to **won't/don't need to** or **won't/don't have to** forms. This is particularly common in the first person:
ANN: *I needn't (won't/don't have to) type this report today. Mr Jones said that there was no hurry about it.*

Note, however, that though it is possible to use **need not** for a future habitual action:
I'm retiring. After Friday I need never go to the office again.
it is not possible to use it for a present habitual action:
I don't have to queue for my bus. I get on at the terminus. (**need not** could not be used here.)

B Past

Here the distinction between the speaker's authority and external authority disappears, and we have a choice of three forms: **didn't have to, didn't need to** and **hadn't got to**. There is no difference in meaning. **didn't have to** is the most usual:
I didn't have to wait long. He was only a few minutes late.
When he was at university he didn't have to/need to pay anything for his keep, for he stayed with his uncle.

didn't have to/need to can be used for single or habitual actions, **hadn't got to** for single actions only.

C It may help the student to see the various forms grouped according to time:

	Speaker's authority	*External authority*
Future	need not	shan't/won't have to shan't/won't need to
Present	need not	haven't got to (single action only) don't have to / don't need to } (single/habitual action)
Past	didn't have to / didn't need to } (single/habitual action) hadn't got to (single action only)	

145 must, have to and need in the interrogative

need I? etc. can be used instead of **must I?** etc., except when **must** follows an interrogative word (i.e. When? Where? Who? What? etc.), because **need?** cannot be used after interrogatives: in the sentence *Where must I put it?* **need** could not be used.

Both **need?** and **must?** imply that the person addressed is the authority concerned. **need?** also implies that the speaker is hoping for a negative answer: *Must I go, mother?* and *Need I go, mother?* mean the same, but in the second question the speaker is hoping that his mother will say *No*. The other interrogative form of **need**, **do I need?** etc., can be used similarly. Note possible answers:

Question	Affirmative answer	Negative answer
Shall I have to go?	*Yes, you will.*	*No, you won't.*
Have I got to go?	*Yes, you have.*	*No, you haven't.*
Does he have to go?	*Yes, he does.*	*No, he doesn't.*
Need I go?	*Yes, you must.*	*No, you needn't.*
Must I go?	*Yes, you must.*	*No, you needn't.*

146 **needn't** + perfect infinitive is used to express an unnecessary action which was nevertheless performed:

I needn't have written to him because he phoned me shortly afterwards (but I did write, thus wasting my time).

You needn't have brought your umbrella for we are going by car (but you have brought your umbrella unnecessarily).

He needn't have left home so early; the train won't be here for an hour (but the man is already at the station and so will have an hour to wait).

147 needn't have (done) compared with didn't have/need (to do)

A **needn't have done**—no obligation but action performed (unnecessarily), i.e. time wasted.

You needn't have watered the flowers, for it is going to rain (you wasted your time).

You needn't have written such a long essay. The teacher only asked for 300 words, and you have written 600.

He needn't have bought such a large house. His wife would have been quite happy in a cottage (waste of money).

You needn't have carried all these parcels yourself. The shop would have delivered them if you had asked them.

B **didn't have/need to do**—no obligation, and normally no action.

I didn't have to translate it for him for he understands Dutch.

I didn't have to cut the grass myself. My brother did it (no obligation and no action).

Some people do use **didn't have to/didn't need to** for actions which were performed. The **have** or **need** is then usually stressed: *You didn't ˈhave to give him my name* would then mean 'It wasn't

necessary to give him my name, but you gave it to him'. But the student is advised to use **needn't have** + past participle when an unnecessary action was performed:
You needn't have given him my name.

148 needn't have/could have/should have + past participles

A **needn't have** + past participle is often combined with **could have** + past participle. The use of this combination is best shown by example:

A: *I wanted a copy of the letter, so I typed it twice.*
B: *You needn't have typed it twice. You could have used a carbon.*

A: *I walked up six flights of stairs.*
B: *You needn't have walked up; you could have taken the lift.*

A: *She stood in a queue to get a 20p Underground ticket.*
B: *But she needn't have stood in a queue. She could have got a ticket from the machine.*

B **needn't have** and **should have** compared

should or **ought to** could be used instead of **need** or **could** in all the examples in A above:
She shouldn't have stood in a queue. She should have got tickets from the machine.
But there is a difference of meaning:
She shouldn't have stood in a queue = It was wrong or foolish of her to stand in a queue.
She needn't have stood in a queue = It was not necessary to do this (but she did it).
shouldn't have (done) implies criticism.
needn't have (done) does not imply criticism.
Similarly *You should have got tickets from the machine* means 'It was foolish of you not to get tickets from the machine'.
But *You could have got tickets* etc. does not imply criticism. It merely states the fact.

149 to need as an ordinary verb, meaning 'require'

As shown in **143, need** can be conjugated as an ordinary verb. It then has the normal regular forms, but no continuous tense.

Infinitive: *to need*
Future: *will/shall need*
Present: *I/we/you/they need, he/she/it needs*
Past: *needed*
Negative and interrogative forms are shown in **143**.

to need can be used with an infinitive, as shown in **143**, or with a noun/pronoun object:
How much money do you need? I need £5.

need can also be used with the passive infinitive or gerund in such sentences as:
Your hair needs to be cut/needs cutting.
The windows need to be cleaned/need cleaning.
want + gerund can be used instead of **need** here:
Your hair wants cutting.
want + passive infinitive is also possible.

150 Diagram showing **must** (obligation) and **must** (deduction)

must

	Obligation	*Deduction*
Present	must (be)	must (be)
Past	had (to be)	must (have been)

Notes:
1 In the present the same form, **must** + present infinitive, is used for both obligation and deduction.
2 In the past the forms are different: for obligation we use **had to**, for deduction we use **must** + perfect infinitive.
3 **must** for obligation can be used in the affirmative, negative and interrogative. **must** for deduction can be used in the affirmative only.

151 **must** for deduction

This use is best seen by examples:

A Considering a present action or situation: **must** + present infinitive:

A: *Tom has a house in London, a flat in Paris and a bungalow in Miami.*
B: *He must be rich.*

A: *I've had no sleep for 48 hours.*
B: *You must be exhausted.*

A: *My brother develops his own films.*
B: *He must save a lot of money.*

B Considering a past action or situation: **must** + perfect infinitive:

A: *They quarrelled quite often and whenever they quarrelled they threw plates at each other.*
B: *They must have broken a lot of plates.*

A: *I took the Underground to Marble Arch. I'm not sure what line it was.*
B: *It must have been the Central Line; no other line goes through Marble Arch.*

Imagine that Bob shares a flat with his brother, Peter, and that no one else ever enters the flat. Ann meets Bob one day and says:
ANN: *I rang your flat yesterday. A man answered but I didn't recognize the voice.*
BOB: *Oh, it must have been my brother, Peter.*

152 Negative deduction

Negative deductions, however, are normally made with **can't** or **couldn't** + the present infinitive of **to be** or the perfect infinitive of any verb (see also **134**):

He was terribly tired after walking six kilometres. He can't be at all strong.
Tom can't have written this because it is in French and he doesn't know French (present deduction about past action).
Jones couldn't have caught the nine o'clock train for he only left his house at 9.15.

Either **can't** or **couldn't** can be used when the deduction is made in the present. **couldn't**, however, must be used when the deduction is made in the past:

He knew that she couldn't have stolen it as she hadn't been in the house at the time.

153 must (deduction) compared to may/might

The difference is best seen by examples:

1 Imagine that we have four keys on a ring and we know that one of these keys opens the cellar door. We might begin by picking one key and saying:
This may/might be the key = Perhaps this is the key.
But after trying three keys unsuccessfully, we will pick up the fourth key and say:
This must be the key (no other choice remains).

2 A: *I wonder why Tom hasn't answered my letter.*
B: *He may/might be ill* = Perhaps he is ill (but there are other possibilities also: he may be away or too busy to answer).
But imagine that Bill never has any visitors. If an ambulance stops at his door the neighbours will say:
Bill must be ill (this is the only possible explanation of the arrival of the ambulance).

3 Similarly, when considering a past action:
He may have come by train = Perhaps he came by train (but there are other possibilities: he might have come by taxi or bus).

But *He must have come by taxi* implies that he had no choice. There was no other way of making this journey.

15 The auxiliaries **ought, dare, used**

154 ought to

ought has no infinitive and no inflexions (i.e. the same form is used for all persons). **ought** can be used as a present or future tense and in the past when preceded by a verb in the past tense. It is followed by the infinitive with **to**, and to remind students of this it is often referred to as **ought to**. The negative is **ought not (oughtn't)**, the interrogative **ought I? ought you?** etc.:

They ought to do it tomorrow. *Ought we to do it at once?*
I knew that I ought not to open the letter.

In conversation either **ought** or **ought to** can often be used alone, the infinitive being understood but not mentioned:

A: *You ought to paint your hall door.*
B: *Yes, I know I ought/ought to.*

155 ought to compared to must, have to and should

A **ought to** expresses the subject's obligations or duty. But here there is neither the speaker's authority (as with **must**), nor an outside authority (as with **have to**). The speaker is only reminding the subject of his duty, or giving advice or indicating a correct or sensible action. It is usually said without much emphasis.

should can be used in exactly the same way (see **235**) and questions or remarks with **ought to** can be answered with **should**:

A: *You ought to/should finish your work before going out.*
B: *I know I should.*

You ought to obey your parents.

A: *You oughtn't to eat between meals; it will make you fat.*
B: *I know I oughtn't to.*

Compare with **have to** and **must**:
You have to obey Mr Pitt (Mr Pitt insists on it).
You must obey Mr Pitt (the speaker insists on, or approves of, Mr Pitt's authority).
Tom, you ought to obey Mr Pitt (neither the speaker's authority nor Mr Pitt's is involved here, but the speaker thinks that obeying Mr Pitt is advisable or part of Tom's duty).
You have to take these blue pills (the doctor insists on it).
You mustn't drink this; it is poison.
You oughtn't to smoke so much; you are wasting your money.

B Like **must**, **ought to** can also be used in giving advice, but it is much less forceful than **must**: *You ought to go to Paris* is much less emphatic than *You must go to Paris*.

156 **ought to** and the perfect infinitive

This construction is used to express an unfulfilled duty or a sensible action that was neglected:

I ought to have taken those books back to the library last week. Now they are overdue and I shall have to pay a fine.

You ought to have told him that the paint on that seat is wet.

You ought to have waited till the lights were green before crossing the road.

You oughtn't to have crossed the road when the lights were red.

should with the perfect infinitive is used in exactly the same way.

157 **dare**

In the affirmative **dare** is conjugated like an ordinary verb, i.e. **dare/dares** in the present, **dared** in the past. But in the negative and interrogative it can be conjugated either like an ordinary verb or like an auxiliary:

Negative present	do/does not dare	dare not
past	did not dare	dared not
Interrogative present	do you/does he dare?	dare you/he?
past	did you/did he dare?	dared you/he?

Infinitives after **dare**

Negative and interrogative forms with **do/did** are in theory followed by the infinitive with **to**, but in practice the **to** is often omitted:

He doesn't dare (to) say anything.

Did he dare (to) criticize my arrangements?

dare I/he/you etc. and **dare not** forms take the infinitive without **to**:

Dare we interrupt? *They dared not move.*

When **dare** is preceded by *nobody, anybody* etc. the **to** is optional:

Nobody dared (to) speak.

dare is not much used in the affirmative except in the expression **I daresay. I daresay** (or **I dare say**) has two idiomatic meanings:

1 I suppose:

I daresay there'll be a restaurant car on the train.

2 I accept what you say (but it doesn't make any difference):

ENGLISH TOURIST: *But I drive on the left in England!*

SWISS POLICEMAN: *I daresay you do, but you must drive on the right here.*

TRAVELLER: *But the watch was given to me; I didn't buy it.*
CUSTOMS OFFICER: *I daresay you didn't, but you'll have to pay duty on it all the same.*

daresay is used in this way with the first person singular only.

how dare(d) you? how dare(d) he/they? can express indignation:
How dare you open my letters? (I am angry with you for opening them).
How dared he complain? (I am indignant because he complained).

dare is also an ordinary transitive verb meaning 'challenge' (but only to deeds requiring courage). It is followed by object + infinitive with **to**:

MOTHER: *Why did you throw that stone through the window?*
SON: *Another boy dared me (to throw it).*

158 used to

A Form

used to is the past tense of a defective verb which has no present tense.

Affirmative: *used* for all persons
Negative: *used not/usedn't* for all persons
Interrogative: *used you/used he/used they?* etc.
Negative interrogative: *usedn't you/he/they?* etc.

Negative and interrogative can also be formed with **did**:
didn't use to *did you use to?* *didn't you use to?*
This is a more informal form, fairly common in conversation.

used is followed by the infinitive with **to**, and to remind students of this it is often referred to as **used to** (just as **have** used for obligation is referred to as **have to**).

B Use

used to is used:

1 To express a discontinued habit or a past situation which contrasts with the present:
I used to smoke cigarettes; now I smoke a pipe.
He used to drink beer; now he drinks wine.
She usedn't to like Tom but she quite likes him now
or *She used to dislike Tom but she quite likes him now.*

used is not normally stressed, but it can be stressed if the speaker wishes to emphasize the contrast between past and present.

2 To express a past routine or pattern. Here we are not making a contrast between past and present; we are merely describing someone's routine during a certain period. Very often there is a

succession of actions. **used to** here is replaceable by **would** (but **would** cannot replace **used to** for a discontinued habit etc. as in 1 above). **used to** here is always unstressed.

Tom and Ann were a young married couple. Every morning Tom used to kiss Ann and set off for work. Ann used to stand at the window and wave goodbye. In the evening she used to welcome him home and ask him to tell her all about his day.

If we use **would** we have:

Every morning Tom would kiss Ann and set off for work. Ann would stand at the window and wave goodbye etc.

Remember that **used to** has no present form. So for present habits or routines we must use the simple present tense.

159 **used** as an adjective: **to be/become/get used to**

used can also be an adjective meaning 'accustomed'. It is then preceded by **be, become** or **get** in any tense and followed by the preposition **to** + noun/pronoun or gerund:

I am used to noise.
I am used to working in a noisy room.
You will soon get used to the electric typewriters.
You will soon get used to typing on electric typewriters.
They soon got used to the traffic regulations.
They soon got used to driving on the left.

I am used to . . . etc. is a psychological statement. *I am used to working in a noisy room* means that I have worked in a noisy room, so the noise doesn't bother me; I don't mind it. *You'll soon get used to typing on electric typewriters* means that after you have used them for a while you will find them quite easy to use.

Very often *I'm used to it* has the meaning 'I don't mind it/It doesn't give me any trouble', as in the above examples. But it can work the other way. Imagine our canteen serves only tea with its meals. A Frenchman, newly arrived from France, might say:

I'm used to wine with my meals, so I find these lunches rather unsatisfying.

Do not confuse subject + **be/become/get** + **used to** with subject + **used (to)**. In the first **used** is an adjective and **to** is a preposition. In the second **used** is a verb and **to** is part of the following infinitive (see also **260**).

Do not confuse these forms with the regular verb **to use** (/ju:z/) meaning 'employ'.

16 The present tenses

There are two present tenses in English:
The present continuous: *I am working.*
The simple present: *I work.*

The present continuous

160 Form

The present continuous tense is formed with the present tense of the auxiliary verb **to be** + the present participle (the infinitive + **ing**):

I am working *you are working* *he is working* etc.

The negative is formed by putting **not** after the auxiliary:

I am not working, you are not working, he is not working, etc.

The interrogative is formed by inverting subject and auxiliary:

am I working? *are you working?* *is he working?* etc.

Negative interrogative:

am I not working? are you not working? is he not working? etc.

161 The present continuous tense of the verb **to work**

Affirmative	*Negative*	*Interrogative*
I am working	I am not working	am I working?
you are working	you are not working	are you working?
he is working	he is not working	is he working?
we are working	we are not working	are we working?
you are working	you are not working	are you working?
they are working	they are not working	are they working?

Contractions: **to be** can be contracted in the present affirmative, negative and negative interrogative as shown in **109**, so the present continuous tense of any verb can be contracted:

I'm working	*I'm not working*	*aren't I working?*
you're working	*you're not/you aren't working*	*aren't you working?*
he's working	*he's not/he isn't working*	*isn't he working?*

Note the irregular contraction for **am I not.**

162 Note on the spelling of the present participle

A When a verb ends in a single **e**, this **e** is dropped before **ing**:

love, loving *hate, hating* *argue, arguing*

This does not happen when the verb ends in **ee**:
agree, agreeing *see, seeing*

B When a verb of one syllable has one vowel and ends in a single consonant, this consonant is doubled before **ing**:
hit, hitting *run, running* *stop, stopping*
Verbs of two or more syllables whose last syllable contains only one vowel and ends in a single consonant double this consonant if the stress falls on the last syllable:
be'gin, beginning *pre'fer, preferring* *ad'mit, admitting*
but *'enter, entering* (stress not on the last syllable)
A final **l** after a single vowel is, however, always doubled:
travel, travelling *signal, signalling*

C **ing** can be added to a verb ending in **y** without affecting the spelling of the verb:
carry, carrying *hurry, hurrying* *enjoy, enjoying*

163 The present continuous tense is used:

A For an action happening now:
It is raining (now). *I am not wearing a coat as it isn't cold.*
Why are you sitting at my desk?
What is the baby doing? He is tearing up a £5 note.

B For an action happening about this time but not necessarily at the moment of speaking:
I am reading a play by Shaw. (This may mean 'at the moment of speaking' but may also mean 'now' in a more general sense.)
He is teaching French and learning Greek. (He may not be doing either at the moment of speaking.)
When two continuous tenses, having the same subject, are joined by **and**, the auxiliary may be dropped before the second verb, as in the above example. This applies to all pairs of compound tenses.

C For a definite arrangement in the near future (and is the most usual way of expressing one's immediate plans):
I'm meeting Peter tonight. He is taking me to the theatre.
A: *Are you doing anything tomorrow afternoon?*
B: *Yes, I'm playing tennis with Ann.*
Note that the time of the action must always be mentioned, as otherwise there might be confusion between present and future meanings. **go** and **come**, however, can be used in this way without a time expression.
(See **197**.)

164 Other possible uses of the present continuous:

A With a point in time to indicate an action which begins before this point and probably continues after it:
At six I am bathing the baby (i.e. I start bathing him before six).
It can be used similarly with a verb in the simple present:
They are flying over the desert when one of the engines fails.
The present continuous is rarely used in this way except in descriptions of daily routine and in dramatic narrative, but with the past continuous such combinations are very useful. (See **176**.)

B With **always** for a frequently repeated action, often one which annoys the speaker or seems unreasonable to him:
Tom is always going away for weekends (present continuous).
This implies that he goes away very often, probably too often in the speaker's opinion; but it does not necessarily mean that he goes away every weekend. It is not a literal statement. Compare with:
Tom always goes away at weekends (simple present tense)
= *Tom goes away every weekend* (a literal statement).
Similarly, compare:
He is always doing homework (implying that he spends too much time on it in the speaker's opinion)
and *He always does his homework* (simple present tense), which merely means that he does it regularly.
Sometimes, especially when used with the first person, **always** with the continuous tense implies that the action is accidental, while **always** with a simple tense would imply a deliberate action:
I always do that would imply a deliberate routine action but *I am always doing that* would usually imply an accidental action.

165 Verbs not normally used in the continuous tenses

A The continuous tenses are normally used only for deliberate actions. The following groups of verbs are, therefore, not normally used in continuous tenses:

1 Verbs of the senses (involuntary actions): *feel, hear, see, smell*; also *notice* and *observe* (= notice).
Exception: *feel* in some uses (see 2 (2) below) and *enjoy*.
For verbs implying deliberate use of the senses, *listen, look, smell* (= sniff at), *watch,* see B below.

2 Verbs expressing feelings and emotions, e.g. *adore, appreciate* (= value), *care* (= like), *desire, detest, fear, hate, like, loathe, love, mind, value, want, wish.*

Exceptions:

1 *long for*, which follows the normal rules for continuous tenses.

2 *feel,* when followed by an adjective indicating the subject's emotions or physical or mental condition, e.g. *well/ill, hot/cold, tense/relaxed, happy/sad, nervous/confident, anxious/relieved, angry/pleased,* is normally used in the simple tenses, but can be used in the continuous also:

How do you feel/are you feeling?
I feel/am feeling better/quite well.
He feels/is feeling much happier now.

3 Verbs of mental activity, e.g. *agree, appreciate* (=understand), *believe, expect* (=think), *feel* (=think), *feel sure/certain, forget, know, mean, perceive, realize, recall, recognize, recollect, remember, see* (=understand), *see through someone* (=penetrate his attempt to deceive), *think* (=have an opinion), *trust* (=believe/have confidence in), *understand.*

4 Verbs of possession: *belong, owe, own, possess.*

5 The auxiliaries, except *be* and *have* in certain uses.

6 *appear* (=seem), *concern, consist, hold* (=contain), *keep* (=continue), *matter, seem, signify.*

Verbs which cannot be used in the continuous tenses have therefore only one present tense, the simple present:

Don't you feel the house shaking?
Do you see the rainbow? *I value your support.*
I appreciate what you've done for me. *I remember him very well.*
I don't mind waiting. *I think I understand what he wants.*
I suppose you know what this means.
I smell something burning.

B Note on involuntary and deliberate verbs of the senses.

The verbs *see, hear* and *smell* are involuntary actions. If our eyes are open, we see—both pleasant and unpleasant sights. Unless we cover our ears, we hear—both pleasant and unpleasant sounds. But the verbs *listen, look* and *watch* are deliberate actions, entirely under our control. We listen, look or watch because we choose to. These verbs therefore follow the normal rule for continuous tenses:

It's a nuisance if the phone rings when you are watching an interesting programme on TV.

smell can mean 'sniff at' and is then, of course, a deliberate action:

Why are you smelling the fish? Has it gone bad?

But *I smell gas. There must be a leak somewhere.*

166 **see, hear, smell, feel** can also be used in some senses as deliberate actions. They can then be put into continuous tenses:

see can mean 'meet by appointment' (usually for business), 'interview':

The director is seeing the applicants this morning.
I am seeing my solicitor tomorrow (definite future arrangement, see **163** C).

see can mean 'visit' (usually as a tourist):
Tom is seeing the town/the sights.

see about = make arrangements or enquiries:
We are seeing about a work permit for you (trying to arrange this).

see to = arrange, put right, deal with:
The plumber is here. He is seeing to the leak in our tank.

see somebody **out** = escort him/her to the door
see somebody **home** = escort him/her home
see somebody **to** + place = escort him/her to + place
ANN: *Bill is seeing you home after the party, isn't he?*
MARY: *No, he isn't seeing me home. He's just seeing me to my bus.*

see someone **off** = say goodbye to a departing traveller at the starting point of his journey (usually the station, airport etc.):
We're leaving tomorrow. Bill is seeing us off at the airport.

hear can mean 'listen formally to' (complaints/evidence etc.):
The court is hearing evidence this afternoon.

hear meaning 'receive news or letters' is used in the continuous form only in the present perfect and future:
I've been hearing all about your accident.
You'll be hearing about the new scheme at our next meeting.

feel can mean 'touch'.

feel for can mean 'try to find by touching':
Tom was feeling for the keyhole in the dark.

167 Some other verbs listed in **165** can be used in the continuous forms in certain cases:

think when no opinion is given or asked for:
A: *What are you thinking about?*
B: *I'm thinking about the play we saw last night.*

But A: *What do you think of it?* (opinion asked for)
B: *I don't think much of it* (opinion given).
A: *Tom is thinking of emigrating. What do you think of the idea?*
B: *I think it is a stupid idea. He should stay where he is.*

be as part of a passive tense:
The house opposite our college is being pulled down.

be used to imply that the subject is temporarily exhibiting some quality:
You're being very clever today would indicate that this was unusual.
The children are being very quiet; I wonder what they're up to (see **114**).

have except when it implies possession or obligation:
I can't open the door; I'm having a bath.
We are having a wonderful time (enjoying ourselves).
I'm having a tooth (taken) out tomorrow. (See **117** A, **120**.)

like meaning enjoy:
How are you liking this hot weather?

But *How do you like this hot weather?* is equally usual.

It is just possible to use **love, hate** and **loathe** in the affirmative and in the same way:
Are you liking your new job?
No, I'm hating it or *Yes, I'm loving it.*
But it would be safer for the student to use the simple present tenses:
Do you like your new job?
No, I hate it or *Yes, I love it.*

expect when it means 'await':
I am expecting a letter today.
She is expecting a baby in January.

The simple present tense

168 Form

The simple present has the same form as the infinitive but adds an **s** for the third person singular:
Infinitive: *to work*
Simple present: *I work, you work, he/she/it works* etc.

The negative is formed with the present tense negative of the verb **to do** + the infinitive (without **to**) of the main verb:
I do not work *you do not work* *he/she/it does not work* etc.

The interrogative is formed with the present tense interrogative of **to do** + the infinitive (without **to**) of the main verb:
do I work? *do you work?* *does he/she/it work?* etc.

The simple present tense of irregular verbs is formed in exactly the same way.

Spelling notes

Verbs ending in **ss, sh, ch, x** and **o** add **es**, instead of **s** alone, to form the third person singular:

I kiss, he kisses *I rush, he rushes* *I watch, he watches*
I box, he boxes *I go, he goes* *I do, he does*

Verbs ending in **y** following a consonant change the **y** into **i** and add **es**:

I carry, he carries *I hurry, he hurries*

but verbs ending in **y** following a vowel obey the usual rule:

I obey, he obeys *I say, he says*

169 The simple present tense of the verb **to work**

A Form

Affirmative	*Negative*	*Interrogative*	*Negative interrogative*
I work	I do not work	do I work?	do I not work?
you work	you do not work	do you work?	do you not work?
he works	he does not work	does he work?	does he not work?
we work	we do not work	do we work?	do we not work?
you work	you do not work	do you work?	do you not work?
they work	they do not work	do they work?	do they not work?

B Contractions: the verb **to do** is normally contracted in the negative and negative interrogative (see **121**):

I don't work *he doesn't work* *don't I work?*
doesn't he work?

170 The simple present used to express habitual action

The main use of the simple present tense is to express habitual actions:

He smokes. *Dogs bark.* *Cats drink milk.* *Birds fly.*

This tense does not tell us whether or not the action is being performed at the moment of speaking, and if we want to make this clear we must add a verb in the present continuous tense:

My neighbour is practising the violin; she usually practises at about this time.

My dog barks an awful lot, but he isn't barking at the moment.

The simple present tense is often used with adverbs or adverb phrases such as: often, usually, sometimes, never, always, occasionally, on Mondays, twice a year, every week etc.:

It rains in winter. *Birds don't build nests in the autumn.*
I go to church on Sundays. *How often do you wash your hair?*
She goes abroad every year.
I never eat tripe. (**never** + affirmative = negative)

171 Other uses of the simple present tense

A It is used, chiefly with the verb **say**, when we are asking about or quoting from books, notices or very recently received letters:
What does that notice say? It says, 'No parking.'
What does the book say? It says, 'Cook very slowly.'
I see you've got a letter from Ann. What does she say?
She says she is coming to London next week.
Shakespeare says, 'Neither a borrower nor a lender be.'
Other verbs of communication are also possible:
Shakespeare advises us not to borrow or lend.
A notice at the end of the road warns people not to go any further.

B It can be used for dramatic narrative. This is particularly useful when describing the action of a play, opera etc., and is often used by radio commentators at sports events, public functions etc.:
When the curtain rises, Juliet is sitting at her desk. The phone rings. She picks it up and listens quietly. Meanwhile the window opens and a masked man enters the room.

C It can be used for a planned future action or series of actions, particularly when they refer to a journey. Travel agents use it a good deal:
We leave London at 10.00 next Tuesday and arrive in Paris at 13.00. We spend two hours in Paris and leave again at 15.00. We arrive in Rome at 19.30, spend four hours in Rome etc.

D It must be used instead of the present continuous with those verbs which cannot be used in the continuous form, e.g. *love, see, believe* etc., so that we can say *I love you* but not *I am loving you*. (See **165**.)

E It is used in conditional sentences, type 1 (see **215**).

F It is used in time clauses (see **313, 203** C).

17 The past and perfect tenses

The simple past tense

172 Form

A The simple past tense in regular verbs is formed by adding **ed** to the infinitive:

Infinitive: *to work* Simple past: *worked*

Verbs ending in **e** add **d** only:

Infinitive: *to love* Simple past: *loved*

There are no inflexions, i.e. the same form is used for all persons:

I worked *you worked* *he worked* etc.

The negative of regular and irregular verbs is formed with **did not** and the infinitive (without **to**):

I did not work *you did not work* *he did not work* etc.

The interrogative of regular and irregular verbs is formed with **did** + subject + infinitive (without **to**):

did I work? *did you work?* etc.

The simple past tense of the verb **to work**:

Affirmative	*Negative*	*Interrogative*	*Negative interrogative*
I worked	I did not work	did I work?	did I not work?
you worked	you did not work	did you work?	did you not work?
he worked	he did not work	did he work?	did he not work?
we worked	we did not work	did we work?	did we not work?
you worked	you did not work	did you work?	did you not work?
they worked	they did not work	did they work?	did they not work?

B Contractions

did not is normally contracted in the negative and negative interrogative:

I didn't work *didn't I work?* etc.

C Spelling notes

The rules about doubling the final consonant when adding **ing** (see **162**) apply also when adding **ed**:

stop, stopped *admit, admitted* *travel, travelled*

Verbs ending in **y** following a consonant change the **y** into **i** before adding **ed**:

carry, carried but *obeyed* (**y** following a vowel does not change)

173 Irregular verbs

These vary considerably in their simple past form:

Infinitive:	*to speak*	*to eat*	*to see*	*to leave*
Simple past:	*spoke*	*ate*	*saw*	*left*

The simple past form of each irregular verb must therefore be learnt, but once this is done there is no other difficulty, as irregular verbs (like regular verbs) have no inflexions in the past tense: The simple past tense of the verb to speak is *spoke* for all persons. The negative is *did not speak* for all persons.
The interrogative is *did I speak?* etc.

A list of irregular verbs will be found in **317**.

174 The simple past is the tense normally used for the relation of past events.

A It is used for actions completed in the past at a definite time. It is therefore used:

1 for a past action when the time is given:
I met him yesterday.

2 or when the time is asked about:
When did you meet him?

3 or when the action clearly took place at a definite time even though this time is not mentioned:
The train was ten minutes late.
How did you get your present job?
I bought this car in Montreal.

4 Sometimes the time becomes definite as a result of a question and answer in the present perfect:
Where have you been? I've been to the opera. Did you enjoy it?
(See **184** for further examples.)

B The simple past tense is used for an action whose time is not given but which (1) occupied a period of time now terminated, or (2) occurred in a period of time now terminated. These may be expressed diagrammatically thus:

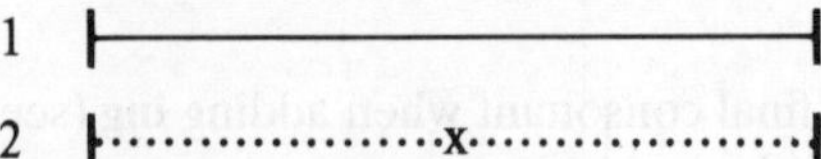

Examples of type 1:
He worked in that bank for four years (but he does not work there now).
She lived in Rome for a long time (but is not living there now).

Examples of type 2:
My grandmother once saw Queen Victoria.
Did you ever hear Maria Callas sing?

These will be clearer when compared with the present perfect (see **181–2**).

C The simple past tense is also used for a past habit:
He always carried an umbrella. *They never drank wine.*
(For **used to** used for past habits see **158**.)

D The simple past is used in conditional sentences, type 2 (see **216**).
(For use after **as if, as though, it is time, if only, wish, would sooner/rather,** see **286–8**.)

The past continuous tense

175 Form

The past continuous tense is formed by the past tense of the verb **to be** + the present participle:

Affirmative	*Negative*	*Interrogative*
I was working	I was not working	was I working?
you were working	you were not working	were you working?
he was working	he was not working	was he working?
we were working	we were not working	were we working?
you were working	you were not working	were you working?
they were working	they were not working	were they working?

Contractions: **was/were not** is usually contracted in the negative, so that we have:
I wasn't working *you weren't working* *wasn't he working?* etc.

Remember that some verbs cannot be used in the continuous tenses (**165–7**).

176 Used for past actions whose exact limits are not known

The past continuous is chiefly used for past actions which continued for some time but whose exact limits are not known and are not important. It might be expressed diagrammatically thus:

A Used without a time expression it can indicate gradual development:
It was getting darker. *The wind was rising.*

B Used with a point in time, it expresses an action which began before that time and probably continued after it. *At eight he was having breakfast* implies that he was in the middle of breakfast at eight, i.e. that he had started it before eight. *He had breakfast at eight* would imply that he started it at eight.

C If we replace the time expression with a verb in the simple past tense:
When I arrived Tom was talking on the telephone

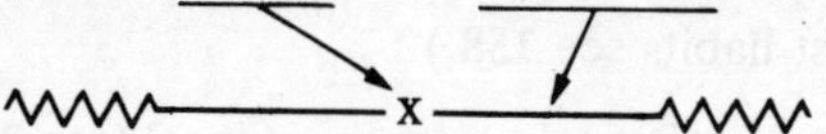

we convey the idea that the action in the past continuous started before the action in the simple past and probably continued after it. The diagram may help to show this relationship. The action in the simple past is indicated by X. Compare this combination with a combination of two simple past tenses, which normally indicates successive actions:
When he saw me he put the receiver down.

D We use the continuous tense in descriptions. Note the combination of description (past continuous) with narrative (simple past):
A wood fire was burning on the hearth, and a cat was sleeping in front of it. A girl was playing the piano and (was) singing softly to herself. Suddenly there was a knock on the door. The girl stopped playing. The cat woke up.

177 The past continuous used in indirect speech, for the future in the past, and with **always**

Here, as in **176**, this tense is used as a past equivalent of the present continuous:

A Direct speech: *He said, 'I am living in London.'*
Indirect speech: *He said he was living in London.*

B Just as the present continuous can be used to express a definite future arrangement:
I'm leaving tonight. I've got my plane ticket.
so the past continuous can express this sort of future in the past:
He was busy packing, for he was leaving that night (the decision to leave had been made some time previously).

C The past continuous with **always**:
He was always ringing me up
expresses a frequently repeated past action, which probably annoyed the speaker (see **164** B).

178 As an alternative to the simple past

The past continuous can be used as an alternative to the simple past to indicate a more casual, less deliberate action:
I was talking to Tom the other day.
The past continuous here gives the impression that the action was in no way unusual or remarkable. It also tends to remove responsibility from the subject. In the above example it is not clear who started the conversation, and it does not matter. Note the contrast with the simple past tense, *I talked to Tom*, which indicates that I took the initiative.

Similarly:
From four to six Tom was washing the car.
This would indicate that this was a casual, possibly routine action. Compare with:
From four to six Tom washed the car (implying a deliberate action by Tom).

Note that continuous tenses are used only for apparently continuous uninterrupted actions. If we divide the action up, or say how many times it happened, we must use the simple past:
I talked to Tom several times. *Tom washed both cars.*
But we may, of course, use the continuous for apparently parallel actions:
Between one and two I was doing the shopping and walking the dog.

This tense is normally used in this way with a time expression such as **today, last night, in the afternoon,** which could either be regarded as points in time or as periods. Periods can also be indicated by exact times as shown above.

In questions about how a period was spent, the continuous often appears more polite than the simple past: *What were you doing before you came here?* sounds more polite than *What did you do before you came here?*

On the other hand *What were you doing in my room?* could indicate a feeling that I think you had no right to be there, but *What did you do in my room?* could never give this impression.

The present perfect tense

179 A Form

The present perfect tense is formed with the present tense of **to have** + the past participle: *I have worked* etc.

The past participle in regular verbs has exactly the same form as the simple past, i.e. *loved, walked* etc. (see spelling rules **172** C). In irregular verbs, the past participles vary (see **317**).

The negative is formed by adding **not** to the auxiliary. The interrogative is formed by inverting the auxiliary and subject. These forms are shown below:

Affirmative	*Negative*
I have worked	I have not worked
you have worked	you have not worked
he has worked	he has not worked
we have worked	we have not worked
you have worked	you have not worked
they have worked	they have not worked

Interrogative	*Negative interrogative*
have I worked?	have I not worked?
have you worked?	have you not worked?
has he worked?	has he not worked?
have we worked?	have we not worked?
have you worked?	have you not worked?
have they worked?	have they not worked?

Contractions: **have** and **have not** can be contracted (see **115**):
I've worked *you haven't worked* *haven't I worked?* etc.

B Use

This tense may be said to be a sort of mixture of present and past. It always implies a strong connexion with the present and is chiefly used in conversations, letters, newspapers and television and radio reports.

180 The present perfect tense is used with **just** to express a recently completed action:

He has just gone out = He went out a few minutes ago.

This is a special idiomatic use of this tense. **just** must be placed between the auxiliary and the main verb. This combination is used chiefly in the affirmative, though the interrogative form is possible:
Has he just gone out?

It is not normally used in the negative.

181 The present perfect is used for past actions whose time is not given and not definite.

A It is used for recent actions when the time is not mentioned:
I have read the instructions but I don't understand them.
Have you had breakfast? No, I haven't had it yet.

Compare with:
I read the instructions last night (time given, so simple past).

Did you have breakfast at the hotel? (i.e. before you left the hotel—simple past).

Note possible answers to questions in the present perfect:

Have you seen my stamps? *Yes, I have/No, I haven't.*
Yes, I saw them on your desk a minute ago.

Have you had breakfast? *Yes, I have/No, I haven't had it yet.*
Yes, I had it at seven o'clock.
Yes, I had it with Mary (time implied).

B It can also be used for actions which occur further back in the past, provided the connexion with the present is still maintained, that is that the action could be repeated in the present:

I have seen wolves in that forest

implies that it is still possible to see them, and

John Smith has written a number of short stories

implies that John Smith is still alive and can write more.

If however the forest has been cut down and John Smith is dead we would say:

I saw wolves in that forest once/several times

or *I used to see wolves here*

and *John Smith wrote a number of short stories.*

Note also that when we use the present perfect in this way we are not necessarily thinking of any one particular action (the action may have occurred several times) or of the exact time when the action was performed. If we are thinking of one particular action performed at a particular time we are more likely to use the simple past.

C It can be used with **lately, recently, never, ever**:

There have been a lot of changes recently.

I've been very busy lately.

Have you ever seen a wolf? No, I've never seen one.

Have you ever made bread? Yes, I made some last week (past tense).

D It can be used with a word or phrase denoting an incomplete period or time, e.g. **this morning/afternoon/evening/week/month/year, today.**

Note that the present perfect can be used with **this morning** only up to about one o'clock, because after that **this morning** becomes a completed period and actions occurring in it must be put into the simple past:

(at 11 a.m.) *Tom has rung three times this morning already.*
(at 2 p.m.) *Tom rang three times this morning.*

Similarly **this afternoon** will end at about five o'clock:
(at 4 p.m.) *I haven't seen Tom this afternoon.*
(at 6 p.m.) *I didn't see Tom this afternoon.*

The present perfect used with an incomplete period of time implies that the action happened or didn't happen at some undefined time during this period:
ANN: *Have you seen him today* (at any time today)?
BILL: *Yes, I have/Yes, I've seen him today* (at some time during the day).

But if we know that an action usually happens at a certain time or in a certain part of our incomplete period we use the simple past tense; if my alarm clock normally goes off at six, I might say at breakfast:
My alarm clock didn't go off this morning.

Imagine that the postman normally comes between nine and ten. From nine till ten we will say:
Has the postman come yet/this morning?
But after this nine to ten period we will say:
Did the postman come this morning?
We use the past tense here because we are thinking about a complete period of time even though we do not mention it.

E The present perfect can be used with **yet** in the interrogative or negative:
Has the postman come yet?
No, he hasn't come yet. We are still expecting him.

182 The present perfect can be used with a time expression.

A It can be used for an action beginning in the past and still continuing:
He has been in the army for two years (he is still in the army).
I have smoked since I left school (I still smoke).
He has lived here all his life (he still lives here).
I have never seen an armadillo.
I have always written with my left hand.
This type of action might be expressed by a diagram thus:
├──────────

Compare the above sentences with:
He was in the army for two years (he is not in the army now).
I smoked for six months (and then stopped smoking).
He lived here all his life (presumably he is now dead).
In each of the last three examples we are dealing with a completed period of time ├──────────┤, so the simple past tense is used (see **174**).

B However the present perfect can sometimes be used for an action which begins in the past and finishes at the moment of speaking. It is chiefly used in this way with the verb **be** and with negative verbs: (on meeting someone) *I haven't seen you for ages* (but I see you now).
This room hasn't been cleaned for months (but we are cleaning it now).
It has been very cold lately but it's beginning to get a bit warmer.
This type of action could be expressed by a diagram thus:
|——|

C Verbs of knowing, believing, understanding etc. cannot be used in the present perfect except as shown in A above:
I have known him for a long time.
We have always believed that this is not possible.
So recent actions, even when the time is not mentioned, must be expressed by the simple past:
Did you know he was going to be married? (*Have you known* would not be possible)
and *Hello! I didn't know you were in London. How long have you been here?*

D Note that questions/answers such as:
How long have you been here? I've been here six months.
will normally be followed by general inquiries in the present perfect about actions occurring within the period mentioned, which is regarded as an incomplete period of time |——
because the action of staying, being etc., is not yet finished:
Have you been to the zoo/the theatre/the museums/the casino?
Have you enrolled in a school/found a job/met many people?
The answers will be in the same tense if no time is mentioned, otherwise they will be in the simple past tense:
Yes, I have (been to the zoo etc.*)*
or *Yes, I went there last week.*
No, I haven't enrolled yet
or *Yes, I enrolled on Monday/this morning.*

E Note the form **it is** + period of time + **since** + past tense or present perfect:
It is three years since I (last) saw Bill
or *It is three years since I have seen Bill.*
This could be replaced by:
I saw Bill three years ago
or *I haven't seen Bill for three years.*

Similarly:
It is two months since Tom (last) smoked a cigarette.
It is two months since Tom has smoked a cigarette.
He last smoked a cigarette two months ago.
He hasn't smoked a cigarette for two months.
We can use the **it is . . . since** construction without the adverb **last**:
It is two years since he left the country.
This, however, is replaceable only by:
He left the country two years ago.
We could not use a negative present perfect as in the sentences about Bill and Tom above.
This construction can be used in the past:
He invited me to go riding with him. But it was two years since I had ridden a horse (=I hadn't ridden a horse for two years previous to the invitation) so I wasn't sure that I would enjoy it.

F Note also sentences of this type:
This is the best wine I have ever drunk.
This is the worst book I have ever read.
This is the easiest job I have ever had.
We can use this construction, without **ever**, with **the first, the second** etc. and **the only**:
It/This is the first time I have seen a mounted band.
It is only the second time he has been in a canoe.
This is the only book he has written.

183 for and since used with the present perfect

for is used with a period of time: *for six days, for a long time*
for used with the simple past tense denotes a terminated period of time: *We lived there for ten years* (but we don't live there now).
for used with the present perfect denotes a period of time extending into the present:
We have lived in London for ten years (and still live there).
for can sometimes be omitted: *We've been here an hour.*
since is used with a point in time and means 'from that point to the time of speaking'. It is always used with a perfect tense:
She has been here since six o'clock (and is still here).
since can never be omitted.
Note that there is a rather confusing difference between **last** and **the last**. We say
I have been here since last week (month, year etc.*)*
but *I have been here for the last week.*

In the first sentence *last week* means a point in time about seven days ago. In the second sentence *the last week* means the period of seven days that has just finished.

184 Further examples of the use of the present perfect and simple past

A A: *Have you ever seen a dinosaur?*
B: *I've seen a model of one in a museum. I've never seen a live one; they've been extinct for millions of years.*
TOM (visiting Philip for the first time): *I didn't know you lived in a houseboat.*
PHILIP: *I've always lived in a houseboat. I was born in one.*
A: *I didn't know you were in England. When did you arrive?*
B: *I arrived last week.*
A: *Did you have a good journey?*
B: *No, I came by air and it was very tiring.*
A: *Have you found a job yet?*
B: *Yes, I've just had an interview for a post and I think I've got it.*

B Note that a conversation about a past action often begins with a question and answer in the present perfect, but normally continues in the simple past, even when no time is given. This is because the action first mentioned has now become definite in the minds of the speakers:
A: *Where have you been?*
B: *I've been to the theatre.*
A: *What was the play?*
B: *'Hamlet.'*
A: *Did you like it/Did you have a good seat/Was the theatre crowded?*
HUSBAND: *Where have you been?*
WIFE: *I've been at the sales.*
HUSBAND: *What have you bought/What did you buy?* (either could be used)
WIFE: *I have bought/I bought you some yellow pyjamas.*
HUSBAND: *Why did you buy yellow? I told you never to buy yellow for me.*
WIFE: *I couldn't resist it. They were very much reduced.*

C The present perfect is often used in newspapers and broadcasts to introduce an action which will then be described in the simple past tense. The time of the action is very often given in the second sentence:

Thirty thousand pounds' worth of jewellery has been stolen from Jonathan Wild and Company, the jewellers. The thieves broke into the flat above some time during Sunday night and entered the shop by cutting a hole in the ceiling.

The Prime Minister has decided to continue with his plan to build X-type aircraft. This decision was announced yesterday and was received with mixed feelings. (Notice that *has been received* would be used if the reporter wished to cover comments made between then and the time of speaking.)

But even if the time of the action is not given the past tense will normally be used in the second sentence:

Two prisoners have escaped from Dartmoor. They used a ladder which had been left behind by some workmen, climbed a twenty-foot wall and got away in a stolen car.

D The present perfect is often used in letters:

I am sorry I haven't written for such a long time, but I've been very busy lately as my partner has been away and I have had to do his work as well as my own. However he came back this morning/has just come back so things are a bit easier now.

My colleagues and I have carefully considered the important issues raised in the report which you sent me on April 26, and we have decided to take the following action.

The present perfect continuous tense

185 Form

This tense is formed by the present perfect of the verb **to be** + the present participle:

Affirmative: *I have been working, he has been working* etc.
Negative: *I have not/haven't been working* etc.
Interrogative: *have you been working?* etc.
Negative interrogative: *haven't you been working?* etc.

186 Use

This tense is used for an action which began in the past and is still continuing ├──────, or has only just finished ├──────┤:

I've been waiting for an hour and he still hasn't turned up.
I'm so sorry I'm late. Have you been waiting long?

Remember that a number of verbs are not normally used in the continuous form (see **165**), but that some of these can be used in this form in certain cases (**166–7**). We can therefore say:

Tom has been seeing about a work permit for you.
She has been having a tooth out. I've been thinking it over.
I've been hearing all about his operation.

In addition, the verb **want** is often used in this tense, and **wish** is also possible:

Thank you so much for the binoculars. I've been wanting a pair for ages.

The present perfect continuous tense is not normally used in the passive. The nearest passive equivalent of a sentence such as *They have been repairing the road* would normally be *The road has been repaired lately*, which is not exactly the same thing.

187 Comparison of the present perfect simple and continuous

A An action which began in the past and is still continuing or has only just finished can, with certain verbs, be expressed by either the present perfect simple or the present perfect continuous. Verbs which can be used in this way include **expect, hope, learn, lie, live, look, rain, sleep, sit, snow, stand, stay, study, teach, wait, want, work**:

He has lived here for six weeks.
He has been living here for six weeks.

How long have you learnt English?
How long have you been learning English?

I've wanted to throw something at him for a long time.
I've been wanting to throw something at him for a long time.

This is not of course possible with verbs which are not used in the continuous forms (see **165–7** and **186**), i.e. the present perfect continuous could not replace the simple present perfect in the following examples:

They've always had a big garden.
How long have you known that?
He's been in hospital since his accident.

Notice also that the present perfect continuous can be used with or without a time phrase. In this way it differs from the simple present perfect, which can only express this type of action if a time phrase is added such as *for six days, since June, never*. When used without a time expression of this kind, the simple present perfect refers to a single completed action.

B A repeated action in the simple present perfect can sometimes be expressed as a continuous action by the present perfect continuous:

I've written six letters since breakfast.
I've been writing letters since breakfast.

I have knocked five times. I don't think anyone's in.
I've been knocking. I don't think anybody's in.

Note that the present perfect continuous expresses an action which is apparently uninterrupted; we do not use it when we mention the number of times a thing has been done or the number of things that have been done.

C There is, however, a difference between a single action in the simple present perfect and an action in the present perfect continuous:

I've put coal on the fire (this job has been done).
I've been putting coal on the fire (this is how I've spent the last five minutes).

TOM: *What have you done with my knife?* (Where have you put it?)
ANN: *I put it back in your drawer.*
TOM (taking it out): *But what have you been doing to it? The blade's all twisted. Have you been sawing wood with it?*

Tom has dug the potato patch, so we can plant the potatoes tomorrow.
He has been digging; that's why he has got such a stiff back.

188 Some more examples of the present perfect and the present perfect continuous

A: *I haven't seen your brother lately. Has he gone away?*
B: *Yes, he's/he has been sent to America.*
A: *When did he go?*
B: *He went last month.*
A: *Have you had any letters from him?*
B: *I haven't, but his wife has been hearing from him regularly.*
A: *Does she intend to go out and join him?*
B: *They've been thinking about it but haven't quite decided yet. I think it would be an excellent idea but they've had a lot of expense lately and perhaps haven't got the money.*

A: *Have you heard that Mr Pitt has been trying to train his Pekinese to obey him? He's/He has been at it all day and is completely exhausted.*
B: *Is the Pekinese exhausted too?*
A: *No, he thoroughly enjoyed it.*
B: *I've always heard that they are naturally disobedient dogs.*
A: *I think poor Mr Pitt has just discovered that for himself.*

A: *Mary has been seeing a lot of Mr Hook lately, hasn't she? Is there anything in it?*
B: *Yes. They have just announced their engagement.*
A: *Are you pleased about it?*
B: *Only moderately. She has been looking for a very rich man all her life and now she's/she has found one, and he's/he has been looking for a really competent secretary all his life and now he's found one, but apart from that they aren't really very well suited.*
A: *I've always heard that Mary has rather a bad temper.*
B: *So has he.*

A: *Do you see those people on that little sandy island? They've been waving handkerchiefs for the last half hour. Do you think they want anything?*
B: *Of course they do. The tide's coming in and very soon that little island will be under water. Have you been sitting here calmly and doing nothing to help them?*
A: *I've never been here before. I didn't know about the tides.*

The past perfect tense

189 A Form

This tense is formed with **had** and the past participle. It is therefore the same for all persons:
Affirmative: *I had/I'd worked* etc.
Negative: *he had not/hadn't worked* etc.
Interrogative: *had they worked?* etc.
Negative interrogative: *hadn't you worked?* etc.

B Use

1 The past perfect is the past equivalent of the present perfect:
Present: *Ann has just left. If you hurry you'll catch her.* (See **180**.)
Past: *When I arrived Ann had just left.*
Present: *I've lost my case.* (See **181**.)
Past: *He had lost his case and had to borrow Tom's pyjamas.*
The past perfect, however, is not, like the present perfect, restricted to actions whose time is not mentioned. We could therefore say:
He had left his case on the 4.40 train.

2 The present perfect can be used with **since/for/always** etc. for an action which began in the past and is still continuing or has only just finished (see **182**). The past perfect can be used similarly for an action which began before the time of speaking in the past, and

1 was still continuing at that time

or 2 stopped at that time or just before it.

But note that the past perfect can also be used

3 for an action which stopped some time before the time of speaking.

Examples of types 1, 2 and 3 are given below:

1 *Bill was in uniform when I met him. He had been a soldier for ten years/since he was seventeen, and planned to stay in the army till he was thirty.*

Ann had lived in a cottage for sixty years/ever since she was born, and had no wish to move to a tower block. (The past perfect continuous tense *had been living* would also be possible here.)

2 *The old oak tree, which had stood in the churchyard for 300 years/since before the church was built, suddenly crashed to the ground.* (The past perfect continuous tense *had been standing* would also be possible here.)

Peter, who had waited for an hour/since ten o'clock, was very angry with his sister when she eventually turned up. (*had been waiting* would also be possible.)

3 *He had served in the army for ten years; then he had retired and married. His children were now at school.*

(Here we cannot use either **since** or the past perfect continuous. Note also that the past perfect here has no present perfect equivalent. If we put the last verb in this sentence into the present tense the other tenses will change to the simple past.

He served in the army for ten years; then retired and married. His children are now at school.)

These structures are shown below in diagram form, with the line AB for the action in the past perfect, and T/S for the time of speaking in the past:

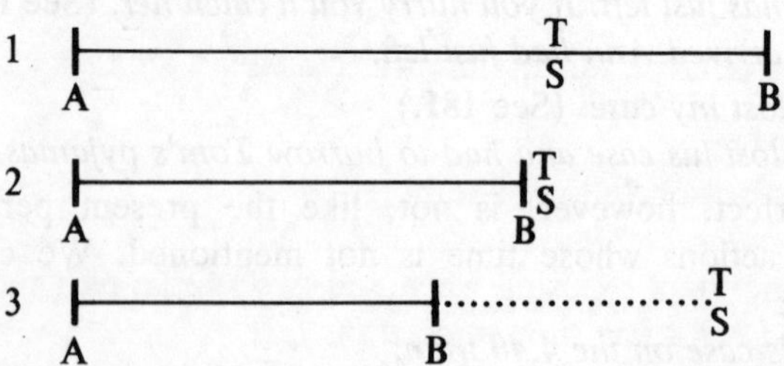

(See also **191** for the use of the past perfect in indirect speech.)

3 The past perfect is also the past equivalent of the simple past tense, and is used when from a certain point in the past the narrator or subject looks back on earlier action:

Tom was 23 when our story begins. His father had died five years before and since then Tom had lived alone. His father had advised him not to get married till he was 35, and Tom intended to follow this advice.

I had just poured myself a glass of beer when the phone rang. When I came back from answering it the glass was empty. Somebody had drunk the beer or thrown it away.

He met her in Paris in 1977. He had last seen her ten years before. Her hair had been grey then; now it was white.

Or *He met her in 1967 and again ten years later. Her hair, which had been grey at their first meeting, was now white.*

But if we merely give the events in the order in which they occurred no past perfect tense is necessary:

Tom's father died when Tom was eighteen. Before he died he advised Tom not to marry till he was 35, and Tom at 23 still intended to follow this advice.

He met her first in 1967 when her hair was grey. He met her again in 1977/He didn't meet her again till 1977. Her hair was now white.

There is no looking back in the above two examples so no reason for a past perfect.

Note the difference of meaning in the following examples:

She heard voices and realized that there were three people in the next room.

She saw empty glasses and cups and realized that three people had been in the room (they were no longer there).

He arrived at 2.30 and was told to wait in the VIP lounge.

He arrived at 2.30. He had been told to wait in the VIP lounge.

In the third example he received his instructions after his arrival. In the fourth he received them before arrival, possibly before the journey started.

190 Past and past perfect tenses in time clauses

A Clauses with **when**

When one past action follows another:

He called her a liar. *She smacked his face.*

we can combine them by using **when** and two simple past tenses:

When he called her a liar she smacked his face

provided that it is clear from the sense that the second action followed the first and that they did not happen simultaneously. When two simple past tenses are used in this way there is usually the idea that the first action led to the second and that the second followed the first very closely:

When he opened the window the bird flew out.
The boys were throwing snowballs through the open window. When I shut the window they stopped throwing them.
When the play ended the audience went home.
When he died he was given a state funeral.

The past perfect is used after **when** when two simple past tenses might give the impression that the two actions happened simultaneously:
When she had sung her song she sat down ('When she sang her song she sat down' might give the impression that she sang seated)

or when we wish to emphasize that the first action was completed before the second one started:
When he had shut the window we opened the door of the cage (we waited for the window to be quite shut before opening the cage).
Similarly:
When he had seen all the pictures he said he was ready to leave (when he had finished looking at them).
Compare with:
When he saw all the pictures he expressed amazement that one man should have painted so many (immediately he saw them he said this).

B Two past actions can also be combined with **till/until, as soon as, before** (for **as** used as a time conjunction see **95**). As above, simple past tenses are used except when it is necessary to emphasize that the first action was completely finished before the second one started:
I waited till it got dark.
He refused to go till he had seen all the papers.
Before I had known him a week he tried to borrow money from me.
As soon as it began to rain we ran indoors.
As soon as his guests had drunk all his brandy they left his house.

C **after**, however, is normally followed by a perfect tense:
After the will had been read there were angry exclamations.

D We have already stated (**189**) that actions viewed in retrospect from a point in the past are expressed by the past perfect tense. If we have two such actions:
He had been to school but he had learnt nothing there, so was now illiterate
and wish to combine them with a time conjunction, we can use **when** etc. with two past perfect tenses:
When he had been at school he had learnt nothing, so he was now illiterate.

But it is more usual to put the verb in the time clause into the simple past:
When he was at school he had learnt nothing, so he was now illiterate.
Similarly:
He had stayed in his father's firm till his father died. Then he had started his own business and was now a very successful man.

E Verbs of knowing, understanding etc. are not normally used in the past perfect tense in time clauses except when accompanied by an expression denoting a period of time:
When she had known me for a year she invited me to tea
but *When I knew the work of one department thoroughly I was moved to the next department.*
Compare with:
When I had learnt the work of one department I was moved.

F Time clauses containing past perfect tenses can be combined with a main verb in the conditional tense, but this is chiefly found in indirect speech, and some examples will be given in the next paragraph.

191 Use of the past perfect in indirect speech

A Present perfect tenses in direct speech become past perfect tenses in indirect speech provided the introductory verb is in the past tense:
He said, 'I've been in England for ten years.'
= *He said that he had been in England for ten years.*
He said, 'When you have worked for me for six months you'll get a rise.'
= *He said that when I had worked for him for six months I would get a rise.*
She said, 'I'll lend you the book as soon as I have read it myself.'
= *She said that she would lend me the book as soon as she had read it herself.*

B Simple past tenses in direct speech usually change similarly:
He said, 'I knew her well.'
= *He said that he had known her well.*
But there are a number of cases where past tenses remain unchanged (see **294**).

(For the past perfect after **if** (conditional) see **217**, after **wish** and **if only** see **286**, after **as if, as though** see **287**.)

192 The past perfect continuous tense

A Form

This tense is formed with **had been** + the present participle. It is therefore the same for all persons:

I had been working   *they had not (hadn't) been working*
had you been working?   *hadn't you been working?*

It is not used with verbs which are not used in the continuous forms, except with **want** and sometimes **wish**:

The boy was delighted with his new knife. He had been wanting one for a long time.

Note that this tense has no passive form. The nearest passive equivalent of a sentence such as *They had been picking apples* would be *Apples had been picked*, which is not the same thing (see B3 below).

B Use

The past perfect continuous bears the same relation to the past perfect that the present perfect continuous bears to the present perfect (see **187**).

1 When the action began before the time of speaking in the past, and continued up to that time, or stopped just before it, we can often use either form (see **187** A):

It was now six and he was tired because he had worked since dawn
= *It was now six and he was tired because he had been working since dawn.*

2 A repeated action in the past perfect can sometimes be expressed as a continuous action by the past perfect continuous (see **187** B):

He had tried five times to get her on the phone.
He had been trying to get her on the phone.

3 But there is a difference between a single action in the simple past perfect and an action in the past perfect continuous (see **187** C):

By six o'clock he had mended the puncture and we were ready to start (i.e. this job had been done)

but *He had been mending the puncture* tells us how he had spent the previous fifteen minutes.

Similarly:

He had looked through the keyhole and seen that there was nobody in the room (one single action)

but *When I opened the door I found him on his knees outside. I knew that he had been looking through the keyhole (for the last half hour).*

Also *They had sawn up the fallen tree so we had a good store of firewood*
but *They had been sawing; that was why they were covered in sawdust.*

18 The future

193 Future forms

The future tense is **will/shall** + infinitive, but it is not used nearly as often as students naturally expect. In fact, it is only one of a number of ways of expressing the future. These forms are listed below and will be dealt with in the order in which they are given. Students should study them in this order, as otherwise the relationship between them will not be clear.

1 The simple present tense **194**
2 **will** + infinitive (used to express intention at the moment of decision) **196**
3 The present continuous tense **197**
4 The **be going to** form **198–200**
5 The future tense **shall/will** + infinitive **201–3**
6 The future continuous tense **205–7**
7 The future perfect tense **210** A
8 The future perfect continuous tense **210** B

For **be** + infinitive used to express future plans see **111** A.
For **be about** + infinitive and **be on the point of** + gerund see **111** C.

Note: Most of the auxiliary verbs are dealt with in chapters 12–15, but **will** + infinitive is an essential part of the future, so we have placed it here. It may seem odd that it has been separated from the future tense but logically it seems best to place it before the present continuous and the **be going to** form.

194 The simple present tense used for the future (not a very important form)

This tense can be used with a time expression for a definite future arrangement:

The boys start school on Monday. *I leave tonight.*
instead of the more normal present continuous tense:
The boys are starting school etc.

The difference between them is:

1 The simple present is more impersonal than the continuous: *I'm leaving tonight* would probably imply that I have decided to leave, but *I leave tonight* could mean that this is part of a plan not necessarily made by me.

2 The simple present can also sound more formal than the

continuous. A big store planning to open a new branch is more likely to say *Our new branch opens next week* than *Our new branch is opening next week.*

3 The simple present is sometimes used where the continuous would sound a bit clumsy, e.g. when speaking of a series of proposed future actions like plans for a journey; i.e. we say:

We leave at six, arrive in Dublin at ten and take the plane on . . . instead of

We are leaving at six, arriving in Dublin at ten and taking the plane on . . .

Note, however, that in a sentence such as *My train **leaves at six***, we are using the simple present for a habitual action. Here, therefore, the simple present is not replaceable by the continuous.

195 A note on the meaning of future with intention

When we say that a form expresses future with intention we mean that it expresses a future action which will be undertaken by the speaker in accordance with his wishes. **will** + infinitive and the **be going to** form can be used in this way.

When we say that a form expresses future without intention we mean that it merely states that a certain action will happen. We don't know whether it was arranged by the subject or by some other person and we don't know what the subject thinks of it. The present tense and the future continuous tense can be used in this way.

The present continuous tense in the second or third person conveys no idea of intention, though there may be a hint of intention when the first person is used.

The future tense (apart from **will** used as in **196, 199**) normally conveys no idea of intention; but see **shall, 202, 233–4**.

196 will + infinitive used to express intention at the moment of decision

1 A: *The phone is ringing.* B: *I'll answer it.*

2 BILL (to waiter): *I'll have cress soup and steak, please.* (*would like* is also possible.)

3 ANN: *I'd better order a taxi for tonight.*
TOM: *Don't bother. I'll drive you.*

4 MARY (looking at a pile of letters): *I'll answer them tonight.*

5 PAUL (who is getting fat and is tired of paying parking fines): *I know what to do. I'll sell my car and buy a push bike.*

6 ALAN (on receiving a telegram saying his father is ill): *I'll go home tonight/I'll leave tonight.*

For unpremeditated actions, as above, we must use **will** (normally contracted to **'ll**). But note that if after his decision the speaker mentions the action again, he will use not **will**, but **be going to** or the present continuous. (**be going to** is always possible; the present continuous has a more restricted use. See **197**.)

For example, imagine that in (2) above a friend, Tom, joins Bill before his food has arrived:

TOM: *What are you having/going to have?*

BILL: *I'm having/going to have cress soup and steak.*

Similarly, at a later time, in:

3 Ann might say:

Tom is driving me/going to drive me to the airport tonight.

4 Mary, however, could only say:

I'm going to answer these letters tonight. (She hasn't made an arrangement with anybody.)

5 Paul, similarly, could say:

I'm going to sell the car

though when he finds a buyer he can say:

I'm selling the car.

6 Alan, however, could say:

I'm going home tonight

even though this is, as yet, only a decision. (See **197** B and D.)

197 The present continuous as a future form

Note that the time must be mentioned, or have been mentioned, as otherwise there may be confusion between present and future.

A The present continuous can express a definite arrangement in the near future:

I'm taking an exam in October implies that I have entered for it; and

Bob and Bill are meeting tonight implies that Bob and Bill have arranged this. If there has merely been an expression of intention, as in **196** (4) and (5) above, we use the **be going to** form.

B But with verbs of movement from one place to another, e.g. **go, come, drive, fly, travel, arrive, leave, start,** and verbs indicating position, e.g. **stay, remain,** and the verbs **do** and **have** (food or drink), the present continuous can be used more widely. It can express a decision or plan without any definite arrangement; Alan in **196** (6) can therefore say *I'm going home tonight/I'm leaving tonight* even before he has arranged his journey.

Note also:

What are you doing next Saturday? (This is the usual way of asking people about their plans.) Possible answers:

I'm going to the seaside (by myself or with someone else).
The neighbours are coming in to watch television.
I'm not doing anything. I'm staying at home. I'm going to write letters. (*I'm writing* . . . would not be possible.)

C This method of expressing the future cannot be used with verbs which are not normally used in the continuous tenses (see **165**). These verbs should be put into the future tense (**will/shall**):
I am meeting him tonight
but *I will/shall know tonight.* (**know** cannot be used in the continuous.)
They will be there tomorrow. (**be** is not normally used in the continuous.)
We'll think it over. (**think** is not normally used in the continuous.)
Note, however, that **see**, when it is used for a deliberate action (**see to/about, see someone out/off/home** etc., **see** meaning 'meet by appointment'), can be used in the continuous tenses (see **167**):
I'm seeing him tomorrow (I have an appointment with him).
to be can be used in the continuous tenses when it forms part of a passive verb:
He is being met at the station.
Our new piano is being delivered this afternoon.

D More examples of combinations of **will** + infinitive used at the moment of decision (see **196**) and the present continuous tense used as a future form:

TRAVEL AGENT: *Now, how do you want to go to Rome, sir? By air or by train?*
TRAVELLER (making up his mind): *The trains are too slow. I'll fly.*
But afterwards, talking about his plans for his journey, this traveller will say:
I'm flying to Rome next week.

ANN: *I'll have to pay £150 rent at the end of this month and I don't know where to find the money.*
TOM: *Don't worry. I'll lend you £150.*
Later, but before Tom has actually lent the money, Ann will say:
Tom is lending me £150.

TOM: *Would you like to come to the opera tonight?*
ANN: *I'd love to. Shall I meet you there?*
TOM: *No, I'll call for you. About seven?*
ANN: *O.K.*
Later, Ann, telling a friend about this plan, will say:
Tom is taking me to the opera tonight. He's calling for me at seven.

(The **be going to** form could replace the continuous tense in the above examples.)

198 The **be going to** form

A Form

The present continuous tense of the verb **to go** + infinitive with **to**. (We say **be going *to***, for the same reason that we say **have *to*, used *to*** etc., i.e. to remind students of the **to** in the following infinitive):
I'm going to buy a bicycle. *She is not going to be there.*
Is he going to lecture in English?

B This form is used:
1 For intention (**198–9**).
2 For prediction (**200**).

C Use for intention

The **be going to** form expresses the subject's intention to perform a certain future action. This intention is always premeditated and there is usually also the idea that some preparation for the action has already been made. Actions expressed by the **be going to** form are therefore usually considered very likely to be performed, though there is not the same idea of definite future arrangement that we get from the present continuous.

The following points may be noted:

1 As already shown **be going to** can be used for the near future with a time expression as an alternative to the present continuous, i.e. we can say:
I'm/I am meeting Tom at the station at six.
I'm/I am going to meet Tom at the station at six.
But note that *I'm meeting Tom* implies an arrangement with Tom. *I'm going to meet Tom* does not: Tom may get a surprise!

2 **be going to** can be used with time clauses when we wish to emphasize the subject's intention:
He is going to be a dentist when he grows up.
What are you going to do when you get your degree?
Normally, however, the future tense (**shall/will**) is used with time clauses.

3 **be going to** can be used without a time expression:
I am going to read you some of my own poems.
He is going to lend me his bicycle.
It then usually refers to the immediate or near future.

4 As seen in (2) above, the **be going to** form can be used with the verb **to be**. It is also sometimes found with other verbs not normally used in the continuous tenses:
I am going to think about it. *I'm sure I'm going to like it.*
But on the whole it is safer to use the future tense here.

5 Note that it is not very usual to put the verbs **go** and **come** into the **be going to** form. Instead we generally use the present continuous tense: i.e. instead of *I am going to go* we normally say *I am going* and instead of *I am going to come* we very often say *I am coming*. Note that we can express intention by using **will** + infinitive. This form is compared with **be going to** in **199**.

199 Comparison of the use of **be going to** and **will** + infinitive to express intention

Very often we can use either the **be going to** form or **will** + infinitive, but there are differences between them, as a result of which there are occasions when only one of them is possible.

The chief difference is:

A The **be going to** form always implies a premeditated intention, and often an intention + plan.

will + infinitive implies intention alone, and this intention is usually, though not necessarily, unpremeditated.

If therefore preparations for the action have been made, we must use **be going to**:

I have bought some bricks and I'm going to build a garage.

If the intention is clearly unpremeditated, we must use **will**:

A: *There is somebody at the hall door.* B: *I'll go and open it.*

(See examples in section E.)

When the intention is neither clearly premeditated nor clearly unpremeditated, either **be going to** or **will** may be used:

I will/am going to climb that mountain one day.

I won't/am not going to tell you my age.

But **will** is the best way of expressing determination:

I ˈwill help you (with stress on *will*) = I definitely intend to help you.

Other differences:

B As already noted **will** + infinitive in the affirmative is used almost entirely for the first person. Second and third person intentions are therefore normally expressed by **be going to**:

He is going to resign.

C But in the negative **won't** can be used for all persons. So we can say:

He isn't going to resign or *He won't resign.*

But note that **won't** used for a negative intention normally means 'refuse':

He won't resign = He refuses to resign.

He isn't going to resign normally means 'He doesn't intend to resign'.

D **be going to**, as already stated, usually refers to the fairly immediate future. **will** can refer either to the immediate or to the more remote future.

E More examples of **be going to** and **will**

1 Examples of **be going to** used to express intention:

Tom has just borrowed the axe; he is going to chop some wood.

What are you doing with that spade? I am going to plant some apple trees.

She has bought some cloth; she is going to make herself a dress.

He is studying very hard; he is going to try for a scholarship.

Why are you taking down all the pictures? I am going to repaper the room.

I have given up my flat in Paris because I'm going to live permanently in London.

Some workmen arrived today with a steamroller. I think they are going to repair the road in front of my house.

Why is he carrying his guitar? He is going to play it under Miss Pitt's window.

Note that it would not be possible to substitute **will** for **be going to** in any of the above examples, as in each of them there is clear evidence of premeditation.

2 Examples of **will** + infinitive

ANN: *This is a terribly heavy box.*
TOM: *I'll help you to carry it.*

FATHER: *I've left my watch upstairs.*
SON: *I'll go and get it for you.*

MR X: *My car won't start.*
MR Y: *I'll come and give it a push.*

MOTHER: *Who will post this letter for me?*
SON: *I will.*

MR X: *Will you lend me £100?*
MR Y: *No, I won't.*

3 Some comparisons of **be going to** and **will**

In answer to Tom's remark *There aren't any matches in the house* Ann might reply either *I'm going to get some today* (premeditated decision) or *I'll get some today* (unpremeditated decision). The first would imply that some time before this conversation she realized that there were no matches and decided to buy some. The second would imply that she had not previously decided to buy matches but took the decision now, immediately after Tom's remark.

Similarly, if Ann says *Where is the telephone book?* and Tom says *I'll get it for you* he is expressing a decision made immediately after Ann's question. If he said *I'm going to get it*, it would mean that he had decided to do this before Ann spoke (presumably because he had anticipated that Ann would want it, or needed it for himself).

Note that **will/won't** does not have any meaning of intention when it is used as indicated in **203** A–E, i.e. when it is used as part of the ordinary future tense **will/shall**. So *He won't resign* can mean *He refuses to resign* or *I don't expect that he will resign*; and in *If he hurries he'll catch up with her*, **will** doesn't express intention but merely states a fact.

200 The **be going to** form used for prediction

A The **be going to** form can express the speaker's feeling of certainty. The time is usually not mentioned, but the action is expected to happen in the near or immediate future:

Look at those clouds! It's going to rain.

Listen to the wind. We're going to have a rough crossing.

It can be used in this way after such verbs as **be sure/afraid, believe, think**:

How pale that girl is! I am sure/I believe/I think she is going to faint.

B Comparison of **be going to** (used for prediction) with **will** (used for probable future)

will is a common way of expressing what the speaker thinks, believes, hopes, assumes, fears etc. will happen (see **203** A):

It will probably be cold/I expect it will be cold.

Tomatoes will be expensive this year/I'm sure tomatoes will be expensive.

will and **be going to** are therefore rather similar and often either form can be used:

It will take a long time to photocopy all the documents

= *It is going to take a long time to photocopy all the documents.*

But there are two differences:

1 **be going to** implies that there are signs that something will happen, **will** implies that the speaker thinks/believes that it will happen.

2 **be going to** is normally used about the immediate/fairly immediate future, **will** doesn't imply any particular time and could refer to the remote future. For example:

The lift is going to break down implies it is making strange noises or behaving in a strange way. We had better get out on the next floor. *The lift will break down* implies that this will happen some time in the future (perhaps because we always overload our lifts, perhaps because it is an XYZ Company lift and they don't last).

Similarly (of a sick man), *He is going to get better* implies that there are signs of recovery. Perhaps his temperature has gone down. *He will get better* implies confidence in his doctor or in the course of treatment, but promises eventual rather than immediate recovery.

Note that **will** is used in formal announcements. An official weather forecast:

There will be rain. Fog will persist in these areas.

But the average reader/listener will say:

There is going to be rain. Fog is going to persist. (See **203** E.)

201 The future tense

Form

A The future tense is formed with **shall/will** + infinitive (without **to**) for the first person singular and plural, and **will** + infinitive (without **to**) for the other persons. The negative is formed by putting **not** after the **shall** or **will**. The interrogative is formed by inverting the subject and **shall** or **will** (**will** is not usual in the first person interrogative).

B

Affirmative	*Negative*	*Interrogative*
I shall/will work	I shall/will not work	shall I work?
you will work	you will not work	will you work?
he will work	he will not work	will he work?
we shall/will work	we shall/will not work	shall we work?
you will work	you will not work	will you work?
they will work	they will not work	will they work?

C Negative interrogative:

will he not work? (won't he work?) etc.

D Contractions: **will** is contracted to **'ll**
will not is contracted to **won't**
shall not is contracted to **shan't**

The contraction **'ll** cannot be used when the infinitive is omitted:

Who will go? I will.

The second *will* could not be contracted.

202 First person will and shall

A Formerly **will** was kept for intention:

I will wait for you = I intend to wait for you

and **shall** was used when there was no intention, i.e. for actions where the subject's wishes were not involved:

I shall be 25 next week.

We shall know the result next week (because it will be in the papers).

Unless the taxi comes soon we shall miss our plane.

I'm sure I shan't lose my way.

I shall see Tom tomorrow (perhaps we go to work on the same train).

shall, used as above, is still found in formal English, but is no longer common in conversation. Instead we normally use **will**:

I will be 25 next week. *We'll know the result tomorrow.*

Unless the taxi comes soon we'll miss the plane.

I'm sure I won't lose my way.

Sometimes, however, **will** might change the meaning of the sentence. If in *I shall see Tom tomorrow* we replace **shall** by **will**, we have *I will see Tom tomorrow*, which could be an expression of intention. To avoid ambiguities of this kind we use the future continuous tense:

I'll be seeing Tom tomorrow. (See **205–7**.)

shall, however, is still used in the interrogative:

In question tags after **let's**: *Let's go, shall we?*

In suggestions: *Shall we take a taxi?*

In requests for orders or instructions: *What shall I do with your mail?*

In speculations: *Where shall we be this time next year?* (though here **will** is also possible).

B New function of **shall**: **shall** for determination

We have already noted (see **196, 199**) that determination is normally expressed by **will**. But sometimes people feel that to express determination they should use another word, a 'heavier' word, a word not normally used much, and so they say **shall**:

(in a speech): *We shall fight and we shall win.* (*We will fight and we will win* or *We will fight and we shall win* would be equally possible.)

shall used in this way sometimes carries the idea of promise which we get in second person **shall**:

You shall have a sweet = I promise you a sweet (see **234**).

In *we shall win* the speaker is promising victory.

shall can be used in this way in ordinary conversation:

I shall be there, I promise you.

But **will** here is equally possible and less trouble for the student. When in doubt use **will.**

203 Uses of the future tense

A To express the speaker's opinions, assumptions, speculations about the future. These may be introduced by verbs such as **think, know, believe, doubt, suppose, assume, expect, hope, be afraid, feel sure, wonder, I daresay,** or accompanied by adverbs such as **probably, possibly, perhaps, surely,** but can be used without them:

(I'm sure) he'll come back. *(I suppose) they'll sell the house.*
(Perhaps) we'll find him at the hotel.
They'll (probably) wait for us.

The future tense can be used with or without a time expression. **be going to** is sometimes possible here also, but it makes the action appear more probable and (where there is no time expression) more immediate: *He'll build a house* merely means 'this is my opinion', and gives no idea when the building will start. But *He's going to build a house* implies that he has already made this decision and that he will probably start quite soon.

B The future tense is used similarly for future habitual actions which we assume will take place:

Spring will come again. *Birds will build nests.*
People will make plans.
Other men will climb these stairs and sit at my desk.
(*will be coming/building/making/climbing/sitting* would also be possible.)

C The future tense is used with clauses of condition, time and sometimes purpose.

If I drop this glass it will break (see **215**).
When it gets warmer the snow will start to melt (see **313**).
I'm putting this letter on top of the pile so that he'll read it first (see **309**).

Note that in an **if**-clause or a time clause we don't use the future tense even when the meaning is future, e.g.:

It will get warmer soon but *When it gets warmer . . .*
and *He will probably be late* but *If he is late . . .*

D Verbs of the senses, of emotion, thinking, possessing etc. (see **165**) normally express the future by the future tense, though **be going to** is sometimes possible. These verbs cannot, of course, express the future by the present continuous:

He'll be here at six. *They'll know tonight.*
You'll have time for tea.

E The future tense is used, chiefly in newspapers and news broadcasts, for formal announcements of future plans. In conversations such statements would normally be expressed by the present continuous or **be going to** form:

NEWSPAPER EXTRACT: *The President will open the new heliport tomorrow.*

But the average reader will say:

The President is going to open/is opening . . .

F As shown in **196** and **199, I/we will** is used for intention, particularly at the moment of decision:

A: *I'm not quite ready.* B: *I'll wait for you.*

will can be used with other persons to express intention but does not normally have this meaning.

won't can be used with all persons to express negative intention. *I've invited him but he won't come* means he refuses to come. (But *he won't come* could also mean 'I don't think he'll come'.)

204 **will** contrasted with **want/wish/would like**

A **will** must not be confused with **want/wish/would like. will** expresses an intention + a decision to fulfil it:

I will buy it = I intend to buy it/I'm going to buy it.

want/wish/would like merely expresses a desire. They do not give any information about intended actions.

B Note, however, that **I'd like** is often a possible alternative to **I'll have/take**:

CUSTOMER (in a shop): *I'd like/I'll have a pound of peas, please.*

DINER (in a restaurant): *I'd like/I'll have cress soup, please.*

Both can be used for invitations:

Would you like a drink? or *Will you have a drink?*

When accepting an invitation we can use either form:

I'd like/I'll have a sherry, please.

But the two forms are not interchangeable in the negative, so if we wish to refuse an invitation we must say:

I won't have anything, thanks

or *I don't want anything, thanks.*

wouldn't like means 'would dislike', so obviously could not be used here.

205 The future continuous tense

Form

This tense is made up of the future tense of **to be** + the present participle.

Affirmative	*I/we will/shall be working* (*shall* is not very usual)
	he/she/you/they will be working
Negative	*I/we will/shall not be working* (*shall* is not very usual)
	he/she/you/they will not be working
Interrogative	*shall I/we be working? will I/we be working?* (*will* is possible here but less usual than *shall*)

will, will not, shall not are contracted to *'ll, won't, shan't.*

Interrogative negative: *won't he/you/they be working?* etc. *shan't I/we be working?* or *won't I/we be working?*

Use

This tense has two uses:

It can be used as an ordinary continuous tense.

It can express a future without intention.

206 The future continuous used as an ordinary continuous tense

Like other continuous tenses it is normally used with a point in time, and expresses an action which starts before that time and probably continues after it. This use is best seen by examples. Imagine a class of students at this moment—9.30 a.m. We might say:

Now they are sitting in their classroom. They are listening to a tape. This time tomorrow they will be sitting in the cinema. They will be watching a film. On Saturday there is no class. So on Saturday they will not be sitting in the cinema. They will be doing other things. Bill will be playing tennis. Ann will be shopping. George will still be having breakfast.

A continuous tense can also be used with a verb in a simple tense:

Peter has been invited to dinner with Ann and Tom. He was asked to come at eight but tells another friend that he intends to arrive at seven. The friend tries to dissuade him: 'When you arrive they'll still be cooking the meal!'

207 The future continuous used to express future without intention

Example: *I will be helping Mary tomorrow.*

This does not imply that the speaker has arranged to help Mary or that he wishes to help her. It merely states that this action will happen. The future continuous tense used in this way is somewhat similar to the present continuous, but differs from it in the following points:

The present continuous tense implies a deliberate future action. The future continuous tense usually implies an action which will occur in the normal course of events. It is therefore less definite and more casual than the present continuous:

I am seeing Tom tomorrow. *I'll be seeing Tom tomorrow.*

The first implies that Tom or the speaker has deliberately arranged the meeting, but the second implies that Tom and the speaker will meet in the ordinary course of events (perhaps they work together).

This difference is not always very important, however, and very often either tense can be used. We can say:

He'll be taking his exam next week

or *He is taking his exam next week.*

He won't be coming to the party

or *He isn't coming to the party.*

The present continuous can only be used with a definite time and for the near future, while the future continuous can be used with or without a definite time and for the near or distant future. We can say:

I am meeting him tomorrow

but *I'll be meeting him tomorrow/next year/some time* (or without a time expression at all).

208 The future continuous and **will** + infinitive compared

A There is approximately the same difference between **will** + infinitive and the future continuous as between **will** + infinitive and the present continuous. **will** + infinitive expresses future with intention. The future continuous expresses future without intention.

In this sentence:

*I'll **write** to Mr Pitt and tell him about Tom's new house*

the verb in bold type expresses intention. The speaker announces a deliberate future action in accordance with his own wishes. But in the sentence:

*I'll **be writing** to Mr Pitt and I'll tell him about Tom's new house*

the verb in bold type expresses no intention. It is a mere statement of fact and implies that this letter to Mr Pitt will be written either as a matter of routine or for reasons unconnected with Tom's new house. Similarly:

Tom won't cut the grass means Tom refuses to cut it,

while *Tom won't be cutting the grass* is a mere statement of fact, giving no information about Tom's feelings. Perhaps Tom is away, or ill, or will be doing some other job.

B **will** + infinitive can express invitation:
Will you have a cigarette? (see **204, 224**)
or a polite request:
Will you help me to lift the piano? (see **225**)
or a command:
You will work in this room (see **226**).
The future continuous can have none of the above meanings:
Will you bring the piano in here? (polite request)
Yes, sir (possible answer).

But *Will you be bringing the piano in here?* (question about a future action)
Yes, I think I will
or *No, I think I'll put it upstairs* (possible answers).
You will work in this office under Mr Pitt (command)
but *You will be working here* (only a statement).
As before, the present continuous could be used here instead of the future continuous, provided that a time expression was added.

209 Examples of various future forms

A Imagine that we ask five people about their plans for the following Saturday. We say:
What are you doing/going to do on Saturday?
1 Peter has arranged to play golf with George; so he will say:
I'm playing/going to play golf with George.
2 Mary has decided to stay at home and make jam; so she will say:
I'm staying/going to stay at home. I'm going to make jam.
3 Andrew's plans depend on the weather; so he may say:
If it's fine I'll work/I'm going to work in the garden.
4 Ann hasn't made any plans, but she is an active person so she may say:
Perhaps I'll take/I expect I'll take/I'll probably take/I suppose I'll take my children for a walk.
5 Bill always has to work on Saturdays; so he will say:
Oh, I'll be working as usual (no other form would give this exact meaning).

B Questions about intentions
These are usually expressed by the present continuous, the **be going to** form or the future continuous. This last tense is a particularly useful interrogative form as it is considered more polite than the others. So if we are continuing to ask our five people questions we may say:

1 *Where are you playing/are you going to play/will you be playing golf?*

2 *What kind of jam are you going to make/will you be making?*

will you + infinitive is less usual than the other forms and is rarely found at the beginning of a sentence. (This is to avoid confusion; because **will you** + infinitive at the beginning of a sentence usually introduces a request.) It is however used in conditional sentences and when the speaker is offering something or asking the other person to make a decision:

What will you do if he is not on the plane?
Will you have a drink?
Will you have your meal now or later?

More examples of questions based on the sentences in A above:

3 If we are questioning Andrew we will probably say:
What are you going to do/What will you be doing in the garden?
(though *What will you do?* would be possible)

and *Are you going to cut/Will you be cutting the grass?*
(*Will you cut the grass?* would sound more like a request.)

4 To Mary we would probably say:
If you take them, where will you go? (though *where will you be going?* is possible)

5 To Bill we could say:
Will you be working all day?
This is the only possible form if we wish to convey the idea that Bill works on Saturday because it is the routine, not from choice.

Note that the future continuous must of course be used in questions of the type *What will you be doing this time next week?* regardless of whether the action is intentional or not (see **206**).

210 The future perfect tense and the future perfect continuous

A The future perfect

Form

will/shall + perfect infinitive for first persons, **will** + perfect infinitive for the other persons:

By the end of next month he will have been here for ten years.

Use

This tense is used for an action which at a given future time will be in the past, or will just have finished. Imagine that it is 3 December and David is very worried about an exam that he is taking on 13 December. Someone planning a party might say:

We'd better wait till 14 December. David will have had his exam by then so he'll be able to enjoy himself.

Note also:

I save £50 a month and I started in January. So by the end of the year I will/shall have saved £600.

BILL (looking at Tom's cellar): *You've got over 400 bottles. How long will that last you? Two years?*

TOM: *Not a hope. I drink eight bottles a week. I'll have drunk all these by the end of this year.*

B The future perfect continuous

Form

will/shall have been + present participle for the first persons, **will have been** + present participle for the other persons:

By the end of the month he will have been working/will have worked here for ten years.

The future perfect continuous bears the same relationship to the future perfect that the present perfect continuous bears to the present perfect, i.e. the future perfect continuous can be used instead of the future perfect:

1 When the action is continuous:

By the end of the month he will have been living/working/studying here for ten years.

2 When the action is expressed as a continuous action:

By the end of the month he will have been training horses/climbing mountains for twenty years.

But if we mention the number of horses or mountains, or divide this action in any way, we must use the future perfect:

By the end of the month he will have trained 600 horses/climbed 50 mountains.

19 Sequence of tenses

211 Subordinate clauses

A sentence can contain a main clause and one or more subordinate clauses. A subordinate clause is a group of words containing a subject and verb and forming part of a sentence:

We knew *that the bridge was unsafe.*
He gave it to me *because he trusted me.*
He ran faster *than we did.*
This is the picture *that I bought in Rome.*

(In the above examples only the subordinate clauses are in italics.)

For other examples see under conditional sentences, relative pronouns and clauses of purpose, comparison, time, result and concession. It is not necessary for the student to make a detailed study of clauses or even to be able to recognize the different kinds of clause, but it is necessary for him to learn to know which is the main verb of a sentence because of the important rule given below.

212 The sequence of tenses

When the main verb of a sentence is in a past tense, verbs in subordinate clauses must be in a past tense also:

Tense of verb in main clause		*Tense of verb in subordinate clause*
Present	He thinks that it will rain.	Future
Past	He thought that it would rain.	Conditional
Present	He sees that he has made a mistake.	Pres. perf.
Past	He saw that he had made a mistake.	Past perf.
Present	I work so hard that I am always tired.	Present
Past	I worked so hard that I was always tired.	Past
Pres. perf.	He has done all that is necessary.	Present
Past perf.	He had done all that was necessary.	Past
Present	He says that he is going to eat it.	Pres. continuous
Past	He said that he was going to eat it.	Past continuous

Note that a clause cannot be formed with an infinitive alone and that infinitives, therefore, are not affected by the above rule:

He wants to go to Lyons. *He wanted to go to Lyons.*
(i.e. the infinitive does not change).

The rule about sequence of tenses applies also to indirect speech when the introductory verb is in a past tense. (See chapter 29.)

20 The conditional

The conditional tenses

213 The present conditional tense

A This is formed with **should/would** + infinitive for the first person and **would** + infinitive for the other persons.

Affirmative	*I should/would work*
	you would/you'd work
	he would/he'd work
Negative	*I should/would not work* or
	I shouldn't/wouldn't work
	you would not/wouldn't work etc.
Interrogative	*should I work?*
	would you work? etc.
Negative interrogative	*should I not/shouldn't I work?*
	would you not/wouldn't you work? etc.

B This form is used:

1 In conditional sentences (see **215–23**).

2 In special uses of **should** and **would** (see chapter 21).

3 As a past equivalent of the future tense. **should/would** must be used instead of **shall/will** when the main verb of the sentence is in the past tense:

I hope (that) I shall/will succeed.
I hoped (that) I should/would succeed.
I know (that) he will be in time.
I knew (that) he would be in time.
He thinks (that) they will give him a visa.
He thought (that) they would give him a visa.
I expect (that) the plane will be diverted.
I expected (that) the plane would be diverted.

shall/will, therefore, in direct speech becomes **should/would** in indirect speech when the introductory verb is in the past tense:

I said, 'I shall be there' = I said that I should/would be there.
He said, 'I shall be there' = He said that he would be there. (**shall** becomes **would** when the subject changes from first to second or third person.)
He said, 'Tom will help me' = He said that Tom would help him.
(See also chapter 29.)

214 The perfect conditional tense

A This is formed with **should/would** and the perfect infinitive:

Affirmative	*I should/would have worked* *you would have worked* etc.
Negative	*I should/would not have worked* or *I shouldn't/wouldn't have worked* etc.
Interrogative	*would you have worked?* etc.
Negative interrogative	*should I not/shouldn't I have worked?* *would you not/wouldn't you have worked?* etc.

B This form is used:

1 In conditional sentences (see **215–23**).

2 In special uses of **should** (see **235–8**) and **would** (see **224–32**).

3 As a past equivalent of the future perfect tense:
I hope he will have finished before we get back.
I hoped he would have finished before we got back.

Conditional sentences

Conditional sentences have two parts: the **if**-clause and the main clause. In the sentence
If it rains I shall stay at home
'If it rains' is the **if**-clause, and 'I shall stay at home' is the main clause.
There are three kinds of conditional sentences. Each kind contains a different pair of tenses. With each type certain variations are possible but students who are studying the conditional for the first time should ignore these and concentrate on the basic forms.

215 Conditional sentences type 1: probable

A The verb in the **if**-clause is in the present tense; the verb in the main clause is in the future tense. It doesn't matter which comes first.
If he runs he'll get there in time.
The cat will scratch you if you pull her tail.
This type of sentence implies that the action in the **if**-clause is quite probable.
Note that the meaning here is present or future, but the verb in the **if**-clause is in a present, not a future tense. **if + will/would** is only possible with certain special meanings. (See **218**.)

B Possible variations of the basic form

1 Variations of the main clause

Instead of **if** + present + future, we may have:

1 **if** + present + **may/might** (possibility)
If the fog gets thicker the plane may/might be diverted (perhaps the plane will be diverted).

2 **if** + present + **may** (permission) or **can** (permission or ability)
If your documents are in order you may/can leave at once (permission).
If it stops snowing we can go out (permission or ability).

3 **if** + present + **must, should** or any expression of command, request or advice
If you want to lose weight you must/should eat less bread.
If you want to lose weight you had better eat less bread.
If you want to lose weight eat less bread.
If you see Tom tomorrow could you ask him to ring me?

4 **if** + present + another present tense
if + two present tenses is used to express automatic or habitual results:
If you heat ice it turns to water (*will turn* is also possible).
If there is a shortage of any product prices of that product go up.

[5] When **if** is used to mean **as/since**, a variety of tenses can be used in the main clause:
BILL: *Ann hates London.*
TOM: *If she hates it why does she live there?/she ought to move out/why has she just bought a flat there?*
This is not, of course, a true conditional clause.

[2] Variations of the **if**-clause

Instead of **if** + present tense, we can have:

1 **if** + present continuous, to indicate a present action or a future arrangement
If you are waiting for a bus you'd better join the queue (present action).
If you are looking for Peter you'll find him upstairs (present action).
If you are staying for another night I'll ask the manager to give you a better room (future arrangement).

2 **if** + present perfect
If you have finished dinner I'll ask the waiter for the bill.
If he has written the letter I'll post it.
If they haven't seen the museum we'd better go there today.

216 Conditional sentences type 2

A The verb in the **if**-clause is in the past tense; the verb in the main clause is in the conditional tense.

If I had a map I would lend it to you. (But I haven't a map. The meaning here is present.)

If someone tried to blackmail me I would tell the police. (But I don't expect that anyone will try to blackmail me. The meaning here is future.)

There is no difference in time between the first and second types of conditional sentence. Type 2, like type 1, refers to the present or future, and the past tense in the **if**-clause is not a true past but a subjunctive, which indicates unreality (as in the first example above) or improbability (as in the second example above).

B Type 2 is used:

1 When the supposition is contrary to known facts:
If I lived near my office I'd be in time for work (but I don't live near my office).
If I were you I'd plant some trees round the house (but I am not you).

2 When we don't expect the action in the **if**-clause to take place:
If a burglar came into my room at night I'd throw something at him (but I don't expect a burglar to come in).
If I dyed my hair blue everyone would laugh at me (but I don't intend to dye it).

Some **if**-clauses can have either of the above meanings:
If he left his bicycle outside someone would steal it.
'If he left his bicycle' could imply 'but he doesn't' (present meaning, as in 1 above) or 'but he doesn't intend to' (future meaning, as in 2). But the correct meaning is usually clear from the text.

At one time ambiguity of this kind was avoided by using **were** + infinitive instead of the past tense in type 2 (2):
If a burglar were to come . . .
If I were to dye my hair blue . . .
If he were to leave . . .
Nowadays this use of **were** is considered rather formal but it is sometimes found in written English.

3 Sometimes, rather confusingly, type 2 can be used as an alternative to type 1 for perfectly possible plans and suggestions:
Will Mary be in time if she gets the ten o'clock bus?
No, but she'd be in time if she got the nine-thirty bus
or *No, but she'll be in time if she gets the nine-thirty bus.*

ANN: *We'll never save £20!*

TOM: *If we each saved 50p a week we'd do it in ten weeks*

or *If we each save 50p a week we'll do it in ten weeks.*

A suggestion in type 2 is a little more polite than a suggestion in type 1, just as **would you** is a more polite request form than **will you**. But the student needn't trouble too much over this use of type 2.

C Possible variations of the basic form

1 Variations of the main clause

1 **might** or **could** may be used instead of **would**:

If you tried again you would succeed (certain result).

If you tried again you might succeed (possible result).

If I knew her number I could ring her up (ability).

If he had a permit he could get a job (ability or permission).

[2] The continuous conditional form may be used instead of the simple conditional form:

TOM: *Peter is on holiday; he is touring Italy.*

ANN: *If I were on holiday I would/might be touring Italy too.*

[3] **if** + past tense can be followed by another past tense when we wish to express automatic or habitual reactions in the past: compare **if** + two present tenses, **215** B 1(4). Note that the past tenses here have a past meaning:

If anyone interrupted him he got angry (whenever anyone interrupted him).

If there was a scarcity of anything, prices of that thing went up.

[4] When **if** is used to mean 'as' or 'since', a variety of tenses is possible in the main clause. **if** + past tense here has a past meaning. The sentence is not a true conditional.

ANN: *The pills made him dizzy. All the same he bought some more/has bought some more/is buying some more* etc.

TOM: *If they made him dizzy why did he buy/has he bought/is he buying more?*

BILL: *I knew she was short of money.*

GEORGE: *If you knew she was short of money you should have lent her some/why didn't you lend her some?*

[2] Variations of the **if**-clause

Instead of **if** + simple past we can have:

1 **if** + past continuous

We're going by air and I hate flying. If we were going by boat I'd feel much happier.

If my car was working I would/could drive you to the station.

2 **if** + past perfect
If he had taken my advice he would be a rich man now.
(This is a mixture of type 2 and 3. For more examples see **217**.)
(For **if** + **would**, see **218**.)

217 Conditional sentences type 3

A The verb in the **if**-clause is in the past perfect tense; the verb in the main clause is in the perfect conditional. The time is past and the condition cannot be fulfilled because the action in the **if**-clause didn't happen.
If I had known that you were coming I would have met you at the airport (but I didn't know, so I didn't come).
If he had tried to leave the country he would have been stopped at the frontier (but he didn't try).

B Possible variations of the basic form

1 **could** or **might** may be used instead of **would**:
If we had found him earlier we could have saved his life (ability).
If we had found him earlier we might have saved his life (possibility).
If our documents had been in order we could have left at once (ability or permission).

2 The continuous form of the perfect conditional may be used:
At the time of the accident I was sitting in the back of the car, because Tom's little boy was sitting beside him in front. If Tom's boy had not been there I would have been sitting in front.

3 We can use the past perfect continuous in the **if**-clause:
Luckily I was wearing a seat belt. If I hadn't been wearing one I would have been seriously injured.

4 A combination of types 2 and 3 is possible:
The plane I intended to catch crashed and everyone was killed. If I had caught that plane I would be dead now or *I would have been killed* (type 3).
If I had worked harder at school I would be sitting in a comfortable office now; I wouldn't be sweeping the streets. (But I didn't work hard at school and now I am sweeping the streets.)

5 **had** can be placed first and the **if** omitted:
If you had obeyed orders this disaster would not have happened = Had you obeyed orders this disaster would not have happened.

218 Special uses of will/would and should in if-clauses

Normally these auxiliaries are not used after **if** in conditional sentences. There are, however, certain exceptions.

A **if you will/would** is often used in polite requests. **would** is the more polite form.
If you will/would wait a moment I'll see if Mr Jones is free (please wait).
I would be very grateful if you would make the arrangements for me.

if you will/would + infinitive is often used alone when the request is one which would normally be made in the circumstances. The speaker assumes that the other person will comply as a matter of course.
If you'd fill up this form.
(in a hotel) *If you'd just sign the register.*
(in a shop) *If you'd put your address on the back of the cheque.*
(in a classroom) *If you'd open your books.*

B **if + will/would** can be used with all persons to indicate willingness:
If he'll listen to me I'll be able to help him = If he is willing to listen . . .
If Tom would tell me what he wants for his dinner, I'd cook it for him. (The speaker implies that Tom is unwilling to tell her.)

won't used in this way can mean 'refuse':
If he won't listen to me I can't help him = If he is unwilling to listen/If he refuses to listen . . .
If they won't accept a cheque we'll have to pay cash = If they refuse to accept . . .

C **will** can be used to express obstinate insistence (**227** B):
If you ˈwill play the drums all night no wonder the neighbours complain = If you insist on playing . . .

D **if + would like/care** can be used instead of **if + want/wish** and is more polite:
If you would like to come I'll get a ticket for you.
If you'd care to see the photographs I'll bring them round some evening.
If he'd like to leave his car here he can.

But if we rearrange such sentences so that **would like** has no object, we can drop the **would**:
If you like I'll get a ticket for you
but *If you'd like a ticket I'll get one for you.*
If he likes he can leave his car here
but *If he'd like to leave his car here he can/He can leave it here if he'd like to.*

E **if + should** can be used in type 1 to indicate that the action, though possible, is not very likely. It is usually combined with an imperative and is chiefly used in written instructions:
If you should have any difficulty in getting spare parts, ring this number.
If these biscuits should arrive in a damaged condition, please inform the factory at once.

should can be placed first and the **if** omitted:
Should this machine fail, ring the bell and wait.

219 if + were can be used instead of if + was

If she was/were offered the job she'd take it. (Either can be used.)
If Peter was/were to apply for the post he'd probably get it. (**were** is better.)
If I was/were you I should wait a bit. (**were** is more usual.)
Were I you I should wait. (**were** is the only possible form.)
were to is more usual than **was to**. **were** is better than **was** when the supposition is contrary to fact. **were** is the only possible form when the auxiliary is placed first.

Note that **if I were you I should/would** . . . is a useful way of expressing advice:
If I were you I should/I would/I'd paint it green.
The **if I were you** is often omitted:
I'd paint it green.

In indirect speech such sentences are best reported by **advise**:
He said, 'If I were you I'd tell the police'
= *He advised me to tell the police.*

220 if replaced by unless, but for, otherwise, provided, suppose, or inversion

A **unless** + affirmative verb = **if** + negative
Unless you start at once you'll be late
= *If you don't start . . .*
Unless you had a permit you couldn't get a job
= *If you hadn't a permit . . .*

B **but for** = if it were not for/if it hadn't been for
My father sends me an allowance. But for that I wouldn't be here.
The storm delayed us. But for the storm we would have been in time.

C **otherwise** = if this doesn't happen/didn't happen/hadn't happened
We must be back before midnight; otherwise we'll be locked out
= *If we are not back by midnight we'll be locked out.*
Her father pays her fees; otherwise she wouldn't be here
= *If her father didn't pay her fees she wouldn't be here.*
I used my calculator; otherwise I'd have taken much longer
= *If I hadn't used my calculator I'd have taken much longer.*

D **provided (that)** can replace **if** when there is a strong idea of limitation or restriction. It is chiefly used with permission.
You can camp in my field provided you leave no mess.

E **suppose/supposing . . .? = what if . . .?**
Suppose the plane is late?
= *What if/What will happen if the plane is late?*
Suppose no one had been there?
= *What if no one had been there?*

suppose can also introduce suggestions:
Suppose you ask him/Why don't you ask him?

F Inversion of subject and auxiliary with **if** omitted
if + subject + auxiliary can be replaced by auxiliary + subject:
if I were in his shoes = were I in his shoes
if there should be a delay = should there be a delay
if he had known in time = had he known in time

221 if and in case

in case is followed by a present or past tense or by **should**. It appears similar to **if** and is often confused with it. But the two are completely different.

An **in case** clause gives a reason for the action in the main clause:
Some cyclists carry repair outfits in case they have a puncture = Some cyclists carry repair outfits because they may have/because it is possible they will have a puncture.
I always slept by the phone in case he rang during the night = I always slept by the phone because (I knew) he might ring etc.

An **in case** clause can be dropped without changing the meaning of the main clause. In a conditional sentence, however, the action in the main clause depends on the action in the **if**-clause, and if the **if**-clause is dropped the meaning of the main clause changes.

Compare:
1 BILL: *I'll come tomorrow in case Ann wants me*
and 2 TOM: *I'll come tomorrow if Ann wants me.*

In (1) perhaps Ann will want Bill, perhaps she won't. But Bill will come anyway. His action doesn't depend on Ann's. *in case Ann wants me* could be omitted without changing the meaning of the main verb.

In (2), a conditional sentence, Tom will only come if Ann asks him. His action depends on hers. We cannot remove *if Ann wants me* without changing the meaning of the main verb.

An **in case** clause is normally placed after the main clause, not before it.

(Note, however, that **in case of** + noun = **if there is a/an** + noun:
In case of accident, phone 999 = *If there is an accident, phone 999.*
This may have led to the confusion of **if**-clauses and **in case** clauses.)

(See also **310** for **in case** and **lest**.)

222 if only

only can be placed after **if** and indicates hope, a wish or regret according to the tense used with it.

if only + present tense/**will** expresses hope:
If only he comes in time = We hope he will come in time.
If only he will listen to her = We hope he will be willing to listen to her.

if only + past/past perfect expresses regret (it has the same meaning as **wish** + past or past perfect):
If only he didn't drive so fast = We wish he didn't drive so fast/We are sorry he drives so fast.
If only you hadn't said, 'Liar' = We wish you hadn't said, 'Liar'/We are sorry you said, 'Liar'.

if only + **would** can express regret about a present action as an alternative to **if only** + past tense (it has the same meaning as **wish** + **would**):
If only he would drive more slowly (= We are sorry that he isn't willing to drive more slowly)
or a not very hopeful wish concerning the future:
If only the rain would stop = We wish it would stop, but implies that we think it will go on. (See also **wish**, **231**.)

if only clauses can stand alone as above or form part of a full conditional sentence.

223 Conditional sentences in reported speech

A Type 1

1 Basic form. The tenses here change in the usual way:

He said, 'If I get a seat on the plane I'll be home in five hours'
= *He said that if he got a seat on the plane he'd be home in five hours.*
If the introductory verb is in a present tense there is, of course, no tense change.

2 **if**-clause + requests, commands, expressions of advice and questions

These can be reported by **tell/ask/advise** etc. + object + infinitive (see **301**) or by **say** + subject + **should/be** + infinitive (see **302**):
He said, 'If you have time, clean the windows/could you clean the windows?'
= *He told/asked me to clean the windows if I had time*
or *He said that if I had time I was to clean the windows.*

Note that if we use the object + infinitive construction we must place it before the **if**-clause. This often means changing the order of the original and sometimes leads to a clumsy or confused sentence. In such cases use the **say** construction:
'If you see Ann remind her to ring me,' said Tom
= *Tom said that if we saw Ann we were to remind her to ring him.*
(The **tell** construction here would be very clumsy.)

The **say** construction is also more usual when the introductory verb is in a present tense:
PETER (on phone): *If you miss the last bus get a taxi.*
This would normally be reported:
Peter says that if we miss the last bus we are to get a taxi.

Expressions of advice are normally reported by **advise** + object + infinitive or **say** + subject + **should**:
She said, 'If you're tired why don't you sit down?/you had better sit down'
= *She advised me to sit down if I was tired*
or *She said that if I was tired I should/had better sit down.*

Questions are usually reported with the **if**-clause last:
'If the baby is a girl, what will they call her?' he wondered
= *He wondered what they would call the baby if it was a girl.*
'If the door is locked what shall I do?' she asked
= *She asked what she should do if the door was locked.*

B Type 2

1 Basic form. The tenses here do not change:
He says/said, 'If I had a permit I could get a job'
= *He says/said that if he had a permit he could get a job.*

2 Requests

Complete conditional sentences may be left unchanged, or reported by **ask**:

He said, 'I'd be very grateful if you'd let me know as soon as possible'

= *He said he'd be very grateful if I'd let him know as soon as possible*

or *He asked me to let him know as soon as possible.*

if you would + infinitive used alone as a request form is best reported by **ask**:

He says/said, 'If you'd pay the cashier'

= *He asks/asked me to pay the cashier.*

3 **if I were you I'd . . .** is best reported by **advise**:

He said, 'If I were you I'd buy a new one'

= *He advised me to buy a new one.*

C Type 3

No verb changes are required:

He said, 'If I'd heard the whole story I would have acted differently'

= *He said that if he had heard the whole story he would have acted differently.*

21 Other uses of **will, would, shall, should**

will, would

224 **will** and **would**

Invitations expressed by **will you? would you?** or **would you like?**

A *Will you have a drink?* (sometimes shortened to *Have a drink*)
Would you like a drink?
There is no difference in time between these two forms.
In indirect speech these invitations are normally reported by **offer**:
He offered me a drink
though **would you like . . . ?** can be reported by
He asked if I would like . . .

B *Will you come to lunch tomorrow?* (not very usual)
Would you come to lunch tomorrow? (*Could you come* is also possible)
Would you like to come to lunch tomorrow?
There is no difference in time between these forms.
In indirect speech these invitations are normally reported by **invite/ask**:
He invited me to lunch.

C Invitations expressed by **would you? could you? would you like?** + infinitive can be answered *I'd like to very much* or *I'd love to*, or *I'd like to very much/I'd love to, but I'm afraid I'm not free.*

225 Requests can be expressed by **will you? would you?**

Will you type this, please? *Will you give him this letter?*
Will anyone who saw this accident please telephone the nearest police station? (radio announcement)

would you? can be used for a request in the present:
Would you show me the way to the station?
Would you give him this letter?

would you? is less authoritative and therefore more polite than **will you?**

In the past, i.e. in indirect speech, it is possible to use **would**:

He asked if I would show him the way.
But it is more common to use the object + infinitive construction:
He asked me to show him the way.

Note that **will you?** and **would you?** without infinitives are sometimes placed after an imperative:
Come here, will you? *Shut the door, would you?*
But this is not very polite except when used between people who know each other very well.

226 Commands expressed by **will** in the affirmative

'You will stay here till you are relieved,' said the officer.
All boys will attend roll-call at 9 o'clock (school notice).

This is a formal, impersonal type of command, similar to **must** or **is/are to** but more peremptory. It implies the speaker's confidence that the order will be obeyed and is therefore much used in schools and in military etc. establishments.

Note that if we change **will** + infinitive into the future continuous we remove all idea of command: *You will work here under Mr Pitt* is a command, but *You will be working here under Mr Pitt* is only a statement.

In the past, i.e. in indirect speech, we use the **be** + infinitive construction, or **tell/order** etc., with object + infinitive (see **302, 301**):
He said that she was to work under Mr Pitt
or *He told her to work under Mr Pitt.*
It is not possible to use **would** here.

227 Habits expressed by **will, would**

A Habits in the present are normally expressed by the simple present tense; but **will** + infinitive can be used instead when we wish to emphasize the characteristics of the performer rather than the action performed. It is chiefly used in general statements:
An Englishman will usually show you the way in the street (it is normal for an Englishman to act in this way).

This is not a very important use of **will**, but the past form, **would**, has a much wider use and can replace **used to** when we are describing a past routine:
On Sundays he used to/would get up early and go fishing. He used to/would spend the whole day by the river and in the evening used to/would come home with marvellous stories of the fish he had nearly caught.

Note, however, that when **used to** expresses a discontinued habit, it cannot be replaced by **would**. (See **158**.)

Both **will** and **would** can be contracted when used as above.

B **will** can also express obstinate insistence, usually habitual:
If you ˈwill keep your watch half an hour slow it is hardly surprising that you are late for your appointments.
would is used in the past:
We all tried to stop him smoking in bed but he ˈwould do it.
will and **would** are not contracted here and are strongly stressed.

228 Assumptions introduced by will

will here can be used with the present infinitive, present continuous infinitive or perfect infinitive.

Imagine that Tom leaves home at 1 p.m. for a flight to New York. His plane takes off at 3. If at 2.30 someone asks Ann:
How far do you think Tom has got?
she will answer:
Oh, he'll still be at the airport (I'm sure he is at the airport)
or *He'll be sitting in the airport* (I'm sure he is sitting . . .).
If Bill asks the same question at 11 p.m. Ann will say:
Oh, he'll be in New York by now
or *He'll have arrived by now* (I'm sure he has arrived).

It can be used in negative and interrogative:
It's no use asking John; he won't know (I'm sure he doesn't know).
Will George be at home now? (Do you think he is at home now?)

The assumptions can be pleasing or displeasing to the speaker.

should can also be used to express an assumption, but assumptions with **should** are slightly less confident than assumptions with **will**. **should** here can be used in the negative but not in the interrogative. **should** is not used with assumptions which are displeasing to the speaker. (See also **238** E.)

229 would like and want; would like and would care

A **would like** and **want**

1 Sometimes either can be used:

1 In requests and questions about requests (but **would not like** is not used here: see 2 (2) below):
CUSTOMER: *I'd like some raspberries, please* or *I want some raspberries, please.*
GREENGROCER: *I'm afraid I haven't any. Would you like some strawberries?*

CUSTOMER: *No, I don't want any strawberries, thanks.* (*wouldn't like* is not possible.)
I would like is usually more polite than **I want**.

Would you like? can imply a willingness to satisfy the other person's wishes. **Do you want?** doesn't imply this. A shopkeeper, therefore, will normally use **Would you like?** Similarly:
CALLER: *I'd like/I want to speak to Mr X, please.*
TELEPHONIST: *Mr X is out. Would you like/Do you want to speak to Mr Y?*
(**Would you like?** is much more polite and helpful than **Do you want?**)

2 When we are not making requests, but merely talking about our wishes, we can use either **would like** or **want** in affirmative, interrogative or negative. There is no difference in meaning, though *I want* usually sounds more confident than *I would like* and *I want* is not normally used for unrealizable wishes:
I would like to live on Mars.

2 **would like** and **want** are not interchangeable in the following uses:

1 In invitations we use **Would you like?** not **Do you want?**
Would you like a cup of coffee?
Would you like to go to the theatre?
Do you want? used here would be a question only, not an invitation.

2 In the negative there is a difference between **would like** and **want**. **don't want** = 'have no wish for' but **wouldn't like** = 'would dislike'. **wouldn't like** cannot therefore be used in answer to invitations or offers, as it would be impolite. Instead we use **don't want** or some other form:
Would you like some more coffee?
No, I don't want any more, thanks or *No, thanks.*

3 In the past the two forms behave differently. In indirect speech **want** becomes **wanted**, but **would like** remains unchanged:
Tom said, 'I would like/want to see it'
= *Tom said he would like/wanted to see it.*
But if we don't use a reported speech construction we have to say:
Tom wanted to see it.
(We cannot use **would like** here, as *Tom would like to see it* has a present or future meaning.)
would like has two past forms: **would like** + perfect infinitive or **would have liked** + infinitive. But these forms express unrealized wishes only:
I'd like to have gone = I wanted to go but I didn't get my wish.

B **would like** and **would care**

would you care for? + noun and **would you care?** + infinitive are similar to **would you like?** + noun/infinitive, but the speaker is less confident of a favourable answer:

TOM: *Would you care to see my photos, Ann?* (Tom is not sure that Ann will be interested in his photos.)

would care is not normally used in the affirmative so **would like** replaces it:

A: *Would you care to come?*
B: *Yes, I'd like to very much.*
A: *I wouldn't care to live on the tenth floor.*
B: *Oh, I'd like it.*

In the negative both forms have the same meaning.

230 would rather/sooner

A **would rather/sooner** + infinitive without **to**

There is no difference in meaning between these forms, but **would rather** is more often heard. **would rather/sooner** is a very useful way of expressing preference. **I/he** etc. **would rather/sooner** can be used instead of **I prefer/he prefers**:

He prefers reading to talking = He would rather read than talk.
He prefers wine to beer = He would rather drink wine than beer.

would rather/sooner can also be used instead of **would prefer**:

A: *Would you like to go by train?*
B: *I'd prefer to go/I'd rather go by air.*
A: *Would you like a drink?*
B: *I'd prefer a cup of tea/I'd rather have a cup of tea.*

B **would rather/sooner** + subject + past tense

would prefer + object + infinitive cannot be replaced by a similar **would rather** form. Instead we must use **would rather** + subject + past tense:

A: *Shall I start tomorrow?*
B: *I'd prefer you to start today* or *I'd rather you started today.*

(See also **270, 288**.)

231 wish (that) + subject + would

A **wish** + subject + past tense can express regret for a present situation:

I wish I knew his address = I'm sorry I don't know his address.
I wish that he wrote more regularly = I'm sorry he doesn't write more regularly.

B **wish** + subject + **would** can be used similarly, but only with actions which the subject can control, i.e. actions he could change if he wished.

wish + **would** here expresses interest in the subject's willingness/unwillingness to perform the action:

I wish he would write more often = I'm sorry he isn't willing to write more often.

I wish he would wear a coat = I'm sorry he refuses to wear a coat.

Note that the subject of **wish** cannot be the same as the subject of **would**, as this would be illogical. We cannot therefore have **I wish** + **I would**.

C **wish** + subject + **would** can also be used to express dissatisfaction with the present and a wish for change in the future:

I wish he would answer my letter (I have been waiting for an answer for a long time).

I wish they would change the menu (I'm tired of eating sausages).

I wish they would stop making bombs.

But the speaker is normally not very hopeful that the change will take place, and often, as in the third example above, has no hope at all.

As in B above,

1 **wish** + subject + **would** here is restricted to actions where change is possible, and

2 **wish** and **would** cannot have the same subject.

The action is normally in the subject's control and the idea of willingness/unwillingness is still present, but **wish** + subject + **would** can sometimes be used with inanimate subjects. This is particularly common when talking about the weather etc.:

I wish it would stop raining. *I wish the sun would come out.*

I wish prices would come down.

wish + subject + **would** here is rather like **would like**, but **would like** is not restricted to actions where change is possible and does not imply dissatisfaction with the present situation. Also the **would like** construction does not imply any lack of hope:

TOM: *I would like my son Jack to study art* (I want him to study art/I hope he will study art).

BILL: *I wish my son Peter would study art* (Peter has obviously refused to do this).

D **I wish you would . . .** is a possible request form. Here there is no feeling that the person addressed will refuse to perform the request, but there is a feeling that this person is annoying or disappointing the speaker in some way: *I wish you would help me* often implies 'You should have offered to help me', and *I wish you would stop humming/interrupting/asking silly questions* would imply that the speaker was irritated by the noise/the interruptions/the silly questions.

However, **I wish you would** can be used in answer to an offer of help, and does not then imply any dissatisfaction:

A: *Shall I help you check the accounts?*

B: *I wish you would* (I'd be glad of your help).

E **if only + would** can replace **wish + would** in B and C above. It cannot be used for requests as in D.

if only is more dramatic than **wish**:

If only he would join our party!

(For **wish/if only** + past and perfect tenses see **286**.)

232 **would** for past intention

As has already been noted **would** is the past equivalent of **will** when **will** is used for the ordinary future:

He knows he will be late. *He knew he would be late.*

would similarly is the past equivalent of **will** used to express intention:

I said, 'I will help him.'

I said that I would help him.

He said, 'I won't lend you a penny.'

He said that he wouldn't lend me a penny.

But notice that whereas **would** used for future or intention is restricted to subordinate clauses as in the above examples, **wouldn't** used for negative intention can stand alone:

He won't help me today (he refuses to help).

He wouldn't help me yesterday (he refused to help).

would cannot be used in this way. So to put a sentence such as *I will help him today* into the past, we have to replace **will** by another verb:

I wanted/intended/offered to help him yesterday.

shall

Apart from its use in the future tense **shall** can be used as follows:

233 Requests for orders or advice, offers, suggestions expressed by **shall I? shall we?**

A *How shall I cook it?* *Where shall we put this?*

B When the request is for advice only we use either **shall** or **should**:
Which one shall I buy? or *Which one should I buy?*

C Offers:
Shall I wait for you? *Shall I help you to pack?*

D Suggestions:
Shall we meet at the theatre?

(See **300** for **shall I/we?** in reported speech.)

234 **shall** in the second and third persons is used to express (A) the subject's intention to perform a certain action or to cause it to be performed, and (B) a command. Both these uses are old-fashioned and formal and normally avoided in modern spoken English.

A Examples of **shall** used to express the speaker's intention:
You shall have a sweet = I'll give you a sweet or I'll see that you get a sweet.
He shan't come here = I won't let him come here.
They shall not pass = We won't let them pass.
In the past, i.e. in indirect speech, it is usually necessary to change the wording:
He said, 'You shall have a sweet.'
= *He promised me a sweet.*

B Examples of **shall** used to express a command:
Yachts shall go round the course, passing the marks in the correct order (yacht-racing rules).
Members shall enter the names of their guests in the book provided (club rules).
This construction is chiefly used in regulations or legal documents. In less formal English **must** or **are to** would be used instead of **shall** in the above sentences.
When sentences of this type are reported in indirect speech, **shall** is usually replaced by **must, have/had to, is/was to**:
REGULATIONS: *Each competitor shall wear a number.*
The regulations say that each competitor must/has to/is to/wear a number.
The regulations said that each competitor must/had to/was to/wear a number.
should would be grammatically possible here but would weaken the idea of command.

C **shall you?** is an old-fashioned form which is sometimes still found in serious novels possibly because it is shorter and neater than the future continuous tense.

should

235 **should** is used to express duty and to indicate a correct or sensible action.

It is therefore a usual way of expressing advice:
You should pay your debts (duty).
You shouldn't tell lies (duty).
You should eat more fruit (advice).
You've spelt it wrong. There should be another 's' (correct action).
Shops should remain open till later in the evening (sensible action).
They shouldn't allow parking in this street; it's too narrow.
The mail should be left in the hall.

should here has the same meaning as **ought to** (see **155**). It is less forceful than **must** or **have to** because no authority is involved.

should + present infinitive has a present or future meaning:
You should go today/tomorrow.
It need not change in indirect speech:
He said that I should go that day/the next day.

should + perfect infinitive (*you should have gone*) expresses a past unfulfilled duty or sensible action which was not performed:
You should have stopped at the red lights (but you didn't).
The letters should have been posted yesterday.
Similarly in the negative:
You shouldn't have been rude to him (but you were rude).
The door shouldn't have been locked.

236 **that . . . should** can be used after certain verbs as an alternative to a gerund or infinitive construction.

A **suggest, propose, insist (on)** take either gerund or **that . . . should**:
Tom suggested selling the house.
Tom suggested my selling the house (possessive adjective + gerund).
Tom suggested that I should sell the house (pronoun + **should**).
Tom suggested that Ann should sell the house (noun + **should**).

With an active verb as shown above **should** is one of several alternatives. With a passive verb, however, **should** is the usual construction:
Tom suggested that the house should be sold.
(See also the last example in B-E below.)

Similarly:
He insisted on being present when work started.
He insisted that nothing should start till he arrived.

He proposed (our) postponing the trip.
He proposed that we/Ann and I should postpone the trip.
He proposed that the trip should be postponed.

B **recommend, advise** can take either gerund or infinitive or **should**:
He recommended (my) buying new tyres.
He recommended me/Tom and me to buy new tyres.
He recommended that I/Tom and I should buy new tyres.
He recommended that new tyres should be bought.

C **determined, was determined, agreed** and **demanded** take either infinitive or **should**:
He determined/was determined to get there first.
He determined/was determined that nobody should get there before him.
He agreed to divide the prize between Tom and Ann.
He agreed that Tom and Ann should share the prize.
He agreed that the prize should be shared between Tom and Ann.
With the present tenses of these verbs **that . . . shall** is possible, but the infinitive construction is generally preferred.

D **arrange, stipulate** and **be anxious** can be followed by **for** + object + infinitive or a **should** construction:
I am anxious for nobody to know where I am going.
I am anxious that nobody should know where I am going.
He was anxious for everyone to have a chance to vote.
He was anxious that everyone should have a chance to vote.
He arranged for me to study with his own children.
He arranged that I should study with his own children.
He stipulated for the best materials to be used.
He stipulated that the best materials should be used.

E **order, command, urge** normally take an object + infinitive construction:
He urged the committee to buy the site.
But **that . . . should** is sometimes used, particularly in the passive:
He urged that the site should be bought.
He ordered Tom to go (he spoke directly to Tom).
He ordered that Tom should go (he probably told someone else to tell Tom).
He commanded the men to shut the gates.
He commanded that the men should shut the gates.
He commanded that the gates should be shut.
In the above constructions the **should** is sometimes omitted, particularly before the verb **be**:
He proposed that Sir Francis (should) be made a director.

237 it is/was + adjective + **that . . . should**

A **that . . . should** can be used after **it is/was necessary, advisable, essential, better, vital, important;** after **right, fair, natural, just** (these are often preceded by **only**) and after **reasonable**, as an alternative to a **for** + infinitive construction:

It is better for him to hear it from you.
It is better that he should hear it from you.
It is essential for him to be prepared for this.
It is essential that he should be prepared for this.

should is sometimes omitted, as shown in **236**:

It is essential that he be prepared.

Other examples:

We felt that it was only right that she should have a share.
It is advisable that everyone should have a map.

B **that . . . should** can be used after **it is/was strange, odd, surprising, amazing, annoying, ridiculous, ludicrous, absurd** and similar adjectives as an alternative to **that** + present/past tense:

It is ridiculous that we should be short of water in a country where it is always raining.
It is strange that the car should break down today in exactly the same place where it broke down yesterday.

The perfect infinitive is sometimes used when referring to past events:

It is amazing that she should have said nothing about the murder (amazing that she said).

238 Other uses of **should**

A After **don't know why/see no reason why/can't think why** etc. when the speaker queries the reasonableness or justice of an assumption:

I don't know why you should think that I did it.

The perfect infinitive is usual when the assumption was in the past:

I can't think why he should have said that it was my fault.

B Idiomatically with **who, where, what** in dramatic expressions of surprise:

What should I find but an enormous spider!

Quite often the surprise is embarrassing:

Who should come in but his first wife!

C After **lest** and sometimes after **in case**:

1 **lest** is sometimes placed after expressions of fear or anxiety:

He was terrified lest he should slip on the icy rocks.

The perfect infinitive is used when the anxiety concerns a past action:
She began to be worried lest he should have met with some accident.

2 **lest** can also be used in purpose clauses to mean 'for fear that':
He dared not spend the money lest someone should ask where he had got it.

in case, which is more usual than **lest** here, can be followed by **should** or by an ordinary present or past tense:
in case someone should ask/someone asked (see also **221, 310**)

D **should** is sometimes used in purpose clauses as an alternative to **would/could**:
He wore a mask so that no one should recognize him. (See **309**.)

E To express an assumption:
He should be there now (it is reasonable to assume this).
He should have finished by now (**should** + perfect infinitive).
These assumptions are slightly less confident than assumptions with **will**:
He will be there now (I am quite certain of this). (See **228**.)
Note however that **should** is not used when the action assumed is displeasing or inconvenient to the speaker:
Let's not go shopping today. The shops will be crowded. (**should** could not replace **will**.)

But *Let's go early tomorrow when they will/should be fairly empty.*

F In conditional sentences instead of the present tense:
If you should decide to go on horseback remember to bring food for the horses. (See **218** E.)

G In indirect commands when the recipient of the command is not necessarily addressed directly:
He ordered that Tom should leave the house. (See **302** D.)

22 The infinitive

239 Verbs followed directly by the infinitive

The most useful of these are:

agree**	endeavour	proceed
aim	fail	promise*
appear*	forget*	prove*
arrange**	guarantee*	refuse
attempt	happen*	resolve**
bother (negative)	hesitate	seem*
care (negative)	hope	swear*
choose	learn*	tend
claim**	long	threaten*
condescend	manage	trouble (negative)
consent	neglect	try (= attempt)
decide**	offer	undertake*
demand**	plan	volunteer
determine**	prepare	vow
be determined**	pretend*	

Auxiliary verbs

be	have	ought
can	may	shall
dare	must	will
do	need	used

(For verbs of knowing and thinking followed by the infinitive, see **244**. For verbs taking object + infinitive, see **241–2**.)

The following phrases can also be followed by an infinitive:

occur* + to + object (negative/interrogative)
do one's best/do what one can
make an/every effort
make up one's mind* (decide)
take the trouble (the affirmative equivalent of **not bother/trouble**)
turn out* (prove to be)

A Starred verbs* can also be used with **that** + subject + verb (see **316**):

I promise to wait = I promise that I will wait.
He pretended to be angry = He pretended that he was angry.

But a verb + infinitive does not necessarily have the same meaning as the same verb used with **that** + subject; **forget** does not mean the same thing in the following sentences:

He forgot to leave the car keys on the table (he didn't leave them).
He forgot that his brother wanted to use the car.

occur requires **it** as subject both with an infinitive and a **that** construction:
It didn't occur to me to ask him for proof of his identity (I didn't think of doing this).
It occurred to me that he was trying to conceal something (the idea came to me).

appear, happen, seem, turn out, when used with a **that** construction, require **it** as subject:
It turned out that his 'country cottage' was an enormous bungalow.
His country cottage turned out to be an enormous bungalow.

B Verbs with two stars** take an infinitive or a **that . . . should** construction. **that . . . should** is particularly useful in the passive (see **236**).
They decided to divide the profits equally.
They decided that the profits should be divided equally.
I arranged to meet them.
I arranged for Tom to meet them.
I arranged that Tom should meet them.
I arranged that they should be met by Tom.

C The continuous infinitive is often used after **appear, happen, pretend, seem**:
I happened to be looking out of the window when they arrived.
He seems to be following us.

It is also possible after **agree, arrange, decide, determine, hope, manage, plan** and the auxiliary verbs (see **254**).

D The perfect infinitive is possible after **appear, hope, pretend, seem** and the auxiliary verbs (see **255**).

240 Verbs followed by how/what/when/where/which + noun and whether + infinitive

The most useful of these are **ask, decide, discover, find out, forget, know, learn, remember, see** (= understand/perceive), **show** + object, **think, understand, want to know, wonder**:
He discovered how to open the safe.
I found out where to buy fruit cheaply.
I didn't know when to switch the machine off.
I showed her what to do with the rubbish.
I've been wondering where to hang my new picture.
I'll have to think what to wear.
(Note that this construction is not usual after **think** in the simple present or past, but can be used after other tenses of **think**, or after **think** as a second verb, as in the last example above.)

A **whether** + infinitive can be used similarly after **want to know, wonder**:
I wonder/wondered whether to write or phone
and after **decide, know, remember, think** when these verbs follow a negative or interrogative verb:
You needn't decide yet whether to study arts or science.
He couldn't remember whether to turn left or right.

B **ask, decide, forget, learn, remember** can also be followed directly by the infinitive (see **239**). But the meaning is not necessarily the same:
learn how + infinitive = acquire a skill
She learnt how to make lace
though if the skill is a fairly usual one, the **how** is normally dropped:
She learnt to drive a car.
learn + infinitive (without **how**) can have another meaning:
She learnt to trust nobody = She found from experience that it was better to trust nobody.
Note also:
I decided to do it = I said to myself, 'I'll do it.'
I decided how to do it = I said to myself, 'I'll do it this way.'
and *I remembered to get a ticket* (I got a ticket).
I remembered where to get a ticket (I remembered that the tickets could be obtained from the Festival Office).

241 Verbs followed by the infinitive or by object + infinitive

The most important of these are **ask, beg, expect, would hate, help, intend, like** (= think wise or right), **would like** (= enjoy), **would love, mean, prefer, want, wish**:
He likes to have a good meal at midday.
He likes his staff to have a good meal at midday.
I want to learn German.
I want my children to learn German.

A **ask/beg** + infinitive has a different meaning from **ask/beg** + object + infinitive:
I asked to speak to Mr Jones = I said, 'Could I speak to Mr Jones?'
but *I asked Bill to speak to Mr Jones* = I said, 'Bill, would you speak to Mr Jones?'
Similarly:
I begged (to be allowed) to go with him = I said, 'Please let me go with you.'
I begged him to go = I said, 'Please go.'

B **expect** + infinitive and **expect** + object + infinitive can have the same meaning:

I expect to arrive tomorrow = I think it is likely that I will arrive tomorrow.

I expect him to arrive tomorrow = I think it is likely that he will arrive tomorrow.

But very often **expect** + object + infinitive conveys the idea of duty:

He expects his wife to bring him breakfast in bed at weekends (He thinks it is her duty to do this).

C **wish, want, would like** can all mean 'desire'.

wish is the most formal:

Do you wish to see the manager?

Yes, I wish to make a complaint.

The government does not wish Dr Jekyll Hyde to accept a professorship at a foreign university.

(For **wish** + **that** + subject see **231, 286**.)

To express a desire in the past we normally use **wanted**, though **wished** is also possible:

I wanted to see the exhibition. *I wanted Bill to come with me.*

would like can be made past only by using a perfect infinitive. But note that the meaning then changes:

I would like to climb the mountain = I want to climb the mountain

but *I would like to have climbed/would have liked to climb the mountain* = I wanted to climb the mountain but I didn't get my wish.

i.e. **would like** + perfect infinitive and **would have liked** + infinitive express an unfulfilled wish.

For **would like** see also **204, 224, 229, 270**.

D **hate, intend, like, love, mean, want** (= require) can also be followed by gerunds (see **269**).

E **expect** can also be followed by **that** + subject + verb (any tense).

242 Verbs followed by object + infinitive

The most important of these are:

advise	forbid	persuade
allow	force	remind
ask	induce	request
bribe	implore	show how
compel	instruct	teach/teach how
command	invite	tell/tell how
encourage	oblige	tempt
entitle	order	urge

Object + infinitive without **to** can be used after:

feel	let	see
hear	make	watch

Examples:
He encouraged me to try again.
She reminded him to buy petrol.
They invited us to go with them.

A **ask** can also be followed directly by an infinitive and therefore really belongs to the previous paragraph. But **ask** + object + infinitive has a much wider use than **ask** + infinitive, so we have included it here too.

B **advise, allow, permit** can also be used with gerunds (see **267**).

C **make** in the active and **let** (active and passive) take the infinitive without **to**:
He made me move my car
but *I was made to move my car* (passive).
She let us use her phone.
After looking at our passports they let us go.
After they had looked at our passports we were let go/allowed to go (passive).
(In the passive **let** is frequently replaced by **allow**.)

D Verbs of the senses: **feel, hear, see** and the verb **watch** can be used with object + infinitive without **to**, but **see** and **hear** in the passive require the full infinitive:
I felt the house shake. *I heard her shout, 'Stop!'*
I saw him take the money. *He was seen to take the money.*
But these verbs are more often used with object + present participle:
I heard her shouting. *I saw him taking the money.*
(These constructions will be compared in **272**.)

E **show/teach/tell + how**

show used with an infinitive requires **how**:
He showed me how to change a fuse.

tell how + infinitive = instruct:
He told me how to replace a fuse (He gave me the necessary information or instructions).
But **tell** + object + infinitive = order:
He told me to change the fuse = He said, 'Change the fuse.'
teach how:
We can **teach** someone (**how**) to swim, dance, type, ride etc.:
He taught me how to light a fire without matches.

how is possible, but when the skill is a fairly usual one the **how** is normally dropped:
He taught me to ride.
teach + object + infinitive (without **how**) can also mean to teach or train someone to behave in a certain way:
He taught me to obey all commands without asking questions.

F **remind, show** (without **how**), **teach, tell** can also be followed by **that**:
He reminded me to drive slowly.
He reminded me that the road was dangerous.
He showed me how to open the safe.
He showed me that it was quite easy.
But **tell** + **that** does not have the same meaning as **tell** + infinitive:
He told me to go (**tell** = order).
He told me that I was already late (**tell** = inform).

G **ask** and **request** can also be followed by **that** + **should**. This construction is chiefly used in the passive:
He requested/asked that the matter should be kept secret.

243 Verbs and expressions followed by the infinitive without **to**

A **will, shall, can, do, must, may**

B **need** and **dare**, except when they are conjugated with **do/did** or **will/would**:
You needn't say anything but *You don't/won't need to say anything.*
I dared not wake him but *I didn't/wouldn't dare (to) wake him.*
In theory the **to** is required in the last example but in practice it is often omitted. The theory is that if **dare** and **used** are treated as auxiliaries, they take the infinitive without **to** like most auxiliaries. If they are treated as ordinary verbs, with **do/did** etc., they take the full infinitive like ordinary verbs.

C **would rather/sooner, rather/sooner than:**
Would you like to go today? I'd rather wait till tomorrow.
Rather/Sooner than risk a bad crossing, he postponed his journey.
(See **230, 270**.)

D **had better:**
'You had better start at once,' he said = He advised me to start at once.

E **let** and **make** (but **make** in the passive needs the infinitive with **to**):
Let's ring Peter. *Don't let the children play with matches.*
He made me type it again but *I was made to type it again.*

F **feel, hear, see** and **watch**:
I heard him lock the door. *I saw/watched him drive off.*
But **see** and **hear** in the passive take the infinitive with **to**:
He was seen to enter the office. *He was heard to say that . . .*
(See also **272**.)

G **help** may be followed by an infinitive with or without **to**:
He helped us (to) push it.

H If two infinitives are joined by **and**, the **to** of the second infinitive is normally dropped:
I intend to sit in the garden and write letters.
I want you to stand beside me and hold the torch.

I **but** and **except** take the infinitive without **to** when they follow **do + anything/nothing/everything**:
He does nothing but complain.
My dog does everything but speak.
Can't you do anything but ask silly questions?

244 Verbs of knowing and thinking etc.

A **be sure** can be followed by an infinitive or by a construction with **that**, but there is an important difference in meaning:
He is sure to succeed means that the speaker believes this
but *Tom is sure that he will succeed* means that Tom believes this.

B **assume, believe, consider, feel, know, suppose, think, understand** can be followed by object + **to be**:
I consider him to be the best candidate.
But it is much more common to use **that** + an ordinary tense:
I consider that he is the best candidate.
When, however, these verbs are used in the passive they are more often followed by an infinitive than by the **that** construction:
He is known to be honest = It is known that he is honest.
He is thought to be the best player = It is thought that he is the best player.
Note, however, that **suppose** when used in the passive often conveys an idea of duty:
You are supposed to know the laws of your own country = It is your duty to know . . .
(**expect** could also be used here.)
The continuous infinitive can also be used:
He is thought to be hiding in the woods (people think that he is hiding).
He is supposed to be washing the car (he should be washing it).

When the thought concerns a previous action we use the perfect infinitive:

They are believed to have landed in America (it is believed that they landed).

suppose + perfect infinitive need not necessarily convey an idea of duty:

They are supposed to have discovered America (it is thought that they did).

But *You are supposed to have finished by now* would normally mean 'You should have finished'. (See also **291** B.)

C **estimate** and **presume** in the active normally take a **that** construction. In the passive we can use either **that** or an infinitive:

It is estimated that the vase is 2,000 years old

or *The vase is estimated to be 2,000 years old.*

Other uses of the infinitive

For the **be** + infinitive construction and for **to be about** + infinitive, see **111**. For the infinitive used to express purpose see **308**.

245 Infinitives of purpose after **go** and **come**

Purpose is normally expressed by the infinitive:

They went to Amsterdam to buy diamonds. (See **308**.)

But it is not normal to use an infinitive of purpose after the imperative or infinitive of **go** and **come:**

Instead of *Go to find Bill* we normally say *Go and find Bill*; and instead of *Come to talk to Ann* we normally say *Come and talk to Ann*; i.e. we replace the infinitive by **and** + imperative.

And instead of:

I must go to help my mother.
I'll come to check the accounts.

we normally say:

I must go and help my mother
and *I'll come and check the accounts.*

Here we replace the infinitive of purpose by **and** + infinitive without **to** (see **243** H).

But when **go** and **come** are used as gerunds or in any present or past tense they take the ordinary infinitive of purpose:

I've come to check the accounts. *I went to help my mother.*
I didn't come to talk to Bill; I came to talk to you.
I'm thinking of going to look for mushrooms.

The verb **see**, however, seems to be an exception to the above rules, for we can say either *Come to see me* or *Come and see me*, and *I'd like to go to see 'Macbeth'* or *I'd like to go and see 'Macbeth'*.

246 A The infinitive is used after **only** to express a disappointing sequel:
He hurried to the house only to find that it was empty = He hurried to the house and was disappointed when he found etc.
He survived the crash only to die in the desert = He survived the crash but died etc.

B The infinitive can also be used as a connective link without **only**, and without any idea of misfortune:
He returned home to learn that his daughter had just become engaged.
But this use is mainly confined to such verbs as **learn, find, see, hear, be told** etc., as otherwise there might be confusion between an infinitive used connectively and an infinitive of purpose.

247 The infinitive can be used after **the first, the second** etc., **the last, the only** and sometimes after superlatives to replace a relative clause (see **55** B).
He loves parties; he is always the first to come and the last to leave (the first who comes and the last who leaves).
He is the second man to be killed in this way (the second man who was killed).
She was the only one to survive the crash (the only one who survived).

the first, the last etc. can be used here either by themselves, as in the first example, or followed by a noun or pronoun, as in the other examples.

Note the infinitive here has an active meaning. When a passive sense is required a passive infinitive is used:
the best play to be performed that year = the best play that was performed that year

Compare this with:
the best play to perform = the best play for you to perform/the play you should perform (see **248**)

248 The infinitive can be placed after nouns and pronouns to show how they can be used or what is to be done with them (see also **55** B):
I have letters to write (that I must write).
Would you like something to drink?

She said, 'I can't go to the party; I haven't anything to wear' ('that I can wear').

a house to let = a house that the owner wants to let

Note that the active infinitive here has a passive meaning (compare with **247** above). The passive infinitive is possible after **there is/are** + noun/pronoun; i.e. we can say:

There are sheets to be mended or *There are sheets to mend.*

But the active infinitive is more usual. Note that the passive infinitive conveys only the idea of duty: *sheets to be mended* could mean only *sheets that must be mended*, but *books to read* could mean *books that I must read* or *books that I can read.*

The infinitive can be used in the same way with prepositions:

someone to talk to — *a case to keep my records in*
something to talk about — *a cup to drink out of*
a pen to write with — *a table to write on*
a tool to open it with

(See **78** for the position of prepositions.)

249 Infinitive after adjective + noun/pronoun

A After **it is/was** + adjective + **of you/him** etc.:

It is good of you to help me.
It is stupid of him to smoke so much.
It was careless of me to lose my umbrella.
It was clever of him to find his way here.
It was brave of the policemen to tackle the armed men.

wise, kind, good, nice, honest, generous, cowardly, selfish, silly, wicked etc. can also be used in this way.

B After **it/that** + **is/was/would be** + adjective + noun:

That's a stupid place to park a car.
That would be a very rude thing to say.
It was a queer time to choose.

Adjectives in A above can be used here, and also **strange, crazy, mad, odd, funny** (= odd), **extraordinary, astonishing, amazing, pointless, ridiculous** etc.

Comments of this type can also be expressed as exclamations:

What a terrible night to be out in!
What a funny name to give a dog!
What an odd place to have a picnic!

The adjective is often omitted in expressions of criticism or disapproval:

What a (silly) way to bring up a child!
What a (bad) time to come round knocking on people's doors!

250 The infinitive used after adjectives

A After adjectives expressing emotion:
I was delighted to see him.
He'll be angry to find that nothing has been done.
I'm sorry to say I can't find your key anywhere.
Other adjectives of this type are **happy, glad, relieved, astonished, amazed, surprised, horrified, disgusted, disappointed, sad.**

B **it is/was** + adjective can also be followed by an infinitive in such sentences as:
It is lovely to see so much open country.
It was dreadful to find oneself alone in such a place.
It was dreadful for him to find himself alone in such a place.
It is easy to talk; you haven't got to make the decision.
It is easy for you to talk; you haven't got to make the decision.
for + noun/pronoun can usually be added, as shown. This construction is really a rearrangement of a sentence whose subject is an infinitive or an infinitive phrase. It would be possible in each case to begin with the infinitive:
To see so much open country is lovely.
To find oneself alone in such a place was dreadful.
But the **it is/was** construction is much the more usual (see **252**).

C Sentences of the above type can also follow a verb such as **find, think**:
It was easy for him to leave the house unobserved.
He found that it was easy to leave the house unobserved
or *He found it easy* etc.
He thought it was amusing to have two different identities
or *He thought it amusing to have* etc.

D An infinitive is often placed after the adjectives **easy, hard, difficult, awkward, impossible,** etc.:
The book is easy to read. *This car is hard to park.*
Some questions are awkward to answer.
His actions are impossible to justify.

E **apt, anxious, bound, due, inclined, liable, prepared, ready, reluctant, unwilling, willing** can be followed by the infinitive:
He is bound to win = He is sure to win/I am sure that he will win.
He is reluctant to make any decision.
The train is due to leave in ten minutes.
You are inclined to judge people too hastily.
We are all liable to make mistakes.
I am prepared to help you = I am willing to help you.

Do not confuse **anxious** + infinitive with **anxious + about**:
I am anxious = I am worried.
I am anxious about Peter = I am worried about Peter
but *I am anxious to see Peter* = I have a wish to see him.
Note also **be anxious for** + infinitive:
I am anxious for him to learn music.
be anxious can also be followed by **that** + subject + **should.** This is an alternative to **anxious for** + infinitive and is fairly common with a passive verb:
I am anxious for everything to be done properly
= *I am anxious that everything should be done properly*. (See **236** D.)

251 The infinitive after **too, enough** and **so . . . as**

A **too** + adjective/adverb + infinitive

1 **too** + adjective + infinitive

1 The infinitive can refer to the subject of the sentence. It then has an active meaning:
You are too young to understand = You are so young that you cannot understand.
He was too drunk to drive home = He was so drunk that he couldn't drive home.

2 The infinitive can also refer to the object of a verb. It then has a passive meaning:
The plate was so hot that we couldn't touch it could be expressed:
The plate was too hot to touch (too hot to be touched).
Note that *it*, the object of *touch* in the first sentence, disappears in the infinitive construction, because the infinitive, though active in form, is passive in meaning.
Sometimes either an active or a passive infinitive may be used:
This parcel is too heavy to send/to be sent by post.
But this is not always possible, so students are advised to stick to the active infinitive.

for + noun/pronoun can be placed before the infinitive in this construction:
The case was too heavy (for a child) to carry = The case was too heavy to be carried by a child.

3 The infinitive can refer similarly to the object of a preposition:
The grass was so wet that we couldn't sit on it.
The grass was too wet (for us) to sit on.
The light is so weak that we can't read by it.
The light is too weak to read by.

2 **too** + adjective + **a** + noun + infinitive

He was too shrewd a businessman to accept the first offer = As a businessman he was too shrewd to accept the first offer.

He is too experienced a conductor to mind what the critics say = As a conductor he is too experienced to mind what the critics say.

The infinitive here always refers to the subject of the sentence as in A1 above. A passive infinitive is also possible:

He was too experienced a conductor to be worried by what the critics said.

3 **too** + adverb + infinitive

It is too soon (for me) to say whether the scheme will succeed or not.

He spoke too quickly for me to understand. (*for me* is necessary here.)

She works too slowly to be much use to me.

B Adjective/adverb + **enough** + infinitive

1 Adjective + **enough** + infinitive

1 As with the **too** construction, the infinitive can refer to the subject of the verb:

She is old enough to travel by herself.

He was tall enough to see over the heads of the other people.

2 Or it can refer to the object of a verb:

The case is light enough for me to carry = The case is so light that I can carry it.

After a few minutes the coffee was cool enough (for us) to drink.

3 It can refer to the object of a preposition:

The ice was thick enough to walk on.

The light was strong enough to read by.

2 **enough** may be followed by a noun:

He doesn't earn enough money to live on.

We haven't enough time to do it properly.

She had enough sense to turn off the gas.

have + **enough** + noun here is often replaceable by **have** + **the** + noun:

We haven't the time to do it properly.

She had the sense to turn out the gas.

3 Adverb + **enough** + infinitive

He didn't jump high enough to win a prize.

He spoke slowly enough for everyone to understand.

C **so** + adjective + **as** + infinitive

He was so foolish as to leave his car unlocked.

This is an alternative to the **enough** construction in B1 above, but note that *He was foolish enough to leave his car unlocked* can mean either that he did it or that he was capable of doing it, but *He was so foolish as to leave* etc. implies that he actually did so.

The **so . . . as** construction is not very often used as shown above, but it is quite common as a request form:

Would you be so good as to forward my letters? = Would you be good enough to forward my letters?

There is no difference in meaning here between the two forms. It is important not to forget the **as**.

252 The infinitive as subject

An infinitive or an infinitive phrase can be the subject of the verbs **be, seem, appear**. The infinitive can be placed first:

To hesitate would have been fatal.
To obey the laws is everyone's duty.
To save money now seems practically impossible.
To lean out of the window is dangerous.

But it is more usual to place the pronoun **it** first, and move the infinitive or infinitive phrase to the end of the sentence:

It would have been fatal to hesitate.
It is everyone's duty to obey the laws.
It is practically impossible to save money now.
It is dangerous to lean out of the window.

The gerund can be used instead of the infinitive when the action is being considered in a general sense, but it is always safe to use an infinitive. When we wish to refer to one particular action we must use the infinitive:

He said, 'Do come with me.' It was impossible to refuse.

(Here we are referring to one particular action, so the gerund is not used.)

But *It is not always easy to refuse invitations* can be replaced by *Refusing invitations is not always easy.*

Here the action is considered in a general sense, and either gerund or infinitive is possible. (See also **258**.)

An infinitive may also be the subject of a noun clause placed after **find, discover, believe, think, consider, expect, wonder (if).**

Note that after **find** we can omit the verb **be**, i.e. we can say:

He found that it was easy to earn extra money
or *He found it easy to earn extra money.*
He will find that it is hard to make friends
or *He will find it hard to make friends.*

After other verbs, however, the student is advised not to omit the **be**.

A similar clause construction can be formed with gerunds. See **258**.

Infinitives are used in some well-known sayings:
To know all is to forgive all. *To work is to pray.*
To err is human, to forgive divine.

The perfect infinitive can also be used as a subject of a sentence:
To have made the same mistake twice was unforgivable.

Similarly with **it** first:
It is better to have loved and lost than never to have loved at all.

253 The infinitive represented by its **to**

An infinitive can be represented by **to** alone to avoid repetition. This is chiefly done after such verbs as **want, wish, like, love, hate, hope, try,** after the auxiliaries **have, ought, need,** and with **used, be able,** and the **be going to** form:

Did you see the Pyramids? No, I wanted to (see them) but there wasn't time.
I didn't mean to take a taxi but I had to (take one) as I was late.
Would you like to come with me? Yes, I'd love to.
He wanted to go but he wasn't able to.
Did you get a ticket? No, I tried to, but there weren't any left.
Do you do your own housework? I used to, but now I've got a service flat.
Have you fed the dog? No, but I'm just going to.

254 The continuous infinitive

Form

to be + present participle: *He seems to be following us.*

Use

The continuous infinitive can be used:

A After the auxiliary verbs:
The world may be getting colder.
He may/might be waiting in the station = Perhaps he is waiting in the station.
She said that he might be waiting in the station = She said that perhaps he was waiting in the station.
A: *He may be watching TV.*
B: *He can't/couldn't be watching TV. There are no programmes today because of the strike.* (Negative deduction.)

He must be coming by bus. (Deduction: there is no other way of getting here.)

A: *What are you reading?*

B: *I'm reading a novel.*

A: *You shouldn't be reading a novel. You should be reading a textbook.*

B After **appear, happen, pretend, seem:**

He appears/seems to be living in the area = It appears/seems that he is living in the area.

He appeared/seemed to be living in the area = It appeared/seemed that he was living in the area.

I happened to be standing next to him when he collapsed = It happened that I was standing next to him when he collapsed.

He pretended to be looking for a book = He pretended that he was looking for a book.

C After **hope** and **promise** and, but less usually, after **agree, arrange, decide, determine/be determined, plan, undertake:**

I hope/hoped to be earning my living in a year's time = I hope I will/I hoped I would be earning etc.

determine/be determined, plan could replace **hope** above with slight changes of meaning.

I promised to be waiting at the door when he came out.

agree, arrange, decide, determine/be determined, plan, undertake could be used instead of **promise** above with slight changes of meaning.

D After **believe, consider, suppose, think** etc. in the passive:

He is believed to be living in Mexico. (See **291**.)

255 The perfect infinitive

Form

to have + past participle: *to have worked, to have spoken*

Use

A With auxiliary verbs

1 With **should, would, might** and **could** to form the perfect conditional, which is used in the third type of conditional sentence (see **217**):

If I had seen her I should have invited her.

2 With **should** or **ought** to express unfulfilled obligation:

He should have helped her (but he didn't).

I shouldn't have gone out (but I did).

He oughtn't to have gone near the bull (but he did). (See **156, 235**.)

3 With **was, were** to express an unfulfilled plan or arrangement (see **111** A):
The house was to have been ready today but as there has been a builders' strike it is still only half finished.

4 With **should/would like** to express an unfulfilled wish:
I should like to have seen it (but it wasn't possible).
This could also be expressed:
I should have liked to see it or *I should have liked to have seen it* i.e. we can put either or both verbs into the perfect infinitive without changing the meaning.

would is used in the second and third person:
He would like to have emigrated (but his wife successfully opposed the idea).

5 With **could** to express past unused ability or past possibility:
I could have climbed that mountain (but I didn't).
He could have come by now (perhaps he did).
(See also **132–3**.)

6 With **needn't** to express an unnecessary past action (see also **146–8**):
You needn't have hurried. Now we are too early.
You needn't have cooked it. We could have eaten it raw.

7 With **may/might** in speculations about past actions:
He may have come = It is possible that he came.
He might have come = It is possible that he came (the use of **might** increases the doubt).
He may not/might not have come = It is possible that he didn't come.

might must be used when the main verb is in the past:
She said that he mightn't have come (see also **126** B).

8 With **can't, couldn't** and **must** to express deductions

can't or **couldn't** + perfect infinitive express negative deduction (see **152**). Either **can't** or **couldn't** can be used in the present. **couldn't** is necessary when the main verb is in a past tense:
He can't/couldn't have moved the piano himself; it takes two men to lift it

but *We knew he couldn't have crossed the river, because the bridge was broken and there was no boat.*

must + perfect infinitive expresses an affirmative deduction (see **150–1**):
Someone must have been here recently; these ashes are still warm.
He must have come this way; here are his footprints.

B With certain other verbs

1 With **appear, happen, pretend, seem**

Note the difference between present and perfect infinitives here:

Present infinitive:

He seems to be a great athlete = We think he is etc.

He seemed to be a great athlete = We thought he was etc.

Perfect infinitive:

He seems to have been a great athlete = We think he was etc.

He seemed to have been a great athlete = We thought he had been etc.

i.e. the action of the perfect infinitive is an earlier action; it happens before the time of the main verb.

Other examples:

I happened to have driven that kind of car before = It happened that I had driven that kind of car before.

He pretended to have read the book = He pretended that he had read it.

2 With the following verbs in the passive voice: **acknowledge, believe, consider, find, know, report, say, suppose, think, understand** (see **291**):

He is understood to have left the country.

3 The perfect infinitive is possible but less usual with **claim, expect, hope, promise**:

He expects/hopes to have finished by June = He expects/hopes that he will have finished by June.

256 The perfect infinitive continuous

Form

to have been + present participle

Use

It is used chiefly after auxiliary verbs and after **appear** and **seem**, but it can also be used after **happen, pretend** and the passive of **believe, know, report, say, understand**:

A: *He says he was waiting for a train.*

B: *He couldn't have been waiting for a train. There were no trains that day.*

A: *I was following Peter closely.*

B: *You shouldn't have been following him closely; you should have left a good space between the two cars.*

He appears to have been waiting a long time.

He pretended to have been studying.

23 The gerund

257 Form and use

The gerund has exactly the same form as the present participle: *running, working, speaking* etc.

It can be used in the following ways:

1 as subject of a sentence
2 after prepositions
3 after certain verbs
4 in noun compounds (**12**), e.g. *a diving board* (a board for diving off).

258 The gerund as subject

As already seen (**252**), either infinitive or gerund can be the subject of a sentence when an action is being considered in a general sense. We can say:

It is easier to read French than to speak it

or *Reading French is easier than speaking it.*

(For gerund or infinitive after **than** see **311** B3.)

The gerund, like the infinitive (see **252**), can be the subject of a clause placed after **find, discover, believe, think, consider, expect, wonder (if)** etc.

After **find** we can omit the verb **be**, i.e. we can say:

He found that parking was difficult

or *He found parking difficult.*

But it is safer not to omit **be** after the other verbs.

Note the possible difference between gerund and infinitive here: *He found parking difficult* would mean that he usually/always found it difficult. *He found it difficult to park* could refer to one particular occasion. It could also mean that he always found it difficult, but it is more usual to express this idea by a gerund.

The gerund is used in short prohibitions:

No smoking. *No loitering.* *No spitting.*

But these cannot be followed by an object, so prohibitions involving an object are usually expressed by an imperative:

Do not touch these wires.
Do not feed the lions.

Gerunds are used in the saying *Seeing is believing.*

259 Gerunds after prepositions

A When a verb is placed immediately after a preposition the gerund form must be used:

He insisted on seeing her. *He was accused of smuggling.*
I have no objection to hearing your story again.
Can you touch your toes without bending your knees?
He is good at telling lies. *She is fond of climbing.*
They were charged with driving to the public danger.
He was fined for being drunk in charge of a car.
I am quite used to waiting in queues.
He prefers being neutral to taking sides.
A corkscrew is a tool for taking corks out of bottles.
Do you feel like going for a swim? (For **like** (preposition) see **87**.)
After swimming I felt cold.
What about leaving it here and collecting it on the way back?
He is thinking of emigrating. *I'm sorry for keeping you waiting.*
His wife raised the money by selling her jewellery.
We had a lot of difficulty in finding a parking place.
In spite of starting late, he arrived in good time.
Aren't you interested in making money?
There's no point in waiting. *She doesn't care for cooking.*

B A number of verb + preposition/adverb combinations ('phrasal verbs') take the gerund. The most common of these are **be for/against, care for, give up, keep on, leave off, look forward to, put off, see about, take to** (for **go on** see **271**):

I don't care for standing in queues.
He took to ringing us up in the middle of the night.
Eventually the dogs left off barking.
I have seen the film; now I am looking forward to reading the book.
He put off making a decision till he had more information.

260 The word to

This word often causes confusion as it can be either (A) a part of an infinitive, or (B) a preposition:

A **to** placed after the auxiliary verbs **be, have, ought, used** and after **going** (in expressions such as the **be going to** form) is part of the infinitive of the following verb and is only added to remind students that the preceding verb takes the full infinitive, i.e. the infinitive with **to**.

to is often also placed after **love, like, hate, want, try, hope, mean** and some others (see **253**) to avoid repetition of an infinitive already mentioned:

A: *Did you buy cheese?*
B: *No, I meant to, but the shop was shut* (I meant to buy some).

B Otherwise **to** placed after a verb will probably be a preposition and will be followed by noun/pronoun or gerund. Note particularly the following expressions: **look forward to, take to, be accustomed to, be used to**:
I am looking forward to my holidays/to next weekend/to it.
I am looking forward to seeing you.
I am used to heat/hard work/bad food/noise/dust/it.
I am used to standing in queues.

Be careful not to confuse **I used to/he used to** etc., which expresses a past habit or routine (e.g. *They used to burn coal; now they burn oil fuel only*) with **I am used to/he is used to** etc., which means 'I am accustomed to/familiar with':
I am used to the cold (it doesn't worry me).
He is used to working at night (he doesn't mind it). (See **159**.)

A good way of finding out whether a **to** is a preposition or a part of an infinitive is to see if it is possible to put a noun/pronoun after it. For example a noun/pronoun could be placed after **I am accustomed to**:
I am accustomed to it/the dark.
This **to** therefore is a preposition, and verbs used after **to** must be gerunds. If, however, we put a noun/pronoun after **have to**, it would not make sense. This **to** therefore is part of an infinitive.

261 Verbs followed by the gerund

The most important of these are:

admit	excuse	prevent
anticipate	fancy (= imagine)	propose (= suggest)
appreciate	finish	recollect
avoid	forgive	remember (= recollect)
consider	imagine	resent
defer	involve	resist
delay	keep (= continue)	risk
deny	loathe	save (oneself the trouble of)
detest	mind (= object)	
dislike	miss	stop
dread	pardon	suggest
enjoy	postpone	understand
escape		

The gerund is also used after the expressions:
can't stand = endure *can't help* = prevent/avoid
it's no use/good and after the adjective *worth*.

A 1 **appreciate** requires a possessive adjective:
I appreciate your giving me so much of your time.

2 **excuse, forgive, pardon** take either possessive adjective + gerund or object + **for** + gerund:
Forgive my interrupting you.
Forgive me for interrupting you.

3 **prevent** takes either possessive adjective + gerund or object (+ **from**) + gerund:
I can't prevent his leaving the country.
I can't prevent him (from) leaving (**from** is optional).

4 Many verbs can be followed either by the gerund or by possessive adjective/object + gerund. (See **262**.)

5 **propose** = 'suggest' takes the gerund but **propose** = 'intend' takes the infinitive. See **267–71** for verbs which can take either infinitive or gerund.

6 Note the expression **I dread to think**:
I dread to think what will happen if we're late.
This is much the same as *I'm afraid to think* (so I don't think). (See **271** B.)

B Examples of verb + gerund sentences:
He admitted taking the money. (**admit to** + gerund is also possible.)
I don't anticipate meeting any opposition.
Try to avoid making him angry.
He detests writing letters. *She dreads getting old.*
Do you enjoy teaching? *He narrowly escaped being run over.*
He kept complaining.
Putting in a new window will involve cutting away part of the roof.
He didn't want to risk getting wet as he had only one suit.
If we buy plenty of food now it will save shopping later in the week.
Stop talking. (For **stop** + infinitive of purpose see **271** G.)
I can't understand his leaving his wife.
Is there anything here worth buying?
It's no good/use arguing. *I couldn't help laughing.*

262 Verbs + possessive adjective/pronoun object + gerund

A number of verbs and prepositions can be followed directly by the gerund or by possessive adjective/pronoun object + gerund.

A If the verb or verb + preposition is followed directly by the gerund, the gerund refers to the subject of the verb:
Tom insisted on seeing the document (Tom saw it).
If we put a possessive adjective or pronoun before the gerund, the

gerund refers to the person denoted by the possessive adjective/pronoun:
He insisted on my/me reading the document (I had to read it).

B Useful verbs and expressions which can take either construction are:
dislike and **like** (negative), **dread, fancy, mean, mind, involve, propose, recollect, remember, resent, save, stop, suggest, understand; approve/disapprove of, insist on, object to, it's no good/use, there's no point in, what's the point of.**
He disliked working late.
He disliked me/my working late.
I object to paying twice for the same thing.
I object to his/him making private calls on the office phone.
He resented being passed over for promotion.
He resented my/me being promoted before him.
(For **mind** see **263**, for **suggest** and **propose** see **264**.)

C **excuse, forgive, pardon** and **prevent** are not followed directly by the gerund but take either possessive adjective/pronoun + gerund or pronoun + preposition + gerund:
Forgive my/me ringing you up so early.
Forgive me for ringing you up so early.
You can't prevent his/him spending his own money.
You can't prevent him from spending his own money.

D Possessive adjective and pronoun object compared
In formal English the possessive adjective is used with the gerund. But in spoken and less formal English we very often use the pronoun. The student therefore has a choice of forms, but is recommended to use the pronoun.
With **stop** meaning 'prevent' the pronoun is more usual than the possessive adjective:
I can't stop him writing to the papers.

E Nouns with gerunds
In very formal English the possessive case is used here:
I don't remember my mother's complaining about prices.
But it is much more usual to omit the **'s**:
I don't remember my mother complaining.

263 The verb **mind**

A This verb is used chiefly in the interrogative and negative:
Would you mind waiting a moment? *I don't mind walking.*

B It can be followed directly by a gerund, or by a noun/pronoun or possessive adjective + gerund:
I don't mind living here = I live here and don't object to it.
I don't mind his/him living here = He lives here and I don't object to this.
He didn't mind leaving home = He left home quite happily.
He didn't mind Ann leaving home = Ann left home and he was quite happy about it (see **262** E for case of noun).

C **would you mind?** is one of the most usual ways of making a request:
Would you mind not smoking? = Please don't smoke.
Would you mind moving your car? = Please move it.
Note change of meaning when a possessive adjective precedes the gerund:
Would you mind my moving your car? = Would you object if I moved your car? (This is not a request but a polite query.)
Do you mind if I move it? is a possible alternative to *Would you mind my moving it?*
but *Do you mind my moving it?* may mean that the action has already started.

D **mind** can never be followed by an infinitive.

E The personal pronoun object can be used with gerunds instead of a possessive adjective (see **262** D).

264 suggest and propose with gerund or with that + subject constructions

A **suggest**
As already stated, **suggest** can be followed:
1 directly by a gerund:
He said, 'Let's read the instructions first.'
or *He suggested reading the instructions first.*
2 by possessive adjective/object + gerund:
She said, 'Why don't you apply for a work permit, Tom?'
She suggested his/him applying for a work permit.
She suggested Tom's/Tom applying.
3 **suggest** can also be followed by **that** + subject + **should**:
She suggests/suggested that Tom should apply.
This is particularly useful in the passive:
He suggests/suggested sending out circulars.
He suggests/suggested that circulars should be sent out.
4 **suggest** in a future, present or present perfect tense can be

followed by **that** + subject + present tense. **suggest** in a past tense can be followed by **that** + subject + past tense:
She will suggest/suggests/is suggesting/has suggested that you rent a house.
She would suggest/suggested/was suggesting/had suggested that you rented a house.

B **propose** can be used as in A1–3 above:
He proposed travelling by helicopter.
He proposed your/you travelling by helicopter.
He proposed that you should travel by helicopter.
propose + **that** + present or past tense is, however, less usual.

C Note that the nouns **suggestion** and **proposal** can be followed by **that . . . should**:
The suggestion/proposal that the mayor should present the prizes was accepted by everyone.

265 The perfect gerund (**having worked, having spoken** etc.)

This can be used instead of the present form of the gerund (*working, speaking* etc.) when we are referring to a past action:
He was accused of deserting his ship
or *He was accused of having deserted his ship.*

The perfect gerund is fairly usual after **deny**:
He denied having been there.
Otherwise the present form is much the more usual.

266 The passive gerund

Form

Present: *being written*
Past: *having been written*

He was punished by being sent to bed without any supper.
I remember being taken to Paris as a small child.
The safe showed no signs of having been touched.

24 Infinitive and gerund/present participle constructions

Infinitive or gerund

267 Verbs taking either infinitive or gerund:

A **begin, start, continue, cease**
B **attempt, can't bear, intend**
C **advise, allow, permit, recommend**
D **it needs/requires/wants**

A With **begin, start, continue, cease** either infinitive or gerund may be used without any difference in meaning, but the infinitive is more usual with verbs of knowing and understanding and the verb **matter**:

I began working or *I began to work.*
He continued living above the shop
or *He continued to live above the shop.*
But *I am beginning to understand/see/realize why he acted as he did.*
It ceased to matter whether or not he sold his work.
She never ceased complaining/to complain about the prices.

B After **attempt** and **intend** gerunds are possible but infinitives are more common:

Don't attempt to do it by yourself is more usual than *Don't attempt doing it . . .*

After **can't bear** either gerund or infinitive can be used.

C With **advise, recommend, allow, permit**

If the person concerned is mentioned we use the infinitive:

He advised me to apply at once.
She recommends housewives to buy the big tins.
They don't allow us to park here.

But if this person is not mentioned, the gerund is used:

He advised applying at once.
She recommends buying the big tins.
They don't allow parking.

The gerund after **allow** and **permit** cannot have an object, so if we

want an **allow/permit** + verb + object construction, we must use the infinitive and mention the person concerned:
They allowed their tenants to use the garage.

D **it needs/requires/wants** can be followed either by the gerund or by the passive infinitive, the gerund being the more usual:
The grass wants cutting or *The grass wants to be cut.*

268 regret, remember, forget + gerund or infinitive

A **regret, remember, forget** are used with a gerund when the action expressed by the gerund is the earlier action:
I regret spending so much money
= *I'm sorry I spent so much money.* (*spending* is the first action, *regret* is the second.)
I remember reading about the earthquake in the papers. (*reading* is the first action, *remember* is the second.)

remember can be followed by possessive adjective/object + gerund:
I remember his/him telling me about it.
I remember my father('s) telling me about it.

forget + gerund is possible only when **forget** is in the negative. It is often used after **will never forget**:
I'll never forget waiting for bombs to fall
= *I'll always remember waiting for bombs to fall.*

B When **regret, remember, forget** themselves express the earlier action they are followed by an infinitive:
I regret to say that you have failed your exam. (*regret* is the earlier action.)

regret here is normally followed by a verb such as **say, inform, tell**. It is normally used only in the present tense.

remember can be used in any tense:
I'll remember to ring Bill. (*remember* is the earlier action.)

forget is used similarly:
I often forget to sign my cheques.

269 care (negative or interrogative), love, like (= enjoy), hate, prefer

when used in the conditional are followed by the infinitive:
Would you care/like to come with me or would you prefer to stay here? I'd love to come with you.
I'd hate to spend all my life here.

When used in the present or past they are usually followed by the gerund:
I like riding.   *I liked riding.*   *He hates waiting for buses.*

He hated waiting. *He prefers walking to bicycling.*
Tom doesn't care for shopping (**for** is necessary when **care** is followed by a noun or gerund).

But the infinitive is not impossible and is particularly common in American English:
They love/loved to run on the sands.

Note however that **like** can also mean 'think wise or right', and is then always followed by the infinitive:
She likes them to play in the garden (she thinks they are safe there).
I like to go to the dentist twice a year (I think this wise).

Compare this with *I like going to the dentist*, which implies that I enjoy my visits. Similarly:
I don't like to go = I don't think it right to go
while *I don't like going* = I don't enjoy going.

Notice also another difference between these two negative forms:
I don't like to go usually means 'I don't go' (because I don't think it right).
I don't like going usually means 'I go, although I don't enjoy it'.

270 like, prefer and would rather/sooner to express preference

This use is best shown by examples.

A 1 Answers to **what would you like to do?** type of questions:
A: *Would you like to go today or wait till tomorrow?*
B: *I'd like to go today (rather than tomorrow)* (the phrase *rather than tomorrow* would normally be omitted)
or *I'd prefer to go today*
or *I'd rather/sooner go today (than wait till tomorrow).*
would rather/sooner takes the infinitive without **to** (see **230**).

2 Answers to **which would you like me to do?/shall I do this or do that?** type of questions:
A: *Shall I begin today or tomorrow?*
B: *I'd like you to begin today* (**would like** + object + infinitive)
or *I'd prefer you to begin today* (**would prefer** + object + infinitive)
or *I'd rather/sooner you began today* (**would rather/sooner** + subject + past tense). (See **288**.)

B Answers to **which do you prefer?** type of questions:
I like skiing better than skating
or *I prefer skiing to skating*
or *I'd rather/sooner ski than skate.*

Note that **I'd rather/sooner** can be used in both of the above groups. So *I'd rather drive* can mean 'I'd prefer to drive' or 'I prefer driving' (habitual preference).

C Answers to **which did you prefer?** type of questions:
I liked skiing better than skating
or *I preferred skiing to skating.*
would rather/sooner cannot be used here.

271 **agree/agree to, be afraid (of), be about/on the point of, mean, go on, propose, stop, try, used (to)**

These verbs have different meanings according to whether they are used with gerund or infinitive.

A **agree** and **agree to** (preposition)
agree takes the infinitive:
He agreed to wait = I asked him to wait and he said he would (wait).
agree can be followed by **to** + possessive adjective + gerund
He agreed to my leaving early on Fridays = I asked if I could leave early on Fridays and he said that I could.
agree to can also of course be followed by noun or pronoun.

B **be afraid** + gerund merely expresses a fear. It is normally used with involuntary actions:
He never climbed trees as a boy because he was afraid of falling/afraid that he would fall.
He never criticized his boss because he was afraid of losing his job.
be afraid + infinitive, e.g. *I was afraid to move*, means that the subject was too frightened to perform the action in the infinitive. Note that these will normally be deliberate actions:
He was afraid to jump, so he stayed where he was (but *He was afraid of breaking his leg*).
He was afraid to say anything so he kept quiet.

C **be about** + infinitive = **be on the point of** + gerund:
I was about to strike a match/I was on the point of striking a match when I remembered Tom's warning = I was just going to strike a match . . .

D **mean** meaning 'intend' takes the infinitive:
I mean to get to the top by sunrise.
mean meaning 'involve' (used only with an impersonal subject) takes the gerund:
He is determined to get a seat for the ballet even if it means standing in a queue all night.

E **go on** = continue, and is normally followed by the gerund. But it is used with an infinitive, usually of a verb like **tell, talk, explain** etc.,

when the speaker continues talking about the same topic but introduces a new aspect of it:
He began by showing us where the island was and went on to tell us about its climate.

Compare *He went on talking about his accident,* which implies that he had been talking about it before, with *He went on to talk about his accident,* which implies that he had been speaking about himself or his journey but that the accident was being introduced for the first time.

F **propose** meaning 'intend' usually takes the infinitive:
I propose to start tomorrow.

propose meaning 'suggest' takes the gerund:
I propose waiting till the police get here.

G **stop** (= cease) is followed by the gerund:
Stop talking.
It can be followed by object + gerund:
I can't stop him talking to the press.
A possessive adjective would be possible here but is very seldom used.

stop (= halt) can be followed by an infinitive of purpose:
I stopped to ask the way = I stopped in order to ask the way.

H **try** usually means 'attempt' and is followed by the infinitive:
They tried to put wire netting all round the garden (they attempted to do this).
The sentence doesn't tell us whether they succeeded or not.
try can also mean 'make the experiment' and is then followed by the gerund:
They tried putting wire netting all round the garden.
This means that they put wire netting round the garden to see if it would solve their problem (presumably they were trying to keep out rabbits and foxes). We know that they succeeded in performing the main action; what we don't know is whether this action had the desired effect, i.e. kept the foxes out.

I Subject + **used** + infinitive expresses a past habit or routine:
I used to swim all the year round = At one time I swam all the year round. (See **158**.)

But subject + **be/become/get** + **used** + **to** (preposition) is followed by noun or pronoun or gerund and means 'be/become/get accustomed (to)':
I am used to heat/to living in a hot climate = I have lived in a hot climate for some time so I don't mind it. (See **159**.)

Present participle or infinitive

272 Verbs of the senses

A The basic verbs of the senses: **see, hear, feel, smell,** and the verbs **listen (to), notice, watch** and **find** can be followed by object + present participle.
I see him passing my house every day.
I heard her booking tickets.
They felt the house shaking.
She smelt something burning.
I watched them rehearsing the play.
He found her lying at the foot of the stairs.

The action in the present participle may be either complete or incomplete:
I saw him changing the wheel of his car could mean that I watched the whole action or that I saw only part of it.

B **see, hear, feel** and, but less usually, **listen (to), notice** and **watch** can also be followed by object + infinitive without **to**:
We saw him leave the house.
I heard him make arrangements for his journey.

The infinitive implies that the action is complete. *I saw him change the wheel* means that I saw the whole action.

C Comparison of the two forms

The participle is the more generally useful as it can express both complete and incomplete actions. But the infinitive is useful when we want to emphasize that the action is complete. It is also neater than the participle when there are a succession of actions:
I saw him enter the room, unlock a drawer, take out a document, photograph it and put it back.

D In the passive the full infinitive is used after verbs of the senses:
He was heard to say that the minister had been bribed.

273 **go** and **come**

go and **come** can be followed by infinitives of purpose:
He is going to London to see his mother.
She is coming (here) to learn French.
(See also **245**.)

They can also be followed by the participles of verbs of physical activity and the verb **shop**:
They are going riding/skiing/sailing. *Come dancing.*
I'm going shopping this afternoon.

25 The participles

274 The present (or active) participle

Form

The infinitive + **ing**, e.g. *working, loving, sitting, standing, worrying* (see **162**).

Use

A As an adjective:
running water *floating wreckage* *dripping taps*
growing crops

B To form the continuous tenses:
he is working *you have been dreaming* *we are being followed*

C After verbs of sensation (see **272**):
I saw flames rising and heard people shouting.
I heard him booking seats.
Every day I see them passing the house.
I smell something burning.
I saw him kissing her.
You can hear the clock ticking.
I felt the house shaking.

D **catch/find** + object + present participle:
I caught them stealing my apples (I found them doing this bad thing).
If she catches you reading her diary, she'll be furious.
The action expressed by the participle is always one which displeases the subject.
With **find** there is no feeling of displeasure:
I found him standing at the door = I saw him standing at the door/He was standing at the door when I arrived.
With **find** the object could be inanimate:
He found a tree lying across the road.

E **have** + object + present participle:

1 *I'll have him driving after two lessons* = As a result of my efforts he will be driving after two lessons.
He had me swimming in a week = As a result of his efforts I was swimming in a week.

have here is not normally used in the continuous tenses, or in the negative.

2 **have** + object + present participle can also be used as in:
There is a bus stop outside our door so we have people standing on our steps all day
= *There is a bus stop outside our door so people stand/are standing on our steps all day.*
This is chiefly used of actions which annoy the speaker.
have here can be used in any tense.
(See **118** B.)

3 Note also:
I won't have him cleaning his bicycle in the kitchen = I won't allow him to clean his bicycle in the kitchen.

F **spend/waste** + an expression of time or money + present participle:
He spends two hours travelling a day.
He doesn't spend much time preparing his lessons.
We wasted a whole afternoon trying to repair the car.
He spent a lot of money modernizing the house.

G **be busy** + present participle:
She is/was busy packing.

H A participle may introduce a statement in indirect speech (see **305** C).

275 A present participle can replace a sentence or main clause

A When two actions by the same subject occur simultaneously it is usually possible to express one of them by a present participle. The participle can be before or after the finite verb:
He rode away. He whistled as he went.
= *He rode away whistling.*
He holds the rope with one hand and stretches out the other to the boy in the water
= *Holding the rope with one hand, he stretches* etc.

B When one action is immediately followed by another by the same subject the first action can often be expressed by a present participle. The participle must be placed first:
He opened the drawer and took out a revolver
= *Opening the drawer he took out a revolver.*
She raised the trapdoor and pointed to a flight of steps
= *Raising the trapdoor she pointed to a flight of steps.*
We take off our shoes and creep cautiously along the passage
= *Taking off our shoes we creep cautiously along the passage.*

It would seem more logical here to use the perfect participle and say *Having opened, Having raised, Having taken off,* but this is not necessary except when the use of the present participle might lead to ambiguity. *Eating his dinner he rushed out of the house* would give the impression that he left the house with his plate in his hand. Here therefore it would be better to say *Having eaten his dinner . . .*

C When the second action forms part of the first, or is a result of it, we can express the second action by a present participle:
She went out, slamming the door.
He fired, wounding one of the bandits.
I fell, striking my head against the door and cutting it. (Here we have three actions, the last two expressed by participles.)

The participle need not necessarily have the same subject as the first verb:
The plane crashed, its bombs exploding as it hit the ground.

276 A present participle can replace a subordinate clause

A The present participle can replace **as/since/because** + subject + verb, i.e. it can help to explain the action which follows:
Knowing that he wouldn't be able to buy food on his journey he took large supplies with him = As he knew etc.
Fearing that the police would recognize him he never went out in daylight = As he feared etc.

Note that **being** at the beginning of a sentence will normally mean 'as he is/as he was':
Being a student he was naturally interested in museums = Because/As he was a student etc. It could not mean 'While he was a student'.

The subject of the participle need not be the same as the subject of the following verb:
*The **day** being fine, **we** decided to go swimming*
but in cases like this the participle must follow its noun/pronoun. *Being fine the day, we decided* is incorrect, but *Being athletic, Tom found the climb quite easy* is all right, as Tom is the subject of both the participle and the following verb.

It is possible to use two or more participles, one after the other:
***Realizing** that he hadn't enough money and not **wanting** to borrow from his father, he decided to pawn his watch.*
*Not **knowing** the language and **having** no friends in the country, he found it impossible to get a job.*

B A present participle can frequently replace a relative clause (see **55** C):
People who wish to visit the caves . . .
= *People wishing to visit the caves . . .*
Children who need medical attention . . .
= *Children needing medical attention . . .*
A map which marks the political boundaries . . .
= *A map marking the political boundaries . . .*

277 The perfect participle active

Form: **having** + past participle, e.g. *having done, having seen.*

Use: The perfect participle can be used instead of the present participle in sentences of the type shown in **275** B (i.e. where one action is immediately followed by another with the same subject):
Tying one end of the rope to his bed, he threw the other end out of the window
= *Having tied one end of the rope to his bed, he threw the other end* etc.
The perfect participle emphasizes that the first action is complete before the second one starts, but is not normally necessary in combinations of this kind, except when the use of the present participle might lead to confusion:
Reading the instructions, he snatched up the fire extinguisher might give the impression that the two actions were simultaneous. Here, therefore, the perfect participle would be better:
Having read the instructions, he snatched up the fire extinguisher.
The perfect participle is however necessary when there is an interval of time between the two actions:
Having failed twice, he didn't want to try again.
It is also used when the first action covered a period of time:
Having been his own boss for such a long time, he found it hard to accept orders from another.

278 The past participle (passive) and the perfect participle passive

A Form: the past participle of regular verbs is formed by adding **ed** or **d** to the infinitive, e.g. *worked, loved.* For the past participle of irregular verbs see **317**.
Use:
1 As an adjective:
stolen money *a written report* *fallen trees* *broken glass*

2 To form the perfect tenses/infinitives and participles and the passive voice:
he has seen *to have loved* *it was broken*

3 The past participle can replace a subject + passive verb just as the present participle can replace subject + active verb:
She enters. She is accompanied by her mother.
= *She enters, accompanied by her mother.*
He was aroused by the crash and leapt to his feet
= *Aroused by the crash, he leapt to his feet.*
The bridge had been weakened by successive storms and was no longer safe
= *Weakened by successive storms, the bridge was no longer safe*
or *Having been weakened* etc. (see below).
As he was convinced that they were trying to poison him, he refused to eat anything
= *Convinced that they were trying to poison him, he refused* etc.

B The perfect participle passive (**having been** + past participle) is used when it is necessary to emphasize that the action expressed by the participle happened before the action expressed by the next verb:
Having been warned about the bandits, he left his valuables at home = He had been warned etc.
Having been bitten twice, the postman refused to deliver our letters unless we chained our dog up = He had been bitten etc.

279 Misrelated participles

A participle is considered to belong to the noun/pronoun which precedes it:
***Tom, horrified** at what he had done, could at first say nothing.*
***Romeo, believing** that Juliet was dead, decided to kill himself.*
*A **man carrying** a large parcel got out of the bus.*

Note that the participle may be separated from its noun/pronoun by a main verb:
***Jones** and **Smith** came in, **followed** by their wives.*
***She** rushed past the policeman, **hoping** he wouldn't ask what she had in her suitcase.*

If there is no noun/pronoun in this position the participle is considered to belong to the subject of the following main verb:
***Stunned** by the blow, **Peter** fell heavily* (Peter had been stunned).
***Believing** that he is alone, the **villain** expresses his thoughts aloud.*

If this principle is disregarded confusion results. *Waiting for a bus a brick fell on my head* makes it appear that the brick was waiting for a bus, which is nonsense. A participle linked in this way to the wrong noun/pronoun is said to be 'misrelated'. The above sentence should be rewritten *As I was waiting for a bus a brick fell on my head.*

Other examples of misrelated participles:

When using this machine it must be remembered . . .
Correct form: *When using this machine you must remember . . .*

Believing that I was the only person who knew about this beach, the sight of someone else on it annoyed me very much.
Correct form: *As I believed I was the only person* etc.

280 Present participle adjectives and past participle adjectives

Care must be taken not to confuse these. Present participle adjectives, e.g. *amusing, tiring, horrifying,* are active, and mean 'having this effect'. Past participle adjectives, e.g. *amused, tired, bored,* are passive, and mean 'affected in this way'.

The play was boring. *The audience was bored.*
The work was tiring. *The workers soon became tired.*
The scene was horrifying. *The spectators were horrified.*
An infuriating woman (she made us furious).
An infuriated woman (something had made her furious).

26 Commands, requests, advice

281 Commands expressed by the imperative

A The second person imperative

1 This has the same form as the infinitive without **to**:
Hurry! *Wait!* *Stop!*

For the negative we put **do not (don't)** before the verb:
Don't hurry!

2 The person addressed is very often not mentioned, but can be expressed by a noun placed at the end of the phrase:
Eat your dinner, boys. *Be quiet, Tom.*
These nouns can be placed before the verb, but this is much less usual.

The pronoun **you** is rarely used unless the speaker wishes to be rude, or wishes to make a distinction, as in:
You go on; I'll wait.

3 **do** can be placed before the affirmative imperative:
Do hurry. *Do be quiet.*
This **do** could be persuasive, but could also express irritation.

B The first person imperative

Form: **let us (let's)** + infinitive without **to**:
Let's wait for Bill.

For the negative we normally put **not** before the infinitive:
Let's not tell anyone.
But it is possible in colloquial English to put **don't** before **let's**:
Don't let's tell anyone.

By **let's** the speaker can urge his hearers to act in a certain way, or express a decision which they are expected to accept, or express a suggestion.

shall we? is sometimes added to suggestions. Approval of suggestions can be expressed by **Yes, let's**:
Let's go by taxi, shall we? Yes, let's.

In indirect speech **let's** is usually treated as a suggestion (see **303**).

C The third person imperative

Form: **let him/her/it/them** + infinitive without **to**:
Let them go by train.

But this is not a very common construction in modern English. It would be more usual to say:
They had better go by train/They must go by train.
Similarly in the negative:
They had better not go by train/They must not go by train.
The negative third person imperative: **let him etc. not go** is not used in modern English.
For indirect speech forms see **303**.

282 Other ways of expressing commands

A Subject + **shall** for third person commands (in written English)
shall can be used in very formal written regulations which will normally remain in force for some time. These are very often in the passive:
The Chairman, Secretary and Treasurer shall be elected annually (club regulations).
A record shall be kept of the number of students attending each class (college regulations).

B Subject + **will** mainly for third person commands:
When the alarm rings passengers and crew will assemble at their boat stations (notice on board ship).
will used in this way indicates that the person giving the order is quite certain that he will be obeyed. It is used chiefly in written instructions by people who have some authority, e.g. captains of ships, officers of the services, headmasters of schools, trainers of sports teams etc.:
The team will report to the gymnasium for weight-lifting training.
Note that if we move the **will** and place it before the subject, we turn the command into a request.
It is possible to use **you will** for spoken commands:
You will not mention this meeting to anyone.
But it is more usual and more polite to use **must**:
You must not mention etc.

C Commands are often expressed as obligations by **must**:
You must not smoke in the petrol store.
Passengers must cross the line by the footbridge.
Dogs must be kept on leads in this area.

D Instructions or orders can be conveyed by the **be** + infinitive construction:
You are to report for duty immediately.
The switchboard is to be manned at all times.

E Prohibitions may be expressed in written instructions by **may not**:
Candidates may not bring textbooks into the examination room.

283 Request forms

A **could you** is a very useful request form:
Could you please show me the way to . . . ?

possibly can be added to show that the speaker is asking for something extra:
Could you possibly lend me £500?

couldn't expresses the speaker's hopes for a more favourable answer than has just been indicated:
A: *I can't wait.* B: *Couldn't you wait five minutes?*

B **will you/would you (please)**
Will/Would you please count your change?
would is more polite than **will** and students are advised to use it.

will/would you can be placed at the end of the phrase but this form can only be used in very friendly relaxed situations. Used otherwise, it would sound very rude.

will/would can also be used for third person requests:
Would Mrs Jones, passenger to Leeds, please come to the Enquiry Desk?
Will anyone who saw the accident please phone this number . . . ? (police announcement)

C **perhaps you would . . .** implies confidence that the other person will perform this service. It would not be used at the beginning of a conversation or letter, but would be possible later on:
Perhaps you would let me know when your new stock arrives = Please let me know etc.

D **if you would . . .** is an extremely useful request form. It is used in spoken English for routine-type requests which the speaker is quite sure will be obeyed:
(in an office) *If you'd fill up this form/take a seat/wait a few minutes.*
(in a hotel) *If you'd sign the register/follow the porter.*
(in a shop) *If you'd just put your address on the back of the cheque.*
just can be added to show that the action required is very simple and easy.

E **I should/would be very grateful if you would . . .** is a formal request form found chiefly in letters but possible in speech:
I should be very grateful if you would let me know if you have any vacancies . . .

F **would you be good/kind enough** *to keep me informed . . . ?*
would you be so kind as *to keep me informed . . . ?*

G **would you mind** + gerund:
Would you mind signing this form?

H **you might** can express a very casual request:
You might post these letters for me.
But it can only be used in friendly relaxed situations. Used otherwise it would sound rude.

With a certain intonation **might** can express a reproachful request (see **127**).

284 Advice forms

A **must, ought to** and **should** can be used for advice:
You must read this book. It's very interesting.
More trees should/ought to be planted.

B **you had better** + infinitive without **to**:
You'd better take off your wet shoes.
You'd better not wait any longer.
The verb is in the past but the meaning is present or future.

C **if I were you I should/would . . .**
If I were you I'd buy a small car.
This is often shortened to **I should/would . . .** with a slight stress on the **I**:
ˈI'd buy a small car.

D **why don't you . . . ?** can be either advice or suggestion.

E **it is time you** + past tense:
It is time you bought a new coat. (See **288** B.)

27 The subjunctive

285 Present subjunctive

Form: The present subjunctive has exactly the same form as the infinitive; therefore the present subjunctive of **to be** is **be** for all persons, and the present subjunctive of all other verbs is the same as their present tense except that **s** is not added for the third person singular:
The queen lives here (simple present tense).
Long live the queen! (subjunctive).

Use

A The present subjunctive is used in certain exclamations to express a wish or hope, very often involving supernatural powers:

God bless you!	*God forgive you!*
Heaven help us!	*Heaven be praised!*
Damn you!	*Curse this fog!*

B It is sometimes used in poetry, either to express a wish or in clauses of condition or concession:
STEVENSON: *Fair the day shine as it shone in my childhood* (may the day shine/I hope it will shine).
SHAKESPEARE: *If this be error, and upon me proved* . . . (if this is error).
BYRON: *Though the heart be still as loving* . . . (though the heart is).
Notice also the phrase **if need be**, which means 'if it is necessary':
If need be we can always bring another car.

C As seen in **236** certain verbs are followed by **should** + infinitive constructions. When the infinitive is **be**, the **should** is sometimes omitted:
He suggested that a petition (should) be drawn up.
The infinitive thus left alone becomes a subjunctive. Sometimes the **should** is omitted before other verbs:
I recommended that each competitor (should) receive £1.

286 Unreal past tenses (subjunctives) after **wish** and **if only**

Note that we can say either **I/he/she/it was** or **I/he/she/it were. were** is the more correct form but **was** is often used, especially in conversation. Otherwise there is no difference between unreal past tenses (subjunctives) and ordinary past tenses.

wish (that) + subject + a past tense expresses regret about a present situation:

I wish I knew his address = I'm sorry I don't know his address.
I wish you could drive a car = I'm sorry you can't drive a car.
I wish he was coming with us = I'm sorry he isn't coming with us.

wish can be put into the past without changing the subjunctive:

He wished he knew the address = He was sorry he didn't know the address.

Unreal past tenses do not change in indirect speech:

'I wish I lived nearer my work,' he said
= *He said he wished he lived nearer his work.*

wish (that) + subject + a past perfect tense expresses regret about a past situation:

I wish (that) I hadn't spent so much money = I'm sorry I spent so much money.
I wish you had written to him = I'm sorry you didn't write to him.

wish can be changed to **wished** as above:

I wished I hadn't spent so much money = I was sorry I had spent so much money.

(For **wish + would** see **231**. For **wish** + infinitive see **241** C.)

if only can be used in exactly the same way. **if only** + past tense has the same meaning as **wish** but is more dramatic:

If only we knew where to look for him!
If only she had asked someone's advice!

Past and past perfect tenses can also, of course, be placed directly after **if**. The past tense here indicates unreality or improbability. The past perfect tense indicates unreality.

If Tom were here (unreality) *he could tell us what to do.*
If you jumped (were to jump) from Westminster Bridge (improbability) *it would be almost impossible to rescue you.*
If they had arrived ten minutes earlier (unreality) *they would have caught the plane.* (See **216–17**.)

287 **as if/as though** + unreal past tenses

The past subjunctive can be used similarly after **as if/as though** to indicate unreality or improbability or doubt in the present (there is no difference between **as if** and **as though**):

He behaves as if he owned the place (but he doesn't own it or probably doesn't own it or we don't know whether he owns it or not).

He talks as though he knew where she was (but he doesn't know or he probably doesn't know or we don't know whether he knows or not).
He orders me about as if I were his wife (but I am not).

The verb preceding **as if/though** can be put into a past tense without changing the tense of the subjunctive:
He talks/talked as though he knew where she was.

After **as if/as though** we use a past perfect when referring to a real or imaginary action in the past:
He talks about Rome as though he had been there himself (but he hasn't or probably hasn't or we don't know whether he has or not).

Again, the verb preceding **as if/though** can be put into a past tense without changing the tense of the subjunctive:
He looks/looked as though he hadn't had a decent meal for a month.

288 Past tense (subjunctives) after **would rather/sooner, it is time**

A **would rather/sooner** are followed by the infinitive without **to** when the subject of **would rather/sooner** is the same as the subject of the following action:

A: *Would you like to start today?*
B: *I would rather/sooner wait till tomorrow.*

prefer can be used similarly with the full infinitive:
I would prefer to wait till tomorrow.

If, however, the next action has another subject, **would rather/sooner** requires a past tense:

A: *Shall I give you a cheque for £10?*
B: *I'd rather you gave me £10 in notes.*

A: *Would you like him to paint the door green?*
B: *I'd rather he painted it blue.*

prefer, however, like **like**, can be followed by object + infinitive:
I'd prefer you to give me £10 in notes.
I'd prefer him to paint it blue.
(See also **270**.)

B **it is time** can be followed by the infinitive:
It's time to start
or by **for** + object + infinitive:
It's time for us to go
or by subject + a past tense:
It's time we went. *It's time we were leaving.*

There is a slight difference in meaning between the forms: **it is**

time + infinitive merely states that the correct time has arrived; **it is time** + subject + past tense implies that it is a little late. **high** can be added to emphasize this idea:
It's high time we left.

28 The passive voice

289 A Form

1 The passive of an active tense is formed by putting the verb **to be** into the same tense as the active verb and adding the past participle of the active verb:

Active: *We keep the butter here.*
Passive: *The butter is kept here.*

Active: *They broke the window.*
Passive: *The window was broken.*

Active: *People have seen wolves in the streets.*
Passive: *Wolves have been seen in the streets.*

Note the passive of continuous tenses. This sometimes seems difficult because it requires the present continuous form of **to be**, which is not otherwise much used:

Active: *They are repairing the bridge.*
Passive: *The bridge is being repaired.*

Active: *They were carrying the injured player off the field.*
Passive: *The injured player was being carried off the field.*

Other continuous tenses are exceedingly rarely used in the passive, so that sentences such as:

They have/had been repairing the road
and *They will/would be repairing the road*
are not normally put into the passive.

2 Auxiliary + infinitive combinations are made passive by using a passive infinitive:

Active: *You must shut these doors.*
Passive: *These doors must be shut.*

Active: *You ought to open the windows.*
Passive: *The windows ought to be opened.*

Active: *They should have told him* (perfect infinitive active).
Passive: *He should have been told* (perfect infinitive passive).

Note also constructions such as:

His decision is to be regretted = We regret his decision.
If he is to be believed . . . = If we believe him . . .

3 The passive gerund is **being** + past participle:

Active: *I remember my father taking me to the Zoo.*
Passive: *I remember being taken to the Zoo by my father.*

4 Students may like to see a table of active tenses and their passive equivalents.

Tense/verb form	*Active voice*	*Passive voice*
Simple present	keeps	is kept
Present continuous	is keeping	is being kept
Simple past	kept	was kept
Past continuous	was keeping	was being kept
Present perfect	has kept	has been kept
Past perfect	had kept	had been kept
Future	will keep	will be kept
Conditional	would keep	would be kept
Perfect conditional	would have kept	would have been kept
Present infinitive	to keep	to be kept
Perfect infinitive	to have kept	to have been kept
Present participle/gerund	keeping	being kept
Perfect participle	having kept	having been kept

B Use

The passive voice is used in English when it is more convenient or interesting to stress the thing done than the doer of it, or when the doer is unknown: *My watch was stolen* is much more usual than *Thieves stole my watch.*

Note that in theory a sentence containing a direct and an indirect object, such as *Someone gave her a bulldog*, could have two passive forms:

She was given a bulldog.

A bulldog was given to her.

The first of these is much the more usual, i.e. the indirect object becomes the subject of the passive verb.

290 Prepositions with passive verbs

A In a passive sentence the agent, or doer of the action, is very often not mentioned (see **289**). When the agent is mentioned it is preceded by **by**:

Active: *Dufy painted this picture.*

Passive: *This picture was painted by Dufy.*

Active: *Who wrote it?* *What caused this crack?*

Passive: *Who was it written by?* *What was this crack caused by?*

Note, however, that the passive form of such sentences as:

Smoke filled the room. *Paint covered the lock.*

will be:

The room was filled with smoke.

The lock was covered with paint.

We are dealing here with materials used, not with the agents.

B When a verb + preposition + object combination is put into the passive, the preposition will remain immediately after the verb:

Active: *We must write to him.*
Passive: *He must be written to.*

Active: *You can play with these cubs quite safely.*
Passive: *These cubs can be played with quite safely.*

Similarly with verb + preposition/adverb combinations:

Active: *They threw away the old newspapers.*
Passive: *The old newspapers were thrown away.*

Active: *He looked after the children well.*
Passive: *The children were well looked after.*

291 Infinitive constructions after passive verbs

A After **acknowledge, assume, believe, claim, consider, estimate, feel, find, know, presume, report, say, think, understand** etc.

Sentences of the type *People think/consider/know etc. that he is . . .* have two possible passive forms:

It is thought/considered/known etc. that he is . . .
He is thought/considered/known etc. to be . . .

Similarly:

People said that he was jealous of her
= *It was said that he was jealous of her*
or *He was said to be jealous of her.*

The infinitive construction is the neater of the two. It is chiefly used with **to be** though other infinitives can sometimes be used:

He is thought to have information which will be useful to the police.

When the thought concerns a previous action we use the perfect infinitive so that:

People know that he was . . .
= *It is known that he was . . .*
or *He is known to have been . . .*

People believed that he was . . .
= *It was believed that he was . . .*
or *He was believed to have been . . .*

This construction can be used with the perfect infinitive of any verb.

B After **suppose**

1 **suppose** in the passive can be followed by the present infinitive of any verb but this construction usually conveys an idea of duty and is not therefore the normal equivalent of **suppose** in the active:

You are supposed to know how to drive

= *It is your duty to know/You should know how to drive*
though *He is supposed to be in Paris* could mean either 'He ought to be there' or 'People suppose he is there'.

2 **suppose** in the passive can similarly be followed by the perfect infinitive of any verb. This construction may convey an idea of duty but very often does not:
You are supposed to have finished = You should have finished.
But *He is supposed to have escaped disguised as a woman*
= *People suppose that he escaped* etc.

C Note that an infinitive placed after a passive verb is normally a full infinitive, i.e. an infinitive with **to**:

Active:	*We saw them go out.*	*He made us work.*
Passive:	*They were seen to go out.*	*We were made to work.*

let, however, is used without **to**:
Active: *They let us go.*
Passive: *We were let go.*

D The continuous infinitive can be used after the passive of **think, know, believe, understand, report, say, suppose**:
He is thought/known/believed/said/supposed to be living abroad
= *People think/know/believe/say/suppose that he is living abroad.*
You are supposed to be working = *You should be working.*
The perfect form of the continuous infinitive is also possible:
He is believed to have been waiting for a message
= *People believe that he was waiting for a message.*
You are supposed to have been working
= *You should have been working.*

29 Reported speech

292 Direct and indirect (or reported) speech

There are two ways of relating what a person has said: direct and indirect.

In direct speech we repeat the original speaker's exact words: *He said, 'I have lost my umbrella.'*
Remarks thus repeated are placed between inverted commas, and a comma or colon is placed immediately before the remark. Direct speech is found in conversations in books, in plays, and in quotations.

In indirect speech we give the exact meaning of a remark or a speech, without necessarily using the speaker's exact words: *He said that he had lost his umbrella.*

There is no comma after **say** in indirect speech. **that** can be omitted. Indirect speech is normally used when conversation is reported verbally, though direct speech is sometimes employed here to give a more dramatic effect.

When we turn direct speech into indirect, some changes are usually necessary. These are most easily studied by considering statements, questions, and commands separately.

293 Statements in indirect speech: tense changes necessary

A Indirect speech can be introduced by a verb in a present tense: *He says that . . .* This is usual when we are:

1 reporting a conversation that is still going on
2 reading a letter and reporting what it says
3 reading instructions and reporting them
4 reporting a statement that someone makes very often, e.g. *Tom says that he'll never get married.*

When the introductory verb is in a present, present perfect or future tense we can report the direct speech without any change of tense:

PAUL (phoning from the station): *I'm trying to get a taxi.*
ANN (to Mary, who is standing beside her): *Paul says he is trying to get a taxi.*

B But indirect speech is usually introduced by a verb in the past tense. Verbs in the direct speech have then to be changed into a corresponding past tense. The changes are shown in the following table:

Direct speech	Indirect speech
Simple present→	Simple past
'I never eat meat,' he explained	
= *He explained that he never ate meat.*	
Present continuous→	Past continuous
'I'm waiting for Ann,' he said	
= *He said he was waiting for Ann.*	
Present perfect→	Past perfect
'I have found a flat,' he said	
= *He said he had found a flat.*	
Present perfect continuous→	Past perfect continuous
He said, 'I've been waiting for ages'	
= *He said he had been waiting for ages.*	
Simple past→	Past perfect
'I took it home with me,' he said	
= *He said he had taken it home with him.*	
Future→	Conditional
He said, 'Ann will be in Paris on Monday'	
= *He said that Ann would be in Paris on Monday.*	
Future continuous→	Conditional continuous
'I'll be using the car myself on the 24th,' he said	
= *He said he'd be using the car himself on the 24th.*	

Note, however, that **I/we shall** used as an alternative to **I/we will** normally changes to **would** in indirect speech:

'I shall/will be 21 tomorrow,' said Bill

= *Bill said he would be 21 the following day.*

But if the sentence is reported by the original speaker, **I/we shall** can become either **I/we should** or **I/we would. would** is the more common.

294 Past tenses sometimes remain unchanged

A In theory the past tense changes to the past perfect, but in spoken English it is often left unchanged, provided this can be done without causing confusion about the relative times of the actions. For example, *He said, 'I loved her'* must become *He said he had loved her* as otherwise there would be a change of meaning. But

He said, 'Ann arrived on Monday' could be reported *He said Ann arrived* or *had arrived on Monday.*

B The past continuous tense in theory changes to the past perfect continuous but in practice usually remains unchanged except when it refers to a completed action:

She said, 'We were thinking of selling the house but we have decided not to'

= *She said that they had been thinking of selling the house but had decided not to.*

But *He said, 'When I saw them they were playing tennis'*

= *He said that when he saw them they were playing tennis.*

C In written English past tenses usually do change to past perfect but there are the following exceptions:

1 Past/past continuous tenses used in time clauses do not normally change:

He said, 'When we were living/lived in Paris . . .'

= *He said that when they were living/lived in Paris . . .*

The main verb of such sentences can either remain unchanged or become the past perfect:

He said, 'When we were living/lived in Paris we often saw Paul'

= *He said that when they were living/lived in Paris they often saw/had often seen Paul.*

2 A past tense used to describe a state of affairs which still exists when the speech is reported remains unchanged:

She said, 'I decided not to buy the house because it was on a main road'

= *She said that she had decided not to buy the house because it was on a main road.*

3 Unreal past tenses (subjunctives) after **wish, would rather/sooner** and **it is time** do not change:

'We wish we didn't have to take exams,' said the children

= *The children said they wished they didn't have to take exams.*

'Bill wants to go alone,' said Ann, 'but I'd rather he went with a group'

= *Ann said that Bill wanted to go alone but that she'd rather he went with a group.*

'It's time we began thinking about our holidays,' said Mr Pitt

= *Mr Pitt said that it was time they began thinking about their holidays.*

4 Conditional sentences types 2 and 3 remain unchanged (see **223** B, C):

'If my children were older I would emigrate,' said Andrew

= *Andrew said that if his children were older he would emigrate.*

But note:

1 For the first person conditional we can use either **should** or **would. should** used in this way in direct speech will normally be reported by **would**:

'If I had the instruction manual,' said Bill, 'I should/would know what to do'

= *Bill said that if he had the instruction manual he would know what to do.*

If, however, a sentence with **I should . . .** is reported by the original speaker, the **should** can either remain unchanged or be reported by **would**.

2 The advice form **'If I were you I should/would . . .'** is normally reported by **advise** + object + infinitive:

'If I were you I'd wait,' I said

= *I advised him to wait.*

3 The request form **'I should/would be (very) grateful if you would . . .'** is normally reported by **ask** + object + infinitive:

'I'd be very grateful if you'd keep me informed,' he said

= *He asked me to keep him informed.*

5 **would, should, ought to, had better, might, used to, could** and **must** do not normally change.

For first person **should/would** see 4 (1) above:

'I should/would like to take some photographs,' said Mrs Pitt

= *Mrs Pitt said that she would like to take some photographs.*

should used in other ways remains unchanged:

'They ought to/should widen this road,' said Peter

= *Peter said that they ought to/should widen the road.*

But **you ought to/you should,** if used to express advice rather than obligation, can be reported by **advise** + object + infinitive. **you must** can also express advice and be reported similarly:

'You ought to/should/must read the book,' said Ann. 'It's much better than the film.'

= *Ann advised/urged me to read the book . . .*

I/he/she/we/they had better remains unchanged. **you had better** can remain unchanged or be reported by **advise** + object + infinitive (see **301**):

'The children had better go to bed early,' said Tom

= *Tom said that the children had better go to bed early.*

'You'd better not drink the water till it has been boiled,' she said

= *She advised (or warned) us not to drink the water till it had been boiled.*

you might if used as a request form must be reported by **ask** + object + infinitive (see **127** C). Used otherwise, **might** remains unchanged.

For **could** see **307**, for **must** see **306**.

295 Other changes necessary when turning direct speech into indirect speech

A Pronouns and possessive adjectives normally change from first or second person to third person except when the speaker is reporting his own words:

I said, 'I like my new house'

= *I said that I liked my new house* (speaker reporting his own words).

He said, 'I've forgotton the combination of my safe'

= *He said that he had forgotten the combination of his safe.*

'You've overcooked the steak again, Mary,' he said

= *He told Mary that she had overcooked the steak again.*

But notice that sometimes a noun must be inserted to avoid ambiguity:

Tom said, 'He came in through the window' would not normally be reported

Tom said he had come in through the window.

This might give the impression that Tom himself had come in this way; but if we use a noun there can be no confusion:

Tom said that the man/burglar/cat etc. had come in . . .

Pronoun changes may affect the verb when it is in the future or conditional:

He says, 'I shall be there'

= *He says that he will be there.*

He said, 'I shall be there'

= *He said that he would be there.*

B **this** and **these**

this used in time expressions usually becomes **that**:

He said, 'She is coming this week'

= *He said that she was coming that week.*

Otherwise **this** and **that** used as adjectives usually change to **the**:

He said, 'I bought this pearl/these pearls for my mother'

= *He said that he had bought the pearl/pearls for his mother.*

this, these used as pronouns can become **it, they/them**:

He showed me two bullets. 'I found these embedded in the panelling,' he said.

= *He said he had found them embedded in the panelling.*

He said, 'We will discuss this tomorrow'

= *He said that they would discuss it/the matter the next day.*

this, these used as either adjectives or pronouns to indicate choice or to distinguish some things from others usually become **the one near him/the one(s) that he had chosen** or some such phrase:

'Which will you have?' I asked. 'This (one),' he said.

= *I asked which one he would have and he said he would have the one near him.*

296 Adverbs and adverbial phrases of time change as follows:

Direct	*Indirect*
today	that day
yesterday	the day before
the day before yesterday	two days before
tomorrow	the next day/the following day
the day after tomorrow	in two days' time
next week/year etc.	the following week/year etc.
last week/year etc.	the previous week/year etc.
a year etc. ago	a year before/the previous year

'I saw her the day before yesterday,' he said

= *He said he'd seen her two days before.*

'I'll do it tomorrow,' he promised

= *He promised that he would do it the next day.*

'I'm starting the day after tomorrow, mother,' he said

= *He told his mother that he was starting in two days' time.*

She said, 'My father died a year ago'

= *She said that her father had died a year before/the previous year.*

But if the speech is made and reported on the same day these time changes are not necessary:

At breakfast this morning he said, 'I'll be very busy today'

= *At breakfast this morning he said that he would be very busy today.*

Logical adjustments are of course necessary if a speech is reported one/two days after it is made. On Monday Jack said to Tom:

I'm leaving the day after tomorrow.

If Tom reports this speech on the next day (Tuesday) he will probably say:

Jack said he was leaving tomorrow.

If he reports it on Wednesday, he will probably say:

Jack said he was leaving today.

here can become **there** but only when it is clear what place is meant:

We met at the bridge and he said, 'I'll be here again tomorrow'

= *We met at the bridge and he said that he'd be there again the next day.*

Usually **here** has to be replaced by some phrase:
She said, 'You can sit here, Tom'
= *She told Tom that he could sit beside her on the rug* etc.
But *He said, 'Come here, boys'* would normally be reported
He called the boys.

297 Infinitive and gerund constructions in indirect speech

A **agree, refuse, offer, promise, threaten** + infinitive can sometimes be used instead of **say (that)** . . .

ANN: *Would you wait half an hour?* TOM: *All right.*
= *Tom agreed to wait* or *Tom said he would wait.*

ANN: *Would you lend me another £50?*
TOM: *No, I won't lend you any more money.*
= *Tom refused to lend her any more money*
or *Tom said that he wouldn't lend* etc.

PAUL: *I'll help you if you like*
= *Paul offered to help her/me* or *Paul said that he'd help her/me.*
(See also **shall I? 300**.)

ANN: *I'll pay you back next week. Really I will.*
= *Ann promised to pay him/me etc. back the following week*
or *Ann said that she would pay him back*
or *Ann assured him that she would pay him back.*

KIDNAPPERS: *If you don't pay the ransom at once we'll kill your daughter*
= *The kidnappers threatened to kill his daughter if he didn't pay the ransom at once*
or *The kidnappers said that they would kill* etc.
(For object + infinitive constructions see **301**.)

B **accuse** + object + **of, admit, deny, apologize for, insist on** + gerund can sometimes be used instead of **say that**:
'You took the money!' might be reported by
He accused me of taking the money.

'Yes, I took it' or *'I did take it'* might be reported
I admitted taking it.

'No, I didn't take it' might be reported
I denied taking it.

TOM: *I'll pay for both of us.*
BILL: *Let's each pay our own share.*
TOM: *No, I'll pay.*
'No, I'll pay' could be reported as
Tom insisted on paying.

298 say, tell and alternative introductory verbs

A **say** and **tell** with direct speech

1 **say** can introduce a statement or follow it:
Tom said, 'I've just heard the news'
or *'I've just heard the news,' Tom said.*
Inversion of **say** and noun subject is possible when **say** follows the statement:
'I've just heard the news,' said Tom.
say + to + person addressed is possible, but this phrase must follow the direct statement; it cannot introduce it:
'I'm leaving at once,' Tom said to me.
Inversion is not possible here.

2 **tell** requires the person addressed:
Tell me. *He told us.* *I'll tell Tom.*
except with **tell lies/stories/the truth,** when the person addressed need not be mentioned:
He told (me) lies. *I'll tell (you) a story.*
tell used with direct speech must be placed after the direct statement:
'I'm leaving at once,' Tom told me.
Inversion is not possible with **tell**.

B **say** and **tell** with indirect speech
Indirect statements are normally introduced by **say** or **tell** + object. **say + to** + object is possible but much less usual than **tell** + object:
He said he'd just heard the news.
He told me that he'd just heard the news.
Note also **tell . . . how/about**:
He told us how he had crossed the mountains.
He told us about crossing the mountains.
He told us about his journeys.
(For **say** and **tell** with indirect commands, see **301–2**.)

C Other useful verbs are: **add,* admit,* answer,* argue,* assure** + object, **boast,* complain,* deny,* explain,* grumble,* observe,* point out, promise, remark,* remind** + object, **reply.*** These can be used with direct or indirect speech.
With direct speech they follow direct statements:
'It won't cost more,' Tom assured us.
Starred verbs can be inverted, provided the subject is a noun:
'But it will take longer,' Bill objected/objected Bill.
'It'll cost too much,' Jack grumbled/grumbled Jack.

They can all introduce indirect statements. **that** should be placed after the verb:
Tom assured us that it wouldn't cost more. But Bill objected/pointed out that it would take longer.

D **murmur, mutter, shout, stammer, whisper** can precede or follow direct statements or questions. Noun subjects can be inverted as shown above:
'You're late,' whispered Tom/Tom whispered.
They can introduce indirect statements. **that** is usually necessary:
Tom whispered that we were late.
There are, of course, a lot of other verbs describing the voice or the tone of voice, e.g. *bark, growl, snarl, sneer, roar, scream, shriek, yell.* But these are more common with direct than indirect speech.

299 Questions in indirect speech

Example of a direct question: *He said, 'Where is she going?'*
Example of an indirect question: *He asked where she was going.*

A When we turn direct questions into indirect speech, the following changes are necessary:
Tenses, pronouns and possessive adjectives, and adverbs of time and place change as in statements.
The interrogative form of the verb changes to the affirmative form. The question mark (?) is therefore omitted in indirect questions:
He said, 'Where does she live?' = He asked where she lived.

B If the introductory verb is **say**, it must be changed to a verb of inquiry, e.g. **ask, inquire, wonder, want to know** etc.:
He said, 'Where is the station?' = He asked where the station was.
ask, inquire, wonder can also be used in direct speech. They are then usually placed at the end of the sentence:
'Where is the station?' he inquired.

C **ask** can be followed by the person addressed (indirect object):
He asked, 'What have you got in your bag?'
= *He asked (me) what I had got in my bag.*
But **inquire, wonder, want to know** cannot take an indirect object, so if we wish to report a question where the person addressed is mentioned, we must use **ask**:
He said, 'Mary, when is the next train?'
= *He asked Mary when the next train was.*
If we use **inquire, wonder** or **want to know** we must omit *Mary.*

D If the direct question begins with a question word (**when, where, who, how, why** etc.) the question word is repeated in the indirect question:
He said, 'Why didn't you put on the brake?'
= *He asked (her) why she hadn't put on the brake.*
She said, 'What do you want?'
= *She asked (them) what they wanted.*

E If there is no question word, **if** or **whether** must be used:
'Is anyone there?' he asked
= *He asked if/whether anyone was there.*

if and **whether**

1 Normally we can use either. **if** is more usual than **whether**:
'Do you know Bill?' he said
= *He asked if/whether I knew Bill.*
'Did you see the accident?' the policeman asked
= *The policeman asked if/whether I had seen the accident.*

2 **whether** can emphasize that a choice has to be made:
'Do you want to go by air or sea?' the travel agent asked
= *The travel agent asked whether I wanted to go by air or by sea.*
Note **whether or not**:
'Do you want to insure your luggage or not?' he asked
= *He asked whether or not I wanted to insure my luggage*
or *He asked if I wanted to insure my luggage or not.*

3 **whether** + infinitive is possible after **wonder, want to know**:
'Shall/Should I wait for them or go on?' he wondered
= *He wondered whether to wait for them or go on*
or *He wondered whether he should wait for them or go on.*
inquire + **whether** + infinitive is possible but less usual. (For **whether** + infinitive see also **240**.)

4 **whether** is neater if the question contains a conditional clause as otherwise there would be two **ifs**:
'If you get the job will you move to York?' Bill asked
= *Bill asked whether, if I got the job, I'd move to York.*

300 Questions beginning shall I/we? and will you/would you/could you?

A Questions beginning **shall I/we?** can be of four kinds.

1 Speculations or requests for information about a future event:
'Shall I ever see them again?' he wondered.
'When shall I know the result of the test?' she asked.
These follow the ordinary rule about **shall/will**. Speculations are

usually introduced by **wonder**:
He wondered if he would ever see them again.
She asked when she would know the result of her test.

2 Requests for instructions or advice:
'What shall I do with it?' = 'Tell me what to do with it.'
These are expressed in indirect speech by **ask, inquire** etc., with **should** or the **be** + infinitive construction. Requests for advice are normally reported by **should**:
'Shall we send it to your flat, sir?' he said
= *He asked the customer if they were to send/if they should send it to his flat.*
'What shall I say, mother?' she said
= *She asked her mother what she should say* (request for advice).
When a choice is required we normally use **whether** in indirect speech. **whether** + infinitive is sometimes possible.
'Shall I lock the car or leave it unlocked?' he said
= *He asked whether he should/was to lock the car or leave it unlocked*
or *He asked whether to lock the car* etc. (See **299** E.)

3 Offers:
'Shall I bring you some tea?' could be reported
He offered to bring me some tea.
Note that:
'Would you like me to bring you some tea?'
and *'I'll bring you some tea if you like'*
could also be reported by **offer**.

4 Suggestions:
'Shall we meet at the theatre?' could be reported
He suggested meeting at the theatre.

B Questions beginning **will you/would you/could you?** may be ordinary questions but may also be requests, invitations, or, very occasionally, commands:
He said, 'Will you be there tomorrow?' (ordinary question)
= *He asked if she would be there the next day.*
But *He said, 'Will you help me, please?'* (request)
= *He asked me to help him* (see **301** D).
He said, 'Will you have a drink/Would you like a drink? (invitation)
= *He offered me a drink*
or *He asked if I would have/would like a drink.*
He said, 'Will you have lunch with me tomorrow?'
or *'Would you like to have lunch with me tomorrow?' he said*
or *'Could you have lunch with me tomorrow?' he said* (invitations)

= *He invited me/asked me to lunch with him the following day.*
'Will you post this for me?' he said
= *He asked if I would post it for him*
or *He asked me to post it for him.*
'Could/Would you wait a moment?' he said
= *He asked me to wait a moment.*
(For **could I?** see **307**.)

301 Commands, requests, advice in indirect speech

Direct command: *He said, 'Lie down, Tom.'*
Indirect command: *He told Tom to lie down.*
Indirect commands, requests, advice are usually expressed by a verb of command/request/advice + object + infinitive (= the object + infinitive construction).

A The following verbs can be used: **advise, ask, beg, command, encourage, entreat, forbid, implore, invite, order, recommend, remind, request, tell, urge, warn.**
(Note that **say** is not included in this list. For indirect commands/requests reported by **say**, see **302**.)
He said, 'Get your coat, Tom!' = He told Tom to get his coat.
'You had better hurry, Bill!' she said = She advised Bill to hurry.

B Negative commands, requests etc. are usually reported by **not** + infinitive:
'Don't swim out too far, boys,' I said
= *I warned/told the boys not to swim out too far.*
forbid can also be used for prohibitions, but is more common in the passive than in the active.

C Verbs in A above require object + infinitive, i.e. they must be followed directly by the person addressed without preposition (see also **80**). The person addressed is often not mentioned in direct commands, requests etc.:
He said, 'Go away!'
When reporting such commands/requests therefore we must add a noun or pronoun:
He told me/him/her/us/them/the children to go away.
ask differs from the other verbs in A above in that it can also be followed directly by the infinitive of certain verbs: **see, speak to, talk to**:
He said, 'Could I see Tom, please?'
= *He asked to see Tom* (see also **241**).
But this is quite different from the **ask** + object + infinitive type of request.

Both **ask** and **beg** can be followed by the passive infinitive:
'Do, please, send me to a warm climate,' he asked/begged
= *He asked/begged us to send him to a warm climate*
or *He asked/begged to be sent to a warm climate.*

D Examples of indirect commands, requests, advice

Note that direct commands are usually expressed by the imperative, but that requests and advice can be expressed in a variety of ways (see **284, 224–6, 300** B):

'If I were you, I'd stop taking tranquillizers,' I said
= *I advised him to stop taking tranquillizers* (see also **294** C4 (2)).
'Why don't you take off your coat?' he said
= *He advised me to take off my coat* (**suggest + my/me** + gerund would also be possible here).
'Would/Could you show me your passport, please?' he said
= *He asked me to show him my passport.* (*He asked me for my passport/He asked to see my passport* would also be possible.)
'You might post some letters for me,' said my boss
= *My boss asked me to post some letters for him.*
'Yes, we have a room for you,' said the receptionist. 'If you'd just sign the register!'
= *The receptionist said that they had a room for him and asked him to sign the register.*
'Do sit down,' said my hostess
= *My hostess asked/invited me to sit down.*
'Would you like to come for a drive with me?' said Andrew
= *Andrew asked/invited her to come for a drive with him.* (*He asked/invited her to go for a drive* would also be possible.)
'Please, please don't take any risks,' said his wife
= *His wife begged/implored him not to take any risks.*
'Forget all about this young man,' said her parents. 'Don't see him again or answer his letters.'
= *Her parents ordered her to forget all about the young man and told her not to see him again or answer his letters.*

In the passive we could say:
She was ordered to forget all about the young man and forbidden to see him again or answer his letters.
'Don't forget to order the wine,' said Mrs Pitt
= *Mrs Pitt reminded her husband to order the wine.*
'Try again,' said Ann's friends encouragingly
= *Ann's friends encouraged her to try again.*
'Go on, apply for the job,' said Jack
= *Jack urged/encouraged me to apply for the job.*
'You had better not leave your car unlocked,' said my friends;

'there's been a lot of stealing from cars'

= *My friends warned me not to leave my car unlocked as there had been a lot of stealing from cars.*

'will you . . . ?' sentences are normally treated as requests and reported by **ask**:

'Will all persons not travelling please go ashore, as the gangways are about to be taken away,' said one of the ship's officers over the loudspeaker

= *One of the ship's officers asked all persons not travelling to go ashore . . .*

But if a **will you** sentence is spoken sharply or irritably, and the **please** is omitted, it might be reported by **tell** or **order**:

'Will you be quiet!' he said or *'Be quiet, will you!'*

= *He told/ordered us to be quiet.*

302 Other ways of expressing indirect commands

A The **be** + infinitive construction with **say** or **tell**:

He said/told me that I was to wait.

This is a possible alternative to the **tell** + infinitive construction (**301**) so that:

He said, 'Don't open the door' could be reported

He told me not to open the door

or *He said that I wasn't to open the door.*

The **be** + infinitive construction is particularly useful in the following cases:

1 When the command is introduced by a verb in the present tense:

He says, 'Meet me at the station' would normally be reported

He says that we are to meet him at the station.

(*He tells us to meet him* would be possible but much less likely.)

2 When the command is preceded by a clause (usually of time or condition):

He said, 'If she leaves the house follow her' could be reported

He said that if she left the house I was to follow her.

He told me to follow her if she left the house would be equally possible here but note that if we use the **tell** + infinitive construction we must change the order of the sentence so as to put the command first. Sometimes this would result in a rather confusing sentence. For example, the request *If you see Ann tell her to ring me* would become *He told me to tell Ann to ring him if I saw her.* Such requests can only be reported by the **be** + infinitive construction:

He said that if I saw Ann I was to tell her to ring him.

B **say** or **tell** with a **should** construction can be used similarly, but normally indicates advice rather than command:
He said, 'If your brakes are bad don't drive so fast'
= *He said/told me that if my brakes were bad I shouldn't drive so fast*
or *He advised me not to drive so fast if my brakes were bad.* (Note change of order here, as with **tell** + infinitive above.)

C Advice can also be expressed by **advise, recommend** and **urge** + **should**. This is particularly useful with passive infinitives:
He advised/recommended/urged that the law should be changed (see **236** E).

D **command** and **order** can also be used with **should**, but express command, not advice as in B above (see **236**):
1 *He ordered that the porter should lock the doors* (active)
= 2 *He ordered the porter to lock the doors.*
3 *He ordered that the doors should be locked* (passive)
= 4 *He ordered the doors to be locked.*

E Note that when an indirect command is expressed by an object + infinitive construction, as in D2 above, there is normally the idea that the person who is to obey the command is addressed directly. But when the command is expressed by the **be** + infinitive construction (A above) or by a **should** construction (B and D1, above) the recipient of the command need not necessarily be addressed directly. The command may be conveyed to him by a third person.

303 let's, let him/them and second person suggestions

A **let's**

1 **let's** usually expresses a suggestion and is reported by **suggest** in indirect speech:
He said, 'Let's leave the case at the station' would be reported
He suggested leaving the case at the station
or *He suggested that they/we should leave the case at the station.* (See **264** for constructions with **suggest**.)
He said, 'Let's stop now and finish it later' would be reported
He suggested stopping then and finishing it later
or *He suggested that they/we should stop then and finish it later.*
Similarly in the negative:
He said, 'Let's not say anything about it till we hear the facts'
= *He suggested not saying anything/saying nothing about it till they/we heard the facts*
or *He suggested that they/we shouldn't say anything till they/we heard* etc.

But **let's not** used alone in answer to an affirmative suggestion is often reported by some phrase such as *opposed the idea/was against it/objected.* So that:
'Let's sell the house,' said Tom. 'Let's not,' said Ann
could be reported
Tom suggested selling the house but Ann was against it.

2 **let's/let us** sometimes expresses a call to action. It is then usually reported by **urge/advise** + object + infinitive (see also **301**):
The strike leader said, 'Let's show the bosses that we are united'
= *The strike leader urged the workers to show the bosses that they were united.*
The headmaster said, 'Let us not miss this splendid opportunity'
= *The headmaster urged his staff not to miss the splendid opportunity.*

B **let him/them**

1 In theory **let him/them** expresses a command. But very often the speaker has no authority over the person who is to obey the command:
'It's not my business,' said the postman. 'Let the government do something about it.'
Here, the speaker is not issuing a command but expressing an obligation. Sentences of this type are therefore normally reported by **ought/should**:
He said that it wasn't his business and that the government ought to/should do something about it.

2 Sometimes, however, **let him/them** does express a real command. It is then usually reported by **say + be** + infinitive, or **command/order** with **should** (**302** D):
'Let the gates be left open,' said the commander
= *The commander said the gates were to be left open*
or *The commander ordered that the gates should be left open.*

3 Sometimes **let him/them** is more a suggestion than a command. In such cases it is usually reported by **suggest**, or **say + should** (see **264, 302** B):
She said, 'Let them go to their consul. Perhaps he'll be able to help them.'
= *She suggested their/them going to their consul* etc.
or *She suggested that they should go to their consul*
or *She said that they should go to their consul.*

4 Remember that **let** is also an ordinary verb meaning **allow/permit:**
'Let him come with us, mother; I'll take care of him,' I said
= *I asked my mother to let him come with us and promised to take care of him.*

C Second person suggestions can be expressed by **I suggest (your)** + gerund or **what about (your)** + gerund or **suppose you** + present or past tense. (These constructions can, of course, be used with other persons also.) All would normally be reported by **suggest** with a gerund or **should** construction, or a present or past tense:

He said, 'I suggest (your) waiting till dark'

and *He said, 'What about waiting till dark?'*

and *He said, 'Suppose you wait till dark?'* would all be reported *He suggested my waiting/that I should wait/that I waited till dark.*

why don't you + infinitive is also a very useful way of expressing a suggestion. It is reported by **suggest** or **advise**:

He said, 'The job would suit you. Why don't you apply for it?'

= *He said that the job would suit me and suggested my applying for it/advised me to apply for it.*

But **why don't you** can, of course, be an ordinary question:

'Why don't you play the oboe any more?' I asked

= *I asked him why he didn't play the oboe any more.*

304 Exclamations and **yes** and **no**

A Exclamations must become statements in indirect speech. Various constructions are possible:

Exclamations beginning **what a . . .** and **how . . .** such as *He said, 'What a dreadful thing!'* or *'How dreadful!'* are expressed in indirect speech by *He said that it was . . .* So this example becomes: *He said that it was a dreadful thing/that it was dreadful.*

Exclamations such as **ugh! oh! heavens!** are usually reported by *He exclaimed with/gave an exclamation of disgust/surprise* etc.

Note also:

He said, 'Thank you!'	*He thanked me.*
He said, 'Curse this wind.'	*He cursed the wind.*
He said, 'Welcome!'	*He welcomed me.*
He said, 'Happy Christmas!'	*He wished me a happy Christmas.*
He said, 'Congratulations!'	*He congratulated me.*
He said, 'Liar!'	*He called me a liar.*
He said, 'Damn!'	*He swore.*

B **yes** and **no** are expressed in indirect speech by subject + appropriate auxiliary verb:

He said, 'Can you swim?' and I said 'No'

= *He asked (me) if I could swim and I said that I couldn't.*

He said, 'Will you have time to do it?' and I said 'Yes'

= *He asked if I would have time to do it and I said that I would.*

305 Indirect speech: mixed types

Direct speech may consist of statement + question, question + command, command + statement, or all three together.

A Normally each requires its own introductory verb:

'I don't know the way. Do you?' he asked

= *He said he didn't know the way and asked her if she did/if she knew it.*

'Someone's coming,' he said. 'Get behind the screen.'

= *He said that someone was coming and told me to get behind the screen.*

'I'm going shopping. Can I get you anything?' she said

= *She said she was going shopping and asked if she could get me anything.*

'I can hardly hear the radio,' he said. 'Could you turn it up?'

= *He said he could hardly hear the radio and asked her to turn it up.*

B But sometimes, when the last clause is a statement which helps to explain the first, we can use **as** instead of a second introductory verb:

'You'd better wear a coat. It's very cold out,' he said

= *He advised me to wear a coat as it was very cold out.*

'You'd better not walk across the park alone. People have been mugged there,' he said

= *He warned her not to walk across the park alone as people had been mugged there.*

C Sometimes the second introductory verb can be a participle:

'Please, please, don't drink too much! Remember that you'll have to drive home,' she said

= *She begged him not to drink too much, reminding him that he'd have to drive home.*

'Let's shop on Friday. The supermarket will be very crowded on Saturday,' she said

= *She suggested shopping on Friday, pointing out that the supermarket would be very crowded on Saturday.*

(**as** could be used in both these examples.)

306 **must** and **needn't**

A **must** used for deductions, permanent commands/prohibitions and to express intention or advice remains unchanged:

1 Deductions:

She said, 'I'm always running into him; he must live near here!'

= *She said that she was always running into him and that he must live in the neighbourhood.*

2 Permanent command:
He said, 'People must obey their country's laws'
= *He said that people must obey their country's laws.*

3 **must** used casually to express intention:
She said, 'I must tell you about a dream I had last night'
= *She said that she must tell me about a dream she had had the previous night.*
He said, 'We must have a party to celebrate this'
= *He said that they must have a party to celebrate it.*

4 Advice:
She said, 'You must see Othello; it's marvellous'
= *She said that I must see Othello* etc.
Alternatively **advise/recommend** etc. could be used:
She strongly advised me to see Othello.

B **must** used for obligation can remain unchanged. Alternatively it can change as follows:

I/we must can become **would have to** or **had to**.

would have to is used when the obligation depends on some future action, or when the fulfilment of the obligation appears remote or uncertain, i.e. when **must** is clearly replaceable by **will have to**:

1 When **must** is combined with a time clause or an expression of doubt or condition:
'But perhaps he hasn't got a snorkel,' said Tom. 'In that case, we must (will have to) lend him one,' said Ann.
= *Ann said that in that case they would have to lend him one.*
'If the floods get any worse we must (will have to) leave the house,' he said
= *He said that if the floods got any worse they would have to leave* etc.
'When it stops snowing we must start digging ourselves out,' I said
= *I said that when it stopped snowing we would have to start* etc.

2 When the time for fulfilment of the obligation is fairly remote:
'We must mend the roof properly next year,' he said
= *He said that they would have to mend the roof properly the following year.*

3 When no plans have yet been made for fulfilling the obligation. This occurs chiefly with obligations which have only just arisen:
'I have just received a telegram,' he said. 'I must go home at once.'
= *He said that he had just received a telegram and would have to go* etc.
But **had to** would be more usual here if in fact he did go at once, i.e. **had to** would imply that he went at once.

had to is the usual form for obligations where times for fulfilment have been fixed, or plans made, or when the obligation is fulfilled fairly promptly, or at least by the time the speech is reported:

He said, 'I must wash my hands' (and presumably went off to do this)

= *He said that he had to wash his hands.*

Tom said, 'I must be there by nine tomorrow'

= *Tom said that he had to be there by nine the next day.*

would have to would be possible here also but would imply that the obligation was self-imposed and that no outside authority was involved. **had to** could express either an outside authority (i.e. that someone had told him to be there) or a self-imposed obligation.

All difficulties about **had to/would have to** can of course be avoided by keeping **must** unchanged. In all the above examples **must** could have been used instead of **had to/would have to**.

C **you/he/they must** can always remain unchanged, and usually do. Alternatively, **must** here can become **had to/would have to** just as **I/we must** changes:

He said, 'You must start at once'

= *He said that she must/had to/would have to start at once.*

But **would have to** is less usual in the following example because it removes the idea of the speaker's authority:

Tom said, 'If you want to stay on here you must work harder'

= *Tom said that if she wanted to stay on she must/would have to work harder.*

must implies that Tom himself insists on her working harder: **would have to** merely implies that this will be necessary.

D **must I/you/he?** can change similarly but as **must** in the interrogative usually concerns the present or immediate future it usually becomes **had to**:

'Must you go so soon?' I said

= *I asked him if he had to go so soon.*

E **must not**

I must not usually remains unchanged. **you/he must not** remains unchanged or is expressed as a negative command (see **301** and **302**):

He said, 'You mustn't tell anyone'

= *He said that she mustn't tell/that she wasn't to tell anyone*

or *He told her not to tell anyone.*

F **needn't**

needn't can remain unchanged and usually does. Alternatively it can change to **didn't have to/wouldn't have to** just as **must** changes to **had to/would have to**:

I said, 'If you can lend me the money I needn't go to the bank

= *I said that if he could lend me the money I needn't/wouldn't have to go to the bank.*

He said, 'I needn't be in the office till ten tomorrow morning'

= *He said that he needn't/didn't have to be in the office till ten the next morning.*

He said, 'You needn't wait'

= *He said that I needn't wait.*

need I/you/he? behaves exactly in the same way as **must I/you/he?** i.e. it normally becomes **had to**:

'Need I finish my pudding?' asked the small boy

= *The small boy asked if he had to finish his pudding.*

307 could

A **could you? could I?** with a present or future meaning

1 **could you?** (invitation) is reported by **ask** or **invite**:

'Could you have lunch with me tomorrow?' he said

= *He invited me to have lunch with him the next day.*

(But *Could you have lunch with me tomorrow?* could also be treated as an ordinary question, and reported *He asked if I could have lunch with him/if I would be free to have lunch with him.* It is usually clear from the speaker's tone whether it is an invitation or just a question.)

2 **could you?** (request) is normally reported by **ask** + object + infinitive:

'Could you get tickets?' he said

= *He asked me to get the tickets.*

3 **could I have?/could you give me?** is normally reported by **ask for**:

'Could I have a drink?' he said

= *He asked (me) for a drink.*

4 **could I?** (request for permission) is normally reported unchanged:

'Could I use your phone, please?' she said

= *She asked if she could use my phone.*

But **could I see/speak to/talk to?** can be reported by **ask for/ask to see** etc.

'Could I see Mr Smith, please?' she said

= *She asked for Mr Smith/asked to see Mr Smith.*

5 **could I/you/he/she/they?** can be an ordinary question with a present or future meaning. **could** here would be reported unchanged:
'Could you live in London on £25 a week?' he said
= *He asked if I could live/if anyone could live in London on £25 a week,* i.e. if this would be possible.
'Could you get off early tomorrow?' he said
= *He asked if I could get off early the next day,* i.e. if this would be possible or if this would be allowed.

B **could** with a past meaning

1 **could** for permission can remain the same or change to **was/were allowed to** or **had been allowed to**:
He said, 'When I was young I couldn't interrupt my parents'
= *He said that when he was young he couldn't/wasn't allowed to interrupt his parents.*

C **could** for ability
could for present ability does not change:
I said, 'Could you stand on your head?'
= *I asked him if he could stand on his head.*
could for past ability can remain unchanged or become **had been able**:
He said, 'I could read when I was three'
= *He said that he could read/had been able to read when he was three.*

D **could** in conditional sentences type 2
could in **if**-clauses remains unchanged:
She said, 'If I could drive I'd take you there myself'
= *She said that if she could drive she'd take me there herself.*
could in the main clause remains unchanged when the supposition is contrary to fact:
She said, 'If I had some flour I could make a cake' (but she hasn't any flour)
= *She said that if she had some flour she could make a cake*
but can change to **would be able to** in sentences where the supposition could be fulfilled:
She said, 'If you got out of my light I could see what I was doing'
= *She said that if I got out of her light she would be able to see what she was doing.*

30 Clauses of purpose, comparison, reason, time, result and concession

308 A Purpose is normally expressed by an infinitive:
He went to France to learn French.
They stopped to ask someone the way.
When there is a personal object of the main verb, the infinitive will refer to this and not to the subject:
He sent Tom to the post office to buy stamps (Tom was to buy the stamps).

B **so as** or **in order** are used:

1 With a negative infinitive to express a negative purpose:
He left his gun outside so as not to frighten his wife.
He came in quietly so as not to wake the child.

2 With **to be** and **to have**:
She left work early in order to be at home when he arrived.

3 When the purpose is less immediate:
He is studying mathematics so as to qualify for a higher salary.
She learnt typing in order to help her husband with his work.

4 When there is a personal object but we want the infinitive to refer to the subject:
He sent his sons to a boarding school in order to have some peace. (*He* was going to have some peace.)
Compare with:
He sent his sons to a boarding school to learn to live in a community. (*His sons* were to learn to live in a community.)
But this **in order/so as** construction is not very common. It is more usual to say:
He sent his sons to a boarding school because he wanted to have some peace.

5 **in order** (but not **so as**) can be used:
1 To emphasize that the subject really had this purpose in mind:
A: *He bought diamonds when he was in Amsterdam. Wasn't that extraordinary?* B: *It wasn't extraordinary at all. He went to Amsterdam in order to buy diamonds* (not for any other purpose).
We could also, however, express this idea by stressing the first verb and omitting **in order**:
He ˈwent to Amsterdam to buy diamonds.

2 **in order** can also be used when there are a number of words between the main verb and the infinitive of purpose:
He took much more trouble over the figures than he usually did in order to show his new boss what a careful worker he was.
(But **in order** is not essential and is often omitted.)

3 When the infinitive of purpose precedes the main verb, **in order** may be placed first:
In order to show his boss what a careful worker he was, he took extra trouble over the figures.
(But here also **in order** may be omitted.)

C **for** + gerund is used to express the general purpose of a thing:
A corkscrew is a tool for opening bottles.
But for a particular purpose we use the infinitive:
I'm looking for a corkscrew to open this bottle with.

Also *This is a case for keeping records in*
but *I want a case to keep my records in.*

309 Purpose expressed by clauses of purpose

Clauses are necessary when the person to whom the purpose refers is mentioned, instead of being merely understood as in **308**:
Ships carry lifeboats so that the crew can escape if the ship sinks.

A Purpose clauses are usually expressed by **so that** + **will/would** or **can/could** + infinitive.

can/could is used here to mean **will/would be able to**:
They make £10 notes a different size from £5 notes so that blind people can (= will be able to) *tell the difference between them.*
They wrote the notices in several languages so that foreign tourists could (= would be able to) *understand them.*

can and **will** are used when the main verb is in a present, present perfect or future tense; **could** and **would** are used when the main verb is in a past tense. See the examples above and also:
I light/am lighting/have lit/will light the fire so that the house will be warm when they return.
I have given/will give him a key so that he can get into the house whenever he likes.
I pinned the note to his pillow so that he would be sure to see it.
There were telephone points every kilometre so that drivers whose cars had broken down would be able to/could summon help.

Note that if **that** is omitted from purpose clauses with **can/could**, the idea of purpose may disappear. A sentence such as:
He took my shoes so that I couldn't leave the house would normally mean 'He took my shoes to prevent me leaving etc.'

But *He took my shoes so I couldn't leave the house* would normally mean 'He took my shoes; therefore I wasn't able to leave'.

B Purpose clauses can also be formed by **so that/in order that/that** + **may/might** or **shall/should** + infinitive. These are merely more formal constructions than those shown in A above. There is no difference in meaning.

Note that **so that** can be followed by **will/can/may/shall** or their past forms, while **in order that** or **that** are limited to **may/shall** or their past forms.

that used alone is rarely found except in very dramatic speech or writing, or in poetry:

And wretches hang that jurymen may dine (18th century poem).

The rules about sequences of tenses are the same as those shown above:

We carved their names on the stone so that/in order that future generations should/might know what they had done.

These men risk their lives so that/in order that we may live more safely.

may in the present tense is much more common than **shall**, which is comparatively rarely used. In the past tense either **might** or **should** can be used. In theory **might** expresses ability (replacing **could** above) and **should** is used in other cases (replacing **would** above). In practice, however, this distinction is usually disregarded.

The student should know the above forms but should not normally need to use them, as for all ordinary purposes **so that** + **can/could** or **will/would** should be quite sufficient.

C Negative purpose clauses are made by putting the auxiliary verb (usually **will/would** or **should**) into the negative:

He wrote his diary in cipher so that his wife wouldn't be able to read it.

He changed his name so that his new friends wouldn't/shouldn't know that he had once been accused of murder.

Criminals usually telephone from public telephone boxes so that the police won't be able to trace the call.

Negative purpose clauses can, however, usually be replaced by **to prevent** + noun/pronoun + gerund, or **to avoid** + gerund:

She always shopped in another village so that she wouldn't meet her own neighbours/to avoid meeting her own neighbours.

He dyed his beard so that we shouldn't recognize him/to prevent us recognizing him/to avoid being recognized (passive gerund).

These infinitive phrases are preferred to negative purpose clauses.

310 **in case** and **lest**

A **in case**

1 **in case** + subject + verb can follow a statement or command:
I don't let him climb trees in case he tears his trousers.

in case + present tense normally has the meaning 'because this may happen/because perhaps this will happen' or 'for fear that this may happen'.

in case + past tense normally means 'because this might happen/ because perhaps this would happen' or 'for fear that this would happen'.

Both present tense and past tense here can be replaced by **should** + infinitive, but this construction is less usual.

In sentences consisting of a statement or command + an **in case** clause the first action is a preparation for or a precaution against a possible future action:
Don't let the baby play with your watch in case he breaks it.
I carry a spare wheel in case I have a puncture.
I'll make a cake in case someone drops in at the weekend.

Be careful not to confuse an **in case** clause with an **if** clause (see **221**).

2 Tenses with **in case**

MAIN VERB		
Future *Present* *Present perfect*	+ **in case** +	present tense or **should** + infinitive
Conditional *Past tense* *Past perfect*	+ **in case** +	past tense or **should** + infinitive

I always keep candles in the house in case there is a power cut.
I always kept candles in the house in case there was a power cut.
'in case there should be' would also be possible for both sentences.

B

lest means 'for fear that' and is always followed by **should**:
He doesn't/didn't dare to leave the house lest someone should recognize him.

lest is rarely found except in formal written English.

311 Comparisons

A Comparisons with **like**

like can be followed by noun/pronoun or gerund. It should not be followed by subject + verb:
There was a terrible storm; it was like the end of the world.
Getting money from him is like getting blood from a stone.

B Comparisons with **as . . . as** and **than**

as . . . as and **not so/as . . . as** are used with the positive form of an adverb or adjective. **than** is used with the comparative form. When the same verb is used in both clauses we normally express the second verb as an auxiliary:

I can't run as/so fast as he can.
He runs faster than me/than I do.
It is even darker today than it was yesterday.
She had no sooner left the house than it began to rain.

1 **as/than** can sometimes be followed by a noun/pronoun only, the verb being understood but not mentioned:

She is taller than her brother (is).
Tom drove more carefully than Ann (did).
Small cars are easier to park than big ones (are).

Note however that this is possible only when the same verb and the same tense is used in both clauses, and when each clause has a different subject.

When pronouns are used in this way (without the verb) they are usually put into the object form. This is accepted in colloquial English. In written English it is better to use the subject pronoun and the verb:

She doesn't work as hard as me (as hard as I do).
He is older than you (are).
I can swim better than him (better than he can).
We pay more rent than them (than they do).

2 Note that the verb is necessary and cannot be omitted when both clauses have the same subject, when there is a change of verb or tense and when the second clause is expanded:

The trains are more crowded at nine than (they are) at eight.
He is stronger than he looks.
He works harder than I did at his age.
She makes more money in a week than I do/make in a fortnight.

3 **as/than** can also be followed by an infinitive or a gerund:

It is better to say too little than (to) say too much.
He found riding as tiring as walking.

The infinitive is used if the verb before **than/as** is, or contains, an infinitive:

He finds it easier to do the cooking himself than (to) teach his wife to cook.
It is as easy to do it right as (to) do it wrong.
Even lazy people would rather work than starve.

When **than/as** is preceded by an infinitive without **to** it is followed by an infinitive without **to**. Otherwise the **to** is optional.

The gerund is used in other cases, i.e. when the verb preceding **than/as** is a gerund or when the action is represented by a pronoun:
This is more amusing than sitting in an office.
Skiing is more exciting than skating.
It is as easy as falling off a log.
He cleaned his shoes, which was better than doing nothing.

C Comparisons with superlatives present no difficulty:
Is this the best you can offer me?
This is the highest mountain I have ever climbed.
It was the most beautiful house that I had ever seen.

312 Clauses of reason

These are introduced by **because, as** and **since** and sometimes **if** (for **because** and **for** see **93**):
We camped there because it was too dark to go on.
As we hadn't any money we couldn't buy anything to eat. (See also **95**.)
Since you won't take advice there is no point in asking for it.
If (= Since) *you wanted to go to sea, why didn't you?*

These sentences could also be expressed by two clauses joined by **so** or **therefore**:
It was too dark to go on, so we camped there.
We hadn't any money so we couldn't buy anything to eat.
You don't take advice so there's no point in asking for it.

therefore could replace **so** above but is normally used in more formal English:
The delegate from Finland has not yet arrived; we have therefore decided to postpone the meeting till tomorrow morning.

therefore can be placed before the subject of the verb, or before the main verb. The second position is the more usual.

313 Time clauses

These are introduced by conjunctions of time such as **when, as, while** (see **95, 190**), **until/till** (see **83**), **after, as soon as, the sooner, no sooner . . . than, hardly . . . when, immediately, whenever, since,** etc. They can also be introduced by **the moment, the minute.**

A Remember that we do not use a future tense or form, or a conditional tense, in a time clause:

1 A future tense becomes a present tense when we put it in a time clause:
You'll be back soon. I'll stay till then.
= *I'll stay **till you get back**.*

2 The present continuous, used as a future form, changes similarly:
He's arriving at six
but ***When he arrives** he'll tell us all about the match.*

3 **be going to** also changes:
The parachutist is going to jump and his parachute will open soon afterwards
= ***Soon after he jumps** his parachute will open.*
We'll be landing soon and leaving the plane
but ***Immediately we leave the plane** mechanics will start work on it.*

4 The continuous tense can of course be used when it indicates a continuous action:
Peter and John will be playing/are playing/are going to play tennis tonight.
While they are playing (during this time) *we'll go to the beach.*

5 The future perfect changes to the present perfect, and the future perfect continuous changes to the present perfect continuous:
I'll have finished in the bathroom in a few minutes.
***As soon as I have finished** I'll give you a call.*

6 A conditional tense changes to a past tense:
We knew that he would arrive/would be arriving about six.
*We knew that **till he arrived** nothing would be done.*

A future or conditional tense can be used after **when** provided **when** does not introduce a time clause:
He asked when the train would get in (this is not a time clause but a noun clause, object of *asked*).

B Note **no sooner . . . than, hardly . . . when:**
He had no sooner drunk the coffee than he began to feel drowsy
or *No sooner had he drunk the coffee than he began to feel drowsy.*
The performance had hardly begun when the lights went out
or *Hardly had the performance begun when the lights went out.*

Note also **the sooner . . . the sooner:**
The sooner we start, the sooner we'll be there.

C Other examples:
Immediately he earns any money he spends it.
They've moved house three times since they got married.
He rides whenever he can.

314 Clauses of result

These are expressed by **so . . . that** or **such . . . that** and follow the usual rules about sequence of tenses (see **212**).

such is an adjective and is used before an adjective + noun:

They had such a fierce dog that no one dared to go near their house.
He spoke for such a long time that people began to fall asleep.

so is an adverb and is used before adverbs and with adjectives which are not followed by their nouns:

The snow fell so fast that our footsteps were covered up in a few minutes.
Their dog was so fierce that no one dared come near it.
His speech went on for so long that people began to fall asleep.

Note, however, that **such** is never used before **much** and **many**, therefore **so** is used even when **much** and **many** are followed by nouns:

There was so much dust that we couldn't see what was happening.
So many people complained that in the end they took the programme off.

Note that **such** + **a** + adjective + noun is replaceable by **so** + adjective + **a** + noun, so that 'such a good man' is replaceable by 'so good a man'. This is only possible when a noun is preceded by **a/an**. It is not a very usual form but may be met in literature.

Sometimes for emphasis **so** is placed at the beginning of the sentence. It is then followed by the inverted form of the verb (see **72**):

So terrible was the storm that whole roofs were ripped off.

315 Clauses of concession

These are introduced by **though, although** (see **91**), **even if, no matter, however** + adjective/adverb and sometimes by **whatever**. **as** is also possible, but only in the adjective + **as** + **be** construction:

Even if/Though you don't like him you can still be polite.
No matter what you do, don't touch this switch.
However rich people are, they always seem anxious to make more money.
However carefully you drive, you will probably have an accident eventually.
Whatever you do, don't tell him that I told you this.
Patient as he was, he had no intention of waiting for three hours (though he was patient).

may + infinitive can be used in hypothetical cases:

However frightened you may be yourself, you must remain outwardly calm.

should + infinitive can be used after **even if** just as it can after **if** in conditional sentences, to express the idea that the action expressed by the infinitive is not very likely to take place:

Even if he should find out he won't do anything about it.

316 Noun clauses introduced by **that**

A The **that** + subject + verb construction is possible after a large number of verbs. Some of the most useful are given below.

admit*	forget	prove
agree	guarantee	realize
announce	happen	recognize
appear	hear	recommend
arrange	hope	remark
assume	imagine	remind
be afraid	imply	resolve
be anxious	indicate	reveal
believe	inform	say*
command	insist	see
confess	know	seem
declare	learn	show
decide	make out	stipulate
demand	mean	suggest
demonstrate	notice	teach
determine	observe	tell
be determined	occur + **to** + object	think
discover	order	threaten
estimate	perceive	turn out
expect	presume	vow
fear	pretend	warn
feel	promise	wish
find	propose	

*And alternatives, e.g. assure, explain, complain etc. See **298**.

Most of the above verbs can also take another construction (see chapters on the infinitive, the gerund and present participle). Note however that a verb + **that** + subject construction does not necessarily have the same meaning as the same verb + infinitive/gerund/present participle:

He saw her sweeping under the beds = He watched her sweeping etc.

but *He saw that she swept under the beds* could mean either 'He noticed that she did this' or 'He made sure by supervision that she did this'.

Sequence of tenses (see **212**):

The tense of the main verb will affect the tense in the noun clause:

I hope I haven't made a mistake. *I hoped I hadn't made a mistake.*

I promise I will help you. *I promised I would help you.*

Tom thinks it is going to rain. *Tom thought it was going to rain.*

appear, occur, happen, seem require **it** as subject:

It occurred to me that he might be lying.

It turned out that nobody remembered the address.

It appears that we have come on the wrong day.

that + subject + **should** can be used after **agree, arrange, be anxious, command, decide, demand, determine, be determined, order, resolve** and **urge** instead of an infinitive construction, and after **insist** and **suggest** instead of a gerund:
They decided/agreed to put up a statue.
They decided/agreed that a statue should be put up.
He suggested offering a reward.
He suggested that a reward should be offered. (See **236**.)

B **that** + subject + verb can be used after **be** + adjectives expressing feeling: **astonished, delighted, glad, relieved** etc. (See **250** A.)
I am delighted that you can come.
He was relieved that no one had been hurt.

C **that** + subject + verb can also follow an abstract noun such as **belief, fact, fear, hope, report, rumour**:
The rumour that prices were going to rise led to a rush on the shops.

D For **that** clauses after **so/such . . .** see **314**.

E A **that**-clause can also be the subject of a sentence. Normally the sentence begins with **it** + **be** + adjective/noun:
It is unfortunate that you were not insured.
It is a pity that he didn't come earlier.
For constructions with **that** + **should** see **236** and **237**.

31 List of irregular verbs

317 The verbs in italics are verbs which are not very common in modern English but may be found in literature. When a verb has two possible forms and one is less usual than the other, the less usual one will be printed in italics.

Compounds of irregular verbs form their past tenses and past participles in the same way as the original verb:

come	came	come
overcome	overcame	overcome
set	set	set
upset	upset	upset

Present and infinitive	*Simple past*	*Past participle*
abide	*abode*	*abode*
arise	arose	arisen
awake	awoke/awaked	awoken/*awaked*
be	was	been
bear	bore	borne/born*
beat	beat	beaten
become	became	become
befall	*befell*	*befallen*
beget	*begot*	*begotten*
begin	began	begun
behold	*beheld*	*beheld*
bend	bent	bent
bereave	bereaved	bereaved/bereft*
beseech	*besought*	*besought*
bet	betted/bet	betted/bet
bid (=command)	*bade*	*bidden*
bid (=offer)	bid	bid
bind	bound	bound
bite	bit	bitten
bleed	bled	bled
blow	blew	blown
break	broke	broken
breed	bred	bred
bring	brought	brought
broadcast	broadcast	broadcast
build	built	built
burn	burned/burnt	burned/burnt

*These past participles are not optional but carry different meanings and should be checked by the student in a reliable dictionary.

Present and infinitive	*Simple past*	*Past participle*
burst	burst	burst
buy	bought	bought
can†	could	been able
cast	cast	cast
catch	caught	caught
chide	*chid*	*chidden*
choose	chose	chosen
cleave	*clove/cleft*	*cloven/cleft**
cling	clung	clung
clothe	clothed/clad	clothed/clad
come	came	come
cost	cost	cost
creep	crept	crept
crow	crowed/*crew*	crowed
cut	cut	cut
dare	dared/*durst*	dared/*durst*
deal (/di:l/)	dealt (/delt/)	dealt (/delt/)
dig	dug	dug
do	did	done
draw	drew	drawn
dream (/dri:m/)	dreamed/dreamt (/dremt/)	dreamed/dreamt (/dremt/)
drink	drank	drunk
drive	drove	driven
dwell	*dwelled*/dwelt	*dwelled*/dwelt
eat	ate	eaten
fall	fell	fallen
feed	fed	fed
feel	felt	felt
fight	fought	fought
find	found	found
flee	fled	fled
fling	flung	flung
fly	flew	flown
forbear	forbore	forborne
forbid	forbade	forbidden
forget	forgot	forgotten
forgive	forgave	forgiven
forsake	forsook	forsaken
freeze	froze	frozen
get	got	got
gild	gilded/gilt	gilded/gilt
gird	*girded/girt*	*girded/girt*
give	gave	given

*See footnote on page 290.

†Present only.

Present and infinitive	*Simple past*	*Past participle*
go	went	gone
grind	ground	ground
grow	grew	grown
hang	hanged/hung	hanged*/hung
have	had	had
hear (/hiə/)	heard (/hə:d/)	heard (/hə:d/)
hew	hewed	hewed/hewn
hide	hid	hidden
hit	hit	hit
hold	held	held
hurt	hurt	hurt
keep	kept	kept
kneel	knelt	knelt
knit**	knit	knit
know	knew	known
lay	laid	laid
lead	led	led
lean (/li:n/)	leaned/leant (/lent/)	leaned/leant (/lent/)
leap (/li:p/)	leaped/leapt (/lept/)	leaped/leapt (/lept/)
learn	learned/learnt	learned/learnt
leave	left	left
lend	lent	lent
let	let	let
lie	lay	lain
light	lighted/lit	lighted/lit
lose	lost	lost
make	made	made
may†	might	—
mean (/mi:n/)	meant (/ment/)	meant (/ment/)
meet	met	met
mow	mowed	mowed/mown
must†	had to	—
ought†	—	—
pay	paid	paid
put	put	put
read (/ri:d/)	read (/red/)	read (/red/)
rend	*rent*	*rent*
rid	rid	rid
ride	rode	ridden

*See footnote on page 290.

** = unite/draw together. **knit** (= make garments from wool) is a regular verb.

†Present only.

Present and infinitive	*Simple past*	*Past participle*
ring	rang	rung
rise	rose	risen/(/rizn/)
run	ran	run
saw	sawed	sawed/sawn
say	said	said
see	saw	seen
seek	sought	sought
sell	sold	sold
send	sent	sent
set	set	set
sew	sewed	sewed/sewn
shake	shook	shaken
shall†	should	—
shear	sheared/*shore*	sheared/shorn
shed	shed	shed
shine	shone	shone
shoe	shoed/*shod*	shoed/*shod*
shoot	shot	shot
show	showed	showed/shown
shrink	shrank	shrunk
shut	shut	shut
sing	sang	sung
sink	sank	sunk
sit	sat	sat
slay	*slew*	*slain*
sleep	slept	slept
slide	slid	slid
sling	slung	slung
slink	slunk	slunk
slit	slit	slit
smell	smelled/smelt	smelled/smelt
smite	*smote*	*smitten*
sow	sowed	sowed/sown
speak	spoke	spoken
speed	speeded/sped	speeded/sped
spell	spelled/spelt	spelled/spelt
spend	spent	spent
spill	spilled/spilt	spilled/spilt
spin	spun	spun
spit	spat	spat
split	split	split
spread	spread	spread
spring	sprang	sprung
stand	stood	stood
steal	stole	stolen
stick	stuck	stuck
sting	stung	stung
stink	stank/*stunk*	stunk

†Present only.

Present and infinitive	*Simple past*	*Past participle*
strew	strewed	strewed/strewn
stride	strode	stridden
strike	struck	struck
string	strung	strung
strive	strove	striven
swear	swore	sworn
sweep	swept	swept
swell	swelled	swelled/swollen
swim	swam	swum
swing	swung	swung
take	took	taken
teach	taught	taught
tear	tore	torn
tell	told	told
think	thought	thought
thrive	thrived/throve	thrived/thriven
throw	threw	thrown
thrust	thrust	thrust
tread	trod	trodden/trod
understand	understood	understood
undertake	undertook	undertaken
wake	waked/woke	waked/woken
wear	wore	worn
weave	wove	woven
weep	*wept*	*wept*
wet	wetted/wet	wetted/wet
will†	would	—
win	won	won
wind	wound	wound
wring	wrung	wrung
write	wrote	written

†Present only.

32 Verbs + prepositions/adverbs

318 In modern English it is very usual to place prepositions or adverbs after certain verbs so as to obtain a variety of meanings:

look for = search for, seek
look out = beware
look after = take care of
give up = abandon (a habit or attempt)
give away = give to someone/anyone

The student need not try to decide whether the combination is verb + preposition or verb + adverb, but should consider the expression as a whole. It is also important to learn whether the combination is transitive (i.e. requires an object) or intransitive (i.e. cannot have an object):

look for is transitive: *I am looking for my passport.*
look out is intransitive: *Look out! This ice isn't safe!*

Each of the combinations given in the following pages will be marked 'tr' (= transitive) or 'intr' (= intransitive), and the examples of the use of each will help to emphasize this distinction.

Note that it is possible for a combination to have two or more different meanings, and to be transitive in one/some of these and intransitive in others: e.g. **take off** can mean 'remove'. It is then a transitive expression:

He took off his hat.

take off can also mean 'rise from the ground' (used of aircraft). Here it is intransitive:

The plane took off at ten o'clock.

Transitive expressions

A The position of the object:

Noun objects are usually placed at the end of these expressions:

I am looking for ***my glasses***.

With some expressions, however, they can be placed either at the end or immediately after the verb, i.e. before the short word. We can say:

He took off ***his coat*** or *He took* ***his coat*** *off*.

Pronoun objects are sometimes placed at the end of the expression:

I am looking for ***them***.

But they are more often placed immediately after the verb:
*He took **it** off.*
This position is usual before the following short words: **up, down, in, out, away, off** and **on** (except when used in the expression **call on** = visit).

Examples given of the use of each expression will show all possible positions of noun or pronoun objects in the following way:
*I'll give **this old coat** away (give away **this old coat**/give **it** away).*
i.e. with this expression the noun object can come before or after the *away*; the pronoun object must come before the *away*. When only one example is given the student may assume that the pronoun object has the same position as the noun object.

B When these expressions are followed by a verb object the gerund form of the verb is used:
He kept on blowing his horn.
Where gerunds are usual this will be shown by examples.

Note that some expressions can be followed by an infinitive:
It is up to you to decide this for yourself.
Some of the younger members called on the minister to resign.
The lecturer set out to show that most illnesses were avoidable.
go on can be followed by either infinitive or gerund but there is a considerable difference in meaning.

319 Verb + preposition/adverb combinations

account

account for (tr) = give a good reason for, explain satisfactorily (some action or expenditure):
A treasurer must account for the money he spends.
He has behaved in the most extraordinary way; I can't account for his actions at all/I can't account for his behaving like that.

allow

allow for (tr) = make provision in advance for, take into account (usually some additional requirement, expenditure, delay etc.):
TOM: *It is 800 kilometres and I drive at 100 k.p.h., so I'll be there in eight hours.*
ANN: *But you'll have to allow for delays going through towns and for stops for refuelling.*
Allowing for depreciation your car should be worth £2,000 this time next year.

answer

answer back (intr), **answer** somebody **back** = answer a reproof impudently:

FATHER: *Why were you so late last night? You weren't in till 2 a.m.*
SON: *You should have been asleep.*
FATHER: *Don't answer me back. Answer my question.*

ask

ask after/for somebody = ask for news of:
I met Tom at the party; he asked after you (asked how you were/how you were getting on).

ask for
a = ask to speak to:
Go to the office and ask for my secretary.
b = request, demand:
The men asked for more pay and shorter hours.
ask someone **in** (object before **in**) = invite him to enter the house:
He didn't ask me in; he kept me standing at the door while he read the message.

ask someone **out** (object before **out**) = invite him to an entertainment or to a meal (usually in a public place):
She had a lot of friends and was usually asked out in the evenings, so she very seldom spent an evening at home.

back

back away (intr) = step or move back slowly (because confronted by some danger or unpleasantness):
When he took a snake out of his pocket everyone backed away and stood watching it from a safe distance.

back out (intr) = withdraw (from some joint action previously agreed on), discontinue or refuse to provide previously promised help or support:
He agreed to help but backed out when he found how difficult it was.

back somebody **up** = support morally or verbally:
The headmaster never backed up **his staff** *(backed* **them** *up). If a parent complained about a master he assumed that the master was in the wrong.*

be

be in (intr) = be at home/in this building.

be out (intr) = be away from home/from this building for a short time – not overnight.

be away (intr) = be away from home/from this place for at least a night.

be back (intr) = have returned after a long or short absence:
I want to see Mrs Pitt. Is she in?
No, I'm afraid she's out at the moment
or *No, I'm afraid she's away for the weekend.*
When will she be back?
She'll be back in half an hour/next week.

be for (tr) = be in favour of (often used with gerund).

be against (tr) = be opposed to (often used with gerund):
I'm for doing nothing till the police arrive/I'm against doing anything till the police arrive.

be in for (tr) = be about to encounter (usually something unpleasant):
Did you listen to the weather forecast? I'm afraid we're in for a bumpy flight.
If you think that the work is going to be easy you're in for a shock.

be over (intr) = be finished:
The storm is over now; we can go on.

be up (intr) = be out of bed:
Don't expect her to answer the door bell at eight o'clock on Sunday morning. She won't be up.

be up to (tr) = be physically or intellectually strong enough (to perform a certain action). The object is usually **it**, though a gerund is possible:
After his illness the Minister continued in office though he was no longer up to the work/up to doing the work.

be up to something/some mischief/some trick/no good = be occupied or busy with some mischievous act:
Don't trust him; he is up to something/some trick.
The boys are very quiet. I wonder what they are up to.
Note that the object of **up to** here is always some very indefinite expression such as these given above. It is never used with a particular action.

it is up to someone (often followed by an infinitive) = it is his responsibility or duty:
It is up to parents to teach their children manners.
I have helped you as much as I can. Now it is up to you (you must continue by your own efforts).

bear

bear out (tr) = confirm:

*This report bears out **my** theory (bears **my theory** out/bears **it** out).*

bear up (intr) = support bad news bravely, hide feelings of grief: *The news of her death was a great shock to him but he bore up bravely and none of us realized how much he felt it.*

blow

blow out (tr) = extinguish (a flame) by blowing:
*The wind blew out **the candle** (blew **the candle** out/blew **it** out).*

blow up (tr or intr)

a = destroy by explosion, explode, be destroyed:
*They blew up **the bridges** so that the enemy couldn't follow them (blew **the bridges** up/blew **them** up).*
Just as we got to the bridge it blew up.

b = fill with air, inflate, pump up:
*The children blew up **their balloons** and threw them into the air (blew **the balloons** up/blew **them** up).*

boil

boil away (intr) = be boiled until all (the liquid) has evaporated:
I put the kettle on the gas ring and then went away and forgot about it. When I returned, the water had all boiled away and the flame had burnt a hole in the kettle.

boil over (intr) = to rise and flow over the sides of the container (used only of hot liquids):
The milk boiled over and there was a horrible smell of burning.

break

break down figures = take a total and sub-divide it under various headings so as to give additional information:
You say that 10,000 people use this library. Could you break that down into age-groups? (i.e. say how many of these are under 25, over 50 etc.).

break down a door etc. = cause to collapse by using force:
*The firemen had to break down **the door** to get into the burning house (break **the door** down/break **it** down).*

break down (intr) = collapse, cease to function properly, owing to some fault or weakness:

1 Used of people, it normally implies a temporary emotional collapse:
He broke down when telling me about his son's tragic death (i.e. he was overcome by his sorrow, he wept).

2 It can express collapse of mental resistance:
At first he refused to admit his guilt but when he was shown the evidence he broke down and confessed.
3 When used of health it implies a serious physical collapse:
After years of overwork his health broke down and he had to retire from business.
4 It is very often used of machines:
The car broke down when we were driving through the desert and it took us two days to repair it.
5 It can be used of negotiations:
The negotiations broke down (i.e. were discontinued) *because neither side would compromise.*

break in (intr), **break into** (tr)

a = enter by force:
Thieves broke in and stole the silver.
Thieves broke into the house etc.

b = interrupt someone by some sudden remark:
I was telling them about my travels when he broke in with a story of his own.

break in (a young horse/pony etc.) (tr) = train him for use:
You cannot ride or drive a young horse safely before he has been broken in.

break off (tr or intr) = detach or become detached:
He took a bar of chocolate and broke off ***a bit****/broke* ***a bit*** *off/broke* ***it*** *off.*
A piece of rock broke off and fell into the pool at the foot of the cliff.

break off (tr) = terminate (used of agreements or negotiations):
Ann has broken off ***her engagement*** *to Tom (broken* ***her engagement*** *off/broken* ***it*** *off).*

break off (intr) = stop talking suddenly, interrupt oneself:
They were arguing but broke off when someone came into the room.

break out (intr)

a = begin (used of evils such as wars, epidemics, fires, etc.):
War broke out on August 4th.

b = escape by using force from a prison etc.:
They locked him up in a room but he broke out (smashed the door and escaped).
The police are looking for two men who broke out of prison last night.

break up (tr or intr) = disintegrate, cause to disentegrate:
If that ship stays there she will break up/be broken up by the waves.
The old ship was towed away to be broken up and sold as scrap.
Divorce breaks up a lot of ***families*** *(breaks* ***families*** *up/breaks* ***them*** *up).*

break up (intr) = terminate (used of school terms, meetings, parties etc.):
The school broke up on July 30 and all the boys went home for the holidays.
The meeting broke up in confusion.

bring

bring someone **round** (tr; object usually before **round**)
a = persuade someone to accept a previously opposed suggestion:
After a lot of argument I brought him round to my point of view.
b = restore to consciousness:
She fainted when she heard the news but a little brandy soon brought her round.

bring a person or thing **round** (tr; object usually before **round**) = bring him/it to my/your/his house:
I have finished that book you lent me; I'll bring it round (i.e. to your house) *tonight.*

bring up (tr)
a = educate and train children:
She brought up ***her children*** *to be truthful (brought* ***her children*** *up/brought* ***them*** *up).*
b = mention:
At the last committee meeting, the treasurer brought up ***the question*** *of raising the annual subscription (brought* ***the question*** *up/brought* ***it*** *up).*

burn

burn down (tr or intr) = destroy, or be destroyed, completely by fire (used of buildings):
The mob burnt down ***the embassy*** *(burnt* ***the embassy*** *down/burnt* ***it*** *down).*
The hotel burnt down before help came.

call

1 **call** meaning 'visit' (for a short time)
call at a place
I called at the bank and arranged to transfer some money.

call for = visit a place to collect a person or thing:
I am going to a pop concert with Tom. He is calling for me at eight so I must be ready then.
Let's leave our suitcases in the left luggage office and call for them later on when we have the car.

call in is intransitive, and has the same meaning as **look in** and the colloquial **drop in**:
Call in/Look in on your way home and tell me how the interview went.

call on a person:
He called on all the housewives in the area and asked them to sign the petition.

2 Other meanings of **call on, in, for**

call for (tr) = require, demand (the subject here is often an impersonal word or phrase such as: the situation/this sort of work/this etc.; the object is then usually some quality e.g. courage/patience/a steady hand etc.):
The situation calls for tact.
You've got the job! This calls for a celebration.

But it can also be used with a personal subject:
The workers are calling for strike action.
The relations of the dead men are calling for an inquiry.

call in a person/**call** him **in** = send for him/ask him to come to the house to perform some service. **send for** is more authoritative than **call in**, which is therefore a more polite form:
It was too late to call in ***an electrician*** *(call* ***an electrician*** *in/call* ***him*** *in).*
There is some mystery about his death; the police have been called in.

call on somebody (usually + infinitive) = ask him to do something/ask him to help. This is a rather formal way of making a request and is chiefly used on formal occasions or in speeches etc. There is usually the idea that the person called on will consider it his duty to comply with the request:
The president called on his people to make sacrifices for the good of their country.
The chairman called on the secretary to read the minutes of the last meeting.

3 Other combinations with **call**

call off (tr) = cancel something not yet started, or abandon something already in progress:
They had to call off (cancel) ***the match*** *(call* ***the match*** *off/call* ***it*** *off) as the ground was too wet to play on.*

When the fog got thicker the search was called off (abandoned).

call out (tr) = summon someone to leave his house to deal with a situation outside. It is often used of troops when they are required to leave their barracks to deal with civil disturbances:

The police couldn't control the mob so troops were called out.

The Fire Brigade was called out several times on the night of November 5 to put out fires started by fireworks.

Doctors don't much like being called out at night.

call up (tr)

a = summon for military service:

In countries where there is conscription ***men*** *are called up at the age of eighteen (call up* ***men****/call* ***men*** *up/call* ***them*** *up).*

b = telephone:

I called ***Tom*** *up and told him the news (call up* ***Tom****/call* ***him*** *up).*

care

not to care about (tr) = to be indifferent to:

The professor said that he was interested only in research; he didn't really care about students.

care for (tr)

a = like (seldom used in the affirmative):

He doesn't care for films about war.

b = look after (not much used except in the passive):

The house looked well cared for (had been well looked after/was in good condition).

carry

carry on (intr) = continue (usually work or duty):

I can't carry on alone any longer; I'll have to get help.

carry on with (tr) is used similarly:

The doctor told her to carry on with the treatment.

carry out (tr) = perform (duties), obey (orders, instructions), fulfil (threats):

You are not meant to think for yourself; you are here to carry out my orders.

He carried out his threat to cut off our water supply (he threatened to do it and he did it).

He read the instructions but he didn't carry them out.

catch

catch up with (tr), **catch up** (tr or intr) = overtake, but not pass:

I started last in the race but I soon caught up with ***the others*** *(caught* ***them*** *up/caught up).*

*You've missed a whole term; you'll have to work hard to catch up **with the class** (catch **them** up/catch up).*

clean

clean out (tr) a room/cupboard/drawer etc. = clean and tidy it thoroughly:
*I must clean out **the spare room** (clean **the spare room** out/clean **it** out).*
clean up (tr) a mess e.g. anything spilt:
*Clean up **any spilt paint** (clean the **spilt paint** up/clean **it** up).*
clean up (intr) is used similarly:
These painters always clean up when they've finished (leave the place clean).

clear

clear away (tr) = remove articles, usually in order to make space:
*Could you clear away **these papers** (clear **these papers** away/clear **them** away)?*
clear away (intr) = disperse:
The clouds soon cleared away and it became quite warm.
clear off (intr) from an open space, **clear out** (intr) of a room, building = go away (colloquial; as a command it is definitely rude):
'You clear off,' said the farmer angrily. 'You've no right to put your caravans in my field without even asking permission.'
Clear out! If I find you in this building again, I'll report you to the police.
clear out (tr) a room/cupboard/drawer etc. = empty it, usually to make room for something else:
*I'll clear out **this drawer** and you can put your things in it (clear **this drawer** out/clear **it** out).*
clear up (intr) = become fine after clouds or rain:
The sky looks a bit cloudy now but I think it will clear up.
clear up (tr or intr) = make tidy and clean:
When you are cooking it's best to clear up as you go, instead of leaving everything to the end and having a terrible pile of things to deal with.
*Clear up **this mess** (clear **this mess** up/clear **it** up).*
clear up (tr)
a = finish (some work which still remains to be done):
I have some letters which I must clear up before I leave tonight.
b = solve (a mystery):

In a great many detective stories when the police are baffled an amateur detective comes along and clears up ***the mystery*** *(clears* ***it*** *up).*

close

close down (tr or intr) = shut permanently (of a shop or business):
Trade was so bad that many small shops closed down and big shops closed some of ***their branches*** *down (closed down* ***some branches****/ closed* ***them*** *down).*

close in (intr) = come nearer, approach from all sides (used of mist, darkness, enemies etc.):
As the mist was closing in we decided to stay where we were.

close up (intr) = come nearer together (of people in a line):
If you children closed up a bit there'd be room for another one on this seat.

come

come across/upon (tr) = find by chance:
When I was looking for my passport I came across these old photographs.

come along/on (intr) = come with me, accompany me. 'Come on' is often said to someone who is hesitating or delaying:
Come on, or we'll be late.

come away (intr) = leave (with me):
Come away now. It's time to go home.

come away/off (intr) = detach itself:
When I picked up the teapot the handle came away in my hand.

come in (intr), **come into** (tr) = enter:
Someone knocked at my door and I said, 'Come in.'
Come into the garden and I'll show you my roses.

come off (intr)

a = succeed, of a plan or scheme (used in negative):
She told her husband that she was going to spend the week with her mother in York whereas in fact she was going to Paris. She tried to cover her tracks by writing postcards to her husband and asking a friend in York to post them. But the scheme didn't come off because the friend forgot to post them till the following week.

b = take place; happen as arranged:
'When is the wedding coming off?' 'Next June.'

If we say 'The duchess was to have opened the bazaar' we imply that this plan was made but didn't come off (she arranged to open it but later had to cancel this arrangement).

c = end its run (of a play, exhibition etc.):
Lady Windermere's Fan is coming off next week. You'd better hurry if you want to see it.

come out (intr)

a = be revealed, exposed (the subject here is normally **the truth/the facts/the whole story** etc. and usually refers to facts which the people concerned were trying to keep hidden, i.e. scandals etc.):
They deceived everybody till they quarrelled among themselves; then one publicly denounced the others and the whole truth came out.

b = be published (of books):
Her new novel will be coming out in time for the Christmas sales.

c = disappear (of stains):
Tomato stains don't usually come out.

come round (intr)

a = finally accept a previously opposed suggestion:
Her father at first refused to let her study abroad but he came round (to it) in the end (i.e. said she could go).

b = come to my (your/his etc.) house:
I can't come to dinner but I could come round after dinner and tell you the plan.

come round/to (intr; stress on **to**) = recover consciousness:
When we found him he was unconscious but he came round/to in half an hour and explained that he had been attacked and robbed.

come up (intr)

a = rise to the surface:
A diver with an aqualung doesn't have to keep coming up for air; he can stay underwater for quite a long time.
Weeds are coming up everywhere.

b = be mentioned:
The question of the caretaker's wages came up at the last meeting.

come up (intr), **come up to** (tr) = approach, come close enough to talk:
A policeman was standing a few yards away. He came up to me and said, 'You can't park here.'

crop

crop up (intr) = appear, arise unexpectedly or by accident (the subject is normally an abstract noun such as **difficulties/the subject** etc. or a pronoun):
At first all sorts of difficulties cropped up and delayed us. Later we learnt how to anticipate these.

cut

cut down a tree = fell it:
If you cut down ***all the trees*** *you will ruin the land (cut* ***the trees*** *down/cut* ***them*** *down).*

cut down (tr) = reduce in size or amount:
We must cut down expenses or we'll be getting into debt.
'This article is too long,' said the editor. 'Could you cut it down to 2,000 words?'

cut in (intr) = pass one car when there isn't room to do this safely, as another car is coming from the opposite direction:
Accidents are often caused by drivers cutting in.

cut off (tr) = disconnect, discontinue supply (usually of gas, water, electricity etc.). The object can either be the commodity or the person who suffers:
The Company has cut off our ***electricity supply*** *(cut* ***our supply*** *off/cut* ***it*** *off) because we haven't paid our bill.*
They've cut off the water (our water supply) temporarily because they are repairing one of the main pipes.
We were cut off in the middle of our (telephone) conversation (this might be accidental or a deliberate action by the switchboard operator).

cut someone **off** = form a barrier between him and safety (often used in connexion with the tide, expecially in the passive):
We were cut off by the tide and had to be rescued by boat.

be cut off (intr) = be inconveniently isolated (the subject is usually a place or residents in a certain place):
You will be completely cut off if you go to live in that village because there is a bus only once a week.

cut out (tr)

a = cut from a piece of cloth/paper etc. a smaller piece of a desired shape:
When I am making a dress I mark the cloth with chalk and then cut ***it*** *out (cut out* ***the dress****/cut* ***the dress*** *out).*
Young people often cut out photographs of their favourite film stars and stick them to the walls.

b = omit, leave out:
If you want to get thin you must cut out ***sugar*** *(cut* ***it*** *out).*

be cut out for (tr) = be fitted or suited for (used of people, usually in the negative):
His father got him a job in a bank but it became clear that he was not cut out for that kind of work (he wasn't happy and not good at the work).

cut up (tr) = cut into small pieces:
*They cut down the tree and cut **it** up for firewood (cut **the tree** up/cut up **the tree**).*

die

die away (intr) = become gradually fainter till inaudible:
The prisoners waited till the sound of the warder's footsteps died away.

die down (intr) = become gradually calmer and finally disappear (of riots, fires, excitement, etc.):
When the excitement had died down the shopkeepers took down their shutters and reopened their shops.

die out (intr) = become extinct (of customs, races, species of animals etc.):
Elephants would die out if men were allowed to shoot as many as they wished.

do

do away with (tr) = abolish:
The government should do away with the regulations restricting drinking hours.

do up (tr) = redecorate:
*When I do **this room** up I'll paint the walls in stripes (do up **this room**/do **it** up).*

do without (tr) = manage in the absence of a person or thing:
We had to do without petrol during the fuel crisis.
The object is sometimes understood but not mentioned:
If there isn't any milk we'll have to do without (it).

draw

draw back (intr) = retire, recoil:
It's too late to draw back now; the plans are all made.

draw up (tr) = make a written plan or agreement:
*My solicitor drew up **the lease** and we both signed it (drew **it** up).*

draw up (intr) = stop (of vehicles):
The car drew up at the kerb and the driver got out.

drop

drop in (intr) = pay a short unnannounced visit:
He dropped in for a few minutes to ask if he could borrow your power drill (**drop in** is more colloquial than 'call in').

drop out (intr) = withdraw, retire from a scheme or plan:
We planned to hire a bus for the excursion but now so many people have dropped out that it will not be needed.

enter

enter for (tr) = become a candidate (for a contest, examination, etc.):
Two hundred competitors have entered for the motor-cycle race.

fade

fade away (intr) = disappear, become gradually fainter (usually of sounds):
The band moved on and the music faded away.

fall

fall back (intr) = withdraw, retreat (this is a deliberate action, quite different from **fall behind**, which is involuntary).
As the enemy advanced we fell back.

fall back on (tr) = use in the absence of something better:
We had to fall back on dried milk as fresh milk wasn't available.
He fell back on the old argument that if you educate women they won't be such good wives and mothers.

fall behind (intr) = slip into the rear through inability to keep up with the others, fail to keep up an agreed rate of payments:
At the beginning the whole party kept together but by the end of the day the women and weaker men had fallen behind.
He fell behind with his rent and the landlord began to become impatient.

fall in with someone's plans = accept them and agree to co-operate:
Tom to Harry (with whom he is arranging to share a flat): *I'll fall in with whatever you suggest as regards sharing expenses.*

fall in (intr) of troops etc. = get into line

fall out (intr) of troops etc. = leave the lines:
The troops fell in and were inspected. After the parade they fell out and went back to their barracks.

fall off (intr) = decrease (of numbers, attendance etc.):
Orders have been falling off lately; we must advertise more.
If the price of seats goes up much more theatre attendances will begin to fall off.

fall on (tr) = attack violently (the victim has normally no chance to

defend himself as the attackers are too strong. It is also sometimes used of hungry men who attack their food when they get it):
The wolves fell on the flock of sheep and killed them all.
The starving men fell on the food (devoured it).

fall out (intr) = quarrel:
When thieves fall out honest men get their own (proverb). (i.e. get back their property.)

fall through (intr) = fail to materialize (of plans):
My plans to go to Greece fell through because the journey turned out to be much more expensive than I had expected.

feed

be fed up (intr), **be fed up with** (tr) = be completely bored (slang):
I'm fed up with this wet weather.
I'm fed up with waiting; I'm going home.

feel

feel up to (tr) = feel strong enough (to do something):
I don't feel up to dealing with the matter now. I'll do it in the morning.
I don't feel up to it.

fill

fill in/up forms etc. = complete them:
I had to fill in ***three forms*** *to get my new passport (fill* ***three forms*** *in/fill* ***them*** *in).*

find

find out (tr) = discover as a result of conscious effort:
In the end I found out what was wrong with my hi-fi.
The dog found out the way to open the door/found it out.

find someone **out** = discover that he has been doing something wrong (this discovery is usually a surprise because the person has been trusted):
The cashier had been robbing the till for months before he was found out.

fix

fix up (tr) = arrange:
The club has already fixed up ***several matches*** *for next season (fixed* ***several matches*** *up/fixed* ***them*** *up).*

get

get about (intr) = circulate; move or travel in a general sense:
The news got about that he had won the first prize in the state lottery and everybody began asking him for money.
He is a semi-invalid now and can't get about as well as he used to.
get away (intr) = escape, be free to leave
Don't ask him how he is because if he starts talking about his health you'll never get away from him.
I hooked an enormous fish but it got away.
I had a lot to do in the office and didn't get away till eight.
get away with (tr) = perform some illegal or wrong act without being punished, usually without even being caught:
He began forging cheques and at first he got away with it but in the end he was caught and sent to prison.
get back (tr) = recover possession of:
*If you lend him a book he'll lend it to someone else and you'll never get **it** back (get back **your book**/get **your book** back).*
get back = reach home again:
We spent the whole day in the hills and didn't get back till dark.
get off (intr) = be acquitted or receive no punishment (compare with **get away with it,** which implies that the offender is not even caught):
He was tried for theft but got off because there wasn't sufficient evidence against him (was acquitted).
The boy had to appear before a magistrate but he got off (received no punishment) *as it was his first offence.*
get on (intr), **get on with** (tr)
a = make progress, be successful:
How is he getting on at school?
He is getting on very well with his English.
b = live, work etc., amicably with someone:
He is a pleasant friendly man who gets on well with nearly everybody.
How are you and Mr Pitt getting on?
get out (intr) = escape from, leave (an enclosed place):
Don't worry about the snake. I've put it in a cardboard box. It can't get out.
News of the Budget got out before it was officially announced.
I don't very often get out (out of the house) *because I have too much to do.*
Note that the imperative 'Get out', except when it means 'descend' (from a vehicle), is very rude.

get out of (tr) = free oneself from an obligation or habit:
I said that I'd help him. Now I don't want to but I can't get out of it (free myself from my promise).
He knows that he smokes too much but says that he can't get out of the habit.
Some people live abroad to get out of paying heavy taxes.

get over (tr) = recover from (illness, distress, or mental or physical weakness):
He is just getting over a bad heart attack.
I can't get over her leaving her husband like that (I haven't recovered from the surprise; I am astonished).
He used to be afraid of heights but he has got over that now.

get it over (the object is usually **it**, which normally represents something unpleasant) = deal with it and be finished with it:
If you have to go to the dentist why not go at once and get it over?
(Be careful not to confuse this with **get over it**, which is quite different.)

get round a person = coax him into letting you do what you want:
Girls can usually get round their fathers.

get round a difficulty/regulation = find some solution to it/evade it:
If we charge people for admission we will have to pay entertainment tax on our receipts; but we can get round this regulation by saying that we are charging not for admission but for refreshments. Money paid for refreshments is not taxed.

get through (tr or intr) = finish a piece of work, finish successfully:
He got through his exam all right (passed it).

get through (intr) = get into telephone communication:
I am trying to call London but I can't get through; I think all the lines are engaged.

get up (tr) = organize, arrange (usually an amateur entertainment or a charitable enterprise):
We got up ***a subscription*** *for his widow (got* ***a subscription*** *up).*
They got up ***a concert*** *in aid of cancer research (they got* ***it*** *up).*

get up (intr) = rise from bed, rise to one's feet, mount:
I get up at seven o'clock every morning.
(For **get** used to mean enter/leave vehicles, see **84** D.)

give

give something **away** = give it to someone (who need not be mentioned):
I'll give ***this old coat*** *away (give away* ***this old coat****/give* ***it*** *away).*

give someone **away** (object before **away**) = betray him:
He said that he was not an American but his accent gave him away (i.e. told us that he was an American).

give back (tr) = restore (a thing) to its owner:
*I must call at the library to give back **this book** (to give **this book** back/to give **it** back).*

give in (intr) = yield, cease to resist:
At first he wouldn't let her drive the car but she was so persuasive that he eventually gave in.

give out (intr) = become exhausted (of supplies etc.):
The champagne gave out long before the end of the reception.
His patience gave out and he slapped the child hard.

give out (tr)
a = announce verbally:
*They gave out **the names of the winners** (gave **the names** out/gave **them** out).*
b = distribute, issue:
*The teacher gave out **the books*** (i.e. gave ***one/some*** to each pupil).

give up (tr or intr) = abandon an attempt, cease trying to do something:
*I tried to climb the wall but after I had failed three times I gave up/gave up **the attempt**/gave **the attempt** up/gave **it** up.*
A really determined person never gives up/never gives up trying.

give up (tr) = abandon or discontinue a habit, sport, study, occupation:
Have you given up drinking whisky before breakfast?
*He gave up **cigarettes**/gave **them** up.*
He tried to learn Greek but soon got tired of it and gave it up.

give oneself **up** (object before **up**) = surrender:
I'm tired of being chased by the police; I'm going to give myself up.
He gave himself up to despair.

go

go ahead (intr) = proceed, continue, lead the way:
While she was away he went ahead with the work and got a lot done.
You go ahead and I'll follow; I'm not quite ready.

go away (intr) = leave, leave me, leave this place:
Are you going away for your holiday? No, I'm going to stay at home.
Please go away; I can't work unless I am alone.

go back (intr) = return, retire, retreat:
I have left that hotel and I'm never going back to it. It is a most uncomfortable place.

go back on (tr) = withdraw or break (a promise):
He went back on his promise to tell nobody about this (i.e. he told people about it, contrary to his promise).

go down (intr)

a = be received with approval (usually of an idea):
I suggested that she should look for a job but this suggestion did not go down at all well. She said that it was up to her relations to support her at home, now that she was a widow.

b = become less, be reduced (of wind, sea, weight, prices etc.):
During her illness her weight went down from 50 kilos to 40 kilos.
The wind went down and the sea became quite calm.

go for (tr) = attack:
The cat went for the dog and chased him out of the hall.

go in for (tr) = be especially interested in, practise; enter for a competition:
This restaurant goes in for vegetarian dishes (specializes in them).
She plays a lot of golf and goes in for all the competitions.

go into (tr) = investigate thoroughly:
'We shall have to go into this very carefully,' said the detective.

go off (intr)

a = explode (of ammunition or fireworks), be fired (of guns, usually accidentally):
As he was cleaning his gun it went off and killed him.

b = be successful (of social occasions):
The party went off very well (i.e. everyone enjoyed it).

c = start a journey, leave:
He went off in a great hurry.

go on (intr) = continue a journey:
Go on till you come to the cross-roads.

go on (intr), **go on with** (tr), **go on** + gerund = continue any action:
Please go on playing; I like it.
Go on with the treatment. It is doing you good.

go on + infinitive:
He began by describing the route and went on to tell us what the trip would probably cost (he continued [his speech] and told us etc.).

go out (intr)

a = leave the house:
She is always indoors; she doesn't go out enough.

b = join in social life, leave one's house for entertainments etc.
She is very pretty and goes out a lot.
c = disappear, be discontinued (of fashions):
Crinolines went out about the middle of the last century.
d = be extinguished (of lights, fires etc.):
The light went out and we were left in the dark.
go over (tr) = examine, study or repeat carefully:
He went over the plans again and discovered two very serious mistakes.

go round (intr)
a = suffice (for a number of people):
Will there be enough wine to go round?
b = go to his/her/your etc. house:
I said that I'd go round and see her during the weekend.
I think I'll go round tonight (i.e. go to her house).
go through (tr) = examine carefully (usually a number of things; **go through is** like **look through** but more thorough):
There is a mistake somewhere; we'll have to go through the accounts and see where it is.
The police went through their files, to see if they could find any fingerprints to match those that they had found on the handle of the weapon.

go through (tr or intr) = suffer, endure:
No one knows what I went through while I was waiting for the verdict (i.e. how much I suffered).
go through with (tr) = finish, bring to a conclusion (usually in the face of some opposition or difficulty):
He went through with his plan although all his friends advised him to abandon it.
go up (intr)
a = rise (of prices):
The price of strawberries went up towards the end of the season.
b = burst into flames (and be destroyed), explode (used of whole buildings, ships etc.):
When the fire reached the cargo of chemicals the whole ship went up (blew up).
Someone dropped a cigarette end into a can of petrol and the whole garage went up in flames.
go without (tr) = do without. (But it only applies to things. 'Go without a person' has only a literal meaning i.e. it means 'start or make a journey without him'.)

grow

grow out of (tr) = abandon, on becoming older, a childish (and often bad) habit:
He used to tell a lot of lies as a young boy but he grew out of that later on.

grow up (intr)

a = become adult:
'What are you going to do when you grow up?' I asked. 'I'm going to be a pop star,' said the boy.

b = develop (of customs):
The custom of going away for one's holiday has grown up during the last thirty years.

hand

hand down (tr) = bequeath or pass on (traditions/information/possessions):
This legend has been handed down from father to son.

hand in (tr) = give by hand (to someone who need not be mentioned because the person spoken to knows already):
*I handed in **my resignation*** (i.e. gave it to my employer).
*Someone handed **this parcel** in this morning/handed **it** in.*

hand out (tr) = distribute:
*He was standing at the door of the theatre handing out **leaflets** (handing **leaflets** out/handing **them** out).*

hand over (tr or intr) = surrender authority or responsibility to another:
*The outgoing Minister handed over **his department** to his successor (handed **his department** over/handed **it** over).*

hand round (tr) = give or show to each person present:
*The hostess handed round **coffee** and **cakes** (handed **them** round).*

hang

hang about/around (tr or intr) = loiter or wait (near):
He hung about the entrance all day, hoping for a chance to speak to the director.

hang back (intr) = show unwillingness to act:
Everyone approved of the scheme but when we asked for volunteers they all hung back.

hang on to (tr) = retain, keep in one's possession (colloquial):
I'd hang on to that old coat if I were you. It might be useful.

hold

hold off (intr) = keep at a distance, stay away (used of rain):
The rain fortunately held off till after the school sports day.

hold on (intr) = wait (especially on the telephone):
Yes, Mr Pitt is in. If you hold on for a moment I'll get him for you.

hold on/out (intr) = persist in spite of, endure hardship or danger:
The survivors on the rock signalled that they were short of water but could hold out for another day.
The enemy besieged the town but it held out for six weeks.

hold up (tr)
a = stop by threats or violence (often in order to rob):
The terrorists held up the train and kept the passengers as hostages.
Masked men held up **the cashier** *and robbed the bank (held* **him** *up).*
b = stop, delay (especially used in the passive):
The bus was held up because a tree had fallen across the road.

join

join up (intr) = enlist in one of the armed services:
When war was declared he joined up at once.

jump

jump at (tr) = accept with enthusiasm (an offer or opportunity):
He was offered a place in the Himalayan expedition and jumped at the chance.

keep

keep somebody **back** (object before **back**) = restrain, hinder, prevent from advancing:
Frequent illnesses kept him back (i.e. prevented him from making normal progress).

keep down (tr) = repress, control:
What is the best way to keep down **rats***? (keep* **them** *down).*
Try to remember to turn off the light when you leave the room. I am trying to keep down **expenses***/keep* **expenses** *down.*

keep in a schoolboy = oblige him to remain at school after school hours as a punishment:
The teacher kept Tom in/kept him in because he had been inattentive.

keep off (tr or intr) = refrain from walking on, or from coming too close:
'Keep off the grass' (park notice).

keep on (often followed by gerund) = continue:
I wanted to explain but he kept on talking and didn't give me a chance to say anything.

keep out (tr) = prevent from entering:
My shoes are very old and don't keep out the ***water*** *(keep* ***the water*** *out/keep* ***it*** *out).*

keep out (intr) = stay outside:
'Private. Keep out' (notice on door).

keep up (tr) = maintain (an effort):
He began walking at four miles an hour but he couldn't keep up ***that speed*** *and soon began to walk more slowly (he couldn't keep* ***it*** *up).*
It is difficult to keep up a conversation with someone who only says 'Yes' and 'No'.

keep up (intr), **keep up with** (tr) = remain abreast of someone who is advancing; advance at the same pace as:
A runner can't keep up with a cyclist.
The work that the class is doing is too difficult for me. I won't be able to keep up (or *to keep up with them).*
It is impossible to keep up with the news unless you read the newspapers.

knock

knock off (tr or intr) = stop work for the day (colloquial):
English workmen usually knock off at 5.30 or 6.00 p.m.
We knock off work in time for tea.

knock out (tr) = hit someone so hard that he falls unconscious:
In the finals of the boxing championship he knocked out ***his opponent****, who was carried out of the ring (knocked* ***his opponent*** *out/knocked* ***him*** *out).*

lay

lay in (tr) = provide oneself with a sufficient quantity (of stores etc.) to last for some time:
She expected a shortage of dried fruit so she laid in a large supply.

lay out (tr) = plan gardens, building sites etc.:
Le Nôtre laid out ***the gardens*** *at Versailles (laid* ***the gardens*** *out/laid* ***them*** *out).*

lay up (tr) = store carefully till needed again (used of ships, cars etc.):
Before he went to Brazil for a year, he laid up ***his car****, as he didn't want to sell it (laid* ***it*** *up).*

be laid up (of a person) = be confined to bed through illness:
She was laid up for weeks with a slipped disk.

lead

lead up to (tr) = prepare the way for, introduce (figuratively):
He wanted to borrow my binoculars, but he didn't say so at once. He led up to the subject by talking about his holidays.

leave

leave off (usually intr) = stop (doing something):
He was playing his trumpet but I told him to leave off because the neighbours were complaining about the noise.
leave out (tr) = omit:
We'll sing our School Song leaving out the last ten verses.
They gave each competitor a number; but they left out ***No. 13*** *as no one wanted to have it (left* ***No. 13*** *out/left* ***it*** *out).*

let

let down (tr) = lower:
When she lets ***her hair*** *down it reaches her waist (lets down* ***her hair****/lets* ***it*** *down).*
You can let a coat down (i.e. lengthen it) *by using the hem.*
let someone **down** (object before **down**) = disappoint him by failing to act as well as expected, or by failing to fulfil an agreement:
I promised him that you would work well. Why did you let me down by doing so little?
He said he'd come to help me; but he let me down. He never turned up.
let in (tr) = allow to enter, admit:
They let in the ***ticket-holders*** *(let the* ***ticket-holders*** *in/let* ***them*** *in).*
If you mention my name to the door-keeper he will let you in.
let someone **off** (object before **off**) = refrain from punishing:
I thought that the magistrate was going to fine me, but he let me off (compare with **get off**).
let out (tr)
a = make wider (of clothes):
That boy is getting fatter. You'll have to let out ***his clothes*** *(let* ***his clothes*** *out/let* ***them*** *out).*
b = allow to leave, release:
He opened the door and let out ***the dog*** *(let* ***the dog*** *out/let* ***it*** *out).*

listen

listen in (intr) = listen to the radio:
I only listen in if there is a good concert.

live

live down a bad reputation = live in such a manner that people will forget it:
He has never quite been able to live down a reputation for drinking too much which he got when he was a young man (live ***it*** *down).*

live in (intr) = live in one's place of work (chiefly used of domestic servants):
ADVERTISEMENT: *Cook wanted. £80 a week. Live in.*

live on (tr) = use as staple food:
It is said that for a certain period of his life Byron lived on vinegar and potatoes in order to keep thin.

live up to (tr) = maintain a certain standard moral, economic or behavioural:
He had high ideals and tried to live up to them (i.e. he tried to act in accordance with his ideals).

lock

lock up a house (tr or intr; usually intr) = lock all doors:
People usually lock up before they go to bed at night.

lock up a person or thing = put in a locked place i.e. box, safe, prison:
She locked up ***her diamonds*** *every night (locked* ***her diamonds*** *up/locked* ***them*** *up).*

look

look after (tr) = take care of:
Will you look after my parrot when I am away?

look ahead (intr) = consider the future so as to make provision for it:
Everyone should look ahead and save a little money each year for when he retires.

look at (tr) = regard:
He looked at the clock and said, 'It is midnight.'

look back (intr), **look back on** (tr) = consider the past:
Looking back, I don't suppose we are any worse now than people were a hundred years ago.
Perhaps some day it will be pleasant to look back on these things.

look back/round (intr) = look behind (literally):
Don't look round now, but the woman behind us is wearing the most extraordinary clothes.

look for (tr) = search for, seek:
I have lost my watch. Will you help me to look for it?

look out for (tr) = keep one's eyes open so as to see something (usually fairly conspicuous) if it presents itself:
I am going to the party too, so look out for me.

look out (intr) = be watchful, beware:
(to someone just about to cross the road) *'Look out! There's a lorry coming!'*

look forward to (tr) = expect with pleasure (often used with gerund):
I am looking forward to her arrival/to seeing her.

look in (intr) = pay a short (often unannounced) visit (= call in):
I'll look in this evening to see how she is.

look into (tr) = investigate:
There is a mystery about his death and the police are looking into it.

look on . . . as (tr) = consider:
Most people look on a television set as an essential piece of furniture.
These children seem to look on their teachers as their enemies.

look on (intr) = be a spectator only, not a participator:
Two men were fighting. The rest were looking on.

look on (tr), **look out on** (tr) (used of windows and houses) = be facing:
His house looks (out) on to the sea (i.e. from his house you can see the sea).

look over (tr) = inspect critically, read again, revise quickly (**look over** is similar to **go over** but less thorough):
Look over what you've written before handing it to the examiner.
I'm going to look over a house that I'm thinking of buying.

look through (tr) = examine a number of things, often in order to select some of them; turn over the pages of a book or newspaper, looking for information:
Look through your old clothes and see if you have anything to give away.
Look through these photographs and try to pick out the man you saw.
He looked through the books and decided that he wouldn't like them.

look through someone = look at him without appearing to see him, as a deliberate act of rudeness:
She has to be polite to me in the office but when we meet outside she always looks through me.

look up an address/a name/word/train time/telephone number etc. = look for it in the appropriate book or paper, i.e. address book/dictionary/timetable/directory etc.:
If you don't know the meaning of ***the word*** *look* ***it*** *up (look up* ***the word****/look* ***the word*** *up).*
I must look up the time of your train (look for it in the timetable).

look somebody **up** can mean **visit**. The person visited usually lives at some distance and is not seen very often. **look up** is therefore different from **look in**, which implies that the person visited lives quite close:
Any time you come to London do look me up (come and see me).
I haven't seen Tom for ages. I must find out where he lives and look ***him*** *up (look* ***Tom*** *up/look up* ***Tom****).*

look up (intr) = improve (the subject is usually *things/business/world affairs/the weather,* i.e. nothing very definite):
Business has been very bad lately but things are beginning to look up now.

look someone **up and down** = look at him contemptuously, letting your eyes wander from his head to his feet and back again:
The policeman looked the drunk man up and down very deliberately before replying to his question.

look up to (tr) = respect:
Schoolboys usually look up to great athletes.

look down on (tr) = despise:
Small boys usually look down on little girls and refuse to play with them.
She thinks her neighbours look down on her a bit because she's never been abroad.

make

make for (tr) = travel towards:
The escaped prisoner was making for the coast.

make off (intr) = run away (used of thieves etc.):
The boys made off when they saw the policemen.

make out (tr)

a = discover the meaning of, understand, see, hear etc. clearly:
I can't make out ***the address****, he has written it so badly (make* ***the address*** *out/make* ***it*** *out).*
Can you hear what the man with the loud-hailer is saying? I can't make it out at all.
I can't make out why he isn't here yet.

b = state (probably falsely):
He made out that he was a student looking for a job. We later learnt that this wasn't true at all.
The English climate isn't so bad as some English people like to make out.

c = write a cheque:
CUSTOMER: *Who shall I make it out to?*
SHOPKEEPER: *Make it out to Jones and Company.*

make up one's mind = come to a decision:
In the end he made up his mind to go by train.

make up a quarrel/make it up = end it:
*Isn't it time you and Ann made up **your quarrel**/made **it** up?*

make up a story/excuse/explanation = invent it:
I don't believe your story at all. I think you are just making it up.

make up (tr or intr) = use cosmetics:
*Most women make up/make up **their faces**/make **their faces** up/make **them** up.*
Actors have to be made up before they appear on the stage.

make up (tr) = put together, compound, compose:
*Take this prescription to the chemist's. They will make it up for you there (make up **the prescription**/make **the prescription** up).*
NOTICE (in tailor's window): *Customers' own materials made up.*
The audience was made up of very young children.

make up for (tr) = compensate for (the object is very often it):
You'll have to work very hard today to make up for the time you wasted yesterday or *to make up for being late yesterday.*
We aren't allowed to drink when we are in training but we intend to make up for it after the race is over (i.e. to drink more than usual then).

miss

miss out (tr) = leave out ('leave out' is more usual).

mix

mix up (tr) = confuse:
*He mixed up **the addresses** so that no one got the right letters/mixed **them** up.*

be/get mixed up with = be involved (usually with some rather disreputable person or business):
I don't want to get mixed up with any illegal organization.

move

move in (intr) = move self and possessions into new house, flat, rooms etc.
move out (intr) = leave house/flat etc., with one's possessions, vacate accommodation:
I have found a new flat. The present tenant is moving out this weekend and I am moving in on Wednesday.
move on or **up** (intr) = advance, go higher:
Normally in schools boys move up every year.

order

order somebody **about** (object before **about**) = give him a lot of orders (often regardless of his convenience or feelings):
He is a retired admiral and still has the habit of ordering people about.

pay

pay back (tr), **pay someone back** (tr or intr) = repay:
*I must pay back **the money** that I borrowed (pay **the money** back/pay **it** back).*
*I must pay back **Mr Pitt** (pay **Mr Pitt** back/pay **him** back).*
*I must pay Mr Pitt back **the money** he lent me.*
*I must pay him back **the money**. I must pay **it** back to him.*
pay someone **back/out** = revenge oneself:
I'll pay you back for this (i.e. for the harm you have done me).
pay up (intr) = pay money owed in full:
Unless you pay up I shall tell my solicitor to write to you.

pick

pick out (tr) = choose, select, distinguish from a group:
*Here are six diamonds. Pick out **the one you like best** (pick **it** out).*
*In an identity parade the witness has to try to pick out **the criminal** from a group of about eight men (pick **the criminal** out/pick **him** out).*
*I know that you are in this photograph but I can't pick **you** out.*
pick up (tr)
a = raise or lift a person or thing, usually from the ground or from a table or chair:
*He picked up **the child** and carried him into the house/picked **the child** up.*
*She scatters toys all over the floor and I have to pick **them** up.*

b = call for, take with one (in a vehicle):
I won't have time to come to your house but I could pick you up at the end of your road.
The coach stops at the principal hotels to pick up ***tourists****, but only if they arrange this in advance (pick* ***tourists*** *up/pick* ***them*** *up).*
The crew of the wrecked yacht were picked up by helicopter.

c = receive (by chance) wireless signals:
Their S.O.S. was picked up by another ship, which informed the lifeboat headquarters.

d = acquire cheaply, learn without effort:
Sometimes you pick up wonderful bargains in these markets.
Children usually pick up foreign languages very quickly.

point

point out (tr) = indicate, show:
As we drove through the city the guide pointed out ***the most important buildings*** *(pointed* ***the buildings*** *out/pointed* ***them*** *out).*

pull

pull down (tr) = demolish (used of buildings):
Everywhere elegant old ***buildings*** *are being pulled down and mediocre modern erections are being put up. (pull down* ***houses****/pull* ***them*** *down.)*

pull off (tr) = succeed (the object is normally *it*):
Much to our surprise he pulled off ***the deal****/pulled* ***it*** *off (sold the goods/got the contract).*

pull through (intr or tr) = recover from illness/cause someone to recover:
We thought that she was going to die but her own will power pulled her through (tr).
He is very ill but he'll pull through if we look after him carefully (intr).

pull up (intr) = stop (of vehicles):
A lay-by is a space at the side of a main road, where drivers can pull up if they want a rest.

put

put aside/by (tr) = save for future use (usually money). **put aside** often implies that the money is being saved for a certain purpose:
He puts aside ***£10 a month*** *to pay for his summer holiday* (puts **it** aside).
Don't spend all your salary. Try to put ***something*** *by each month.*

put away (tr) = put tidily out of sight (usually in drawers, cupboards etc.):
Put ***your toys*** *away, childen; it's bedtime (put away* ***the toys****/put* ***them*** *away).*

put something **back** = replace it where you found it/where it belongs:
When you've finished with the book put it back on the shelf.

put back a clock/watch = retard the hands: *put the clock back* is sometimes used figuratively to mean *return to the customs of the past*:
MOTHER: *Your father and I will arrange a marriage for you when the time comes.*
DAUGHTER: *You're trying to put* ***the clock*** *back. Parents don't arrange marriages these days! (put back* ***the clock****/put* ***it*** *back).*

put down (tr)
a = the opposite of **pick up**:
He picked up ***the saucepan*** *and put it down at once because the handle was almost red-hot (put* ***the saucepan*** *down/put* ***it*** *down).*
b = crush rebellions, movements:
Troops were used to put down ***the rebellion*** *(put* ***the rebellion*** *down/put* ***it*** *down).*
c = write:
Put down ***his phone number*** *before you forget it (put* ***the number*** *down/put* ***it*** *down).*
CUSTOMER (to shop assistant): *I'll take that one. Please put it down to me/to my account* (enter it in my account).

put something **down to** (tr) = attribute it to:
The children wouldn't answer him, but he wasn't annoyed as he put it down to shyness.
She hasn't been well since she came to this country; I put it down to the climate.

put forward a suggestion/proposal etc. = offer it for consideration:
The older members of the committee are inclined to veto any ***suggestions*** *put forward by the younger ones (put* ***a suggestion*** *forward/put* ***it*** *forward).*

put forward/on clocks and watches = advance the hands. **put forward** is the opposite of **put back**:
In March people in England put ***their clocks*** *forward/on an hour. When summer time ends they put them back an hour.*

put in a claim = make a claim:
He put in a claim for compensation because he had lost his luggage in the train crash.

put in for a job/a post = apply for it:
They are looking for a lecturer in geography. Why don't you put in for it?

put in (intr) used of ships = call (at a port):
Ships on their way to Australia via the Suez Canal used to put in at Genoa/put in here.

put off an action = postpone it:
Some people put off making their wills till it is too late.
I'll put off **my visit** *to Scotland till the weather is warmer (put* **my visit** *off/put* **it** *off).*

put a person **off**

a = tell him to postpone his visit to you:
I had invited some guests to dinner but I had to put them off because a power cut prevented me from cooking anything.

b = repel, deter him:
I wanted to see the exhibition but the queue put me off.
Many people who want to come to England are put off by the stories they hear about English weather.

put on clothes/glasses/jewellery = dress oneself etc. The opposite is **take off**:
He put on **a black coat** *so that he would be inconspicuous (put* **a coat** *on/put* **it** *on).*
She put on her glasses and took the letter from my hand.

put on an expression = assume it:
He put on an air of indifference, which didn't deceive anybody for a moment.

put on a play = produce/perform it:
The students usually put on a play at the end of the year.

put on a light/gas or electric fire/radio = switch it on:
Put on **the light** *(put the* **light** *on/put* **it** *on).*

put out any kind of light or fire = extinguish it:
Put out **that light**/*(put* **the light** *out/put* **it** *out).*

put someone **out** (inconvenience him):
He is very selfish. He wouldn't put himself out for anyone.

be put out = be annoyed:
She was very put out when I said that her new summer dress didn't suit her.

put up (tr)

a = erect (a building, monument, statue etc.):
He put up **a shed** *in the garden to keep tools in (he put* **a shed** *up/put* **it** *up).*

b = raise (prices):
*When the importation of foreign tomatoes was forbidden, home growers put up **their prices** (they put **their prices** up/put **them** up).*

put someone **up** (object usually before **up**) = give him temporary hospitality:
If you come to Paris I will put you up. You needn't look for an hotel.

put someone **up to** something (usually some trick) = give him the idea of doing it/tell him how to do it:
He couldn't have thought of that trick by himself. Someone must have put him up to it.

put up with (tr) = bear patiently:
We had to put up with a lot of noise when the children were at home.

ring

ring up (tr or intr) = telephone:
*I rang up **the theatre** to book seats for tonight. (I rang **the theatre** up/rang **them** up.)*
If you can't come ring up and let me know.

ring off (intr) = end a telephone call by putting down the receiver:
He rang off before I could ask his name.

round

round up (tr) = drive or bring together (people or animals):
The sheepdog rounded up the sheep (collected them into a group) *and drove them through the gate.*
*On the day after the riots the police rounded up **all suspects**/rounded **them** up* (arrested them).

rub

rub out (tr) = erase pencil or ink marks with an india-rubber:
*The child wrote down the wrong word and then rubbed **it** out. (He rubbed **the word** out/rubbed out **the word**.)*

rub up (tr) = revise one's knowledge of a subject:
*I am going to France next month; I must rub up **my French**/rub **it** up.*

run

run after (tr) = pursue (see example below).

run away (intr) = flee, desert (one's home/school etc.), elope:
The thief ran away and the policeman ran after him.
He ran away from home and got a job as a shelf-filler in a supermarket.

run away with (tr) = become uncontrollable (of emotions), gallop off out of rider's control (of horses):
My tongue ran away with me and I said things that I afterwards regretted.
His horse ran away with him and he had a bad fall.

run away with the idea = accept an idea too hastily:
Don't run away with the idea that I am unsociable; I just haven't time to go out much.

run down (tr) = disparage, speak ill of:
*He is always running down **his neighbours** (running **his neighbours** down/running **them** down).*

run down (intr) = become unwound/discharged (of clocks/batteries etc.):
This torch is useless; the battery has run down.

be run down (intr) = be in poor health after illness, overwork etc.:
He is still run down after his illness and unfit for work.

run in (tr) = drive slowly initially to avoid straining engine (necessary with new or reconditioned engines):
*I can't go more than 50 kilometres an hour as this is a new car and I am still running **it** in (I am running in a **new car**/running a **new car** in).*
Notice on the back window of a new car: 'Running in. Please pass.'

run into (tr) = collide with (of vehicles):
The car skidded and ran into a lamp-post (= struck the lamp-post).

run into/across someone = meet him accidentally:
I ran into my cousin in Harrods recently (I met him).

run out of (tr) = have none left, having consumed all the supply:
I have run out of milk. Put some lemon in your tea instead.

run over (tr) = drive over accidentally (in a vehicle):
The drunk man stepped into the road right in front of the oncoming car. The driver couldn't stop in time and ran over him.

run over (tr or intr) = overflow:
He turned on both taps full and left the bathroom. When he came back he found that the water was running over (or *running over the edge of the bath*).

run over/through (tr) = rehearse, check or revise quickly:
We've got a few minutes before the train goes, so I'll just run through your instructions again.

run through (tr) = consume extravagantly, waste (used of supplies or money):
I laid in a good stock of provisions but he ran through it all in a couple of weeks.

run up clothes = make them quickly:
Do you like this blouse? I ran it up myself this afternoon.

run up bills = incur them and increase them by continuing to buy things and put them down to one's account:
Her husband said that she must pay for things at once and not run up bills.

run up against difficulties/opposition = encounter them/it:
If he tries to change the rules of the club he will run up against a lot of opposition.

see

see about (tr) = make inquiries or arrangements:
I must see about getting a room ready for him.

see somebody **off** = accompany an intending traveller to his train/boat/plane etc.:
The station was crowded with boys going back to school and parents who were seeing them off.

see somebody **out** = accompany a departing guest to the door of the house:
When guests leave the host usually sees them out.
Don't bother to come to the door with me. I can see myself out.

see over a house/a building = go into every room, examine it, often with a view to buying or renting (this combination is chiefly used in the infinitive):
I'm definitely interested in the house. I'd like to see over it as soon as possible.

see through (tr) = discover a hidden attempt to deceive:
She pretended that she loved him but he saw through her, and realized that she was only after his money. (He wasn't taken in by her/by her pretence. For **take in** see page 334.)

see to (tr) = make arrangements, put right, repair:
If you can provide the wine I'll see to the food.
That electric fire isn't safe. You should have it seen to.

sell

sell off (tr) = sell cheaply (what is left of a stock):
ASSISTANT: *This line is being discontinued so we are selling off **the remainder** of our stock; that's why they are so cheap (sell **the rest** off/sell **it** off).*

sell out (intr) = sell all that you have of a certain type of article:
When all the seats for a certain performance have been booked, theatres put a notice saying 'Sold out' outside the booking office.

send

be sent down (intr) = be expelled from a university for misconduct:
He behaved so badly in college that he was sent down and never got his degree.

send for (tr) = summon (the person summoned may be in the building already):
One of our water pipes has burst. We must send for the plumber.
The director sent for me and asked for an explanation.

send in (tr) = send to someone (who need not be mentioned because the person spoken to knows already):
You must send in your ***application*** *for the job before Friday* (send it to the authority concerned) *(send* ***your application*** *in/send* ***it*** *in).*

send on (tr) = forward, send after a person:
If any letters come for you after you have gone I will send ***them*** *on (I'll send on* ***your letters****/send* ***your letters*** *on).*

set

set in (intr) = begin (a period, usually unpleasant):
Winter has set in early this year.

set off (tr) = start (a series of events):
That strike set off ***a series of strikes*** *throughout the country (set* ***them*** *off).*

set off/out (intr) = start a journey:
They set out/off at six and hoped to arrive before dark.
'for' is used when the destination is mentioned:
They set out/off for Rome.

set out + infinitive (often **show/prove/explain** or some similar verb) = begin this undertaking, aim:
In this book the author sets out to prove that the inhabitants of the islands came from South America.

set up (tr) = achieve, establish (a record):
He set up ***a new record*** *when he ran a mile in under four minutes (he set* ***a new record*** *up/set* ***it*** *up).*

set up (intr) = start a new business:
When he married he left his father's shop and set up on his own (i.e. opened his own shop).

settle

settle down (intr) = become accustomed to, and contented in, a new place, job etc.:
He was unhappy when he first went to school but he soon settled down and liked it very much.

settle up (intr) = pay money owed:
Tell me what I owe you at the end of the week and I'll settle up with you then.

shout

shout down (tr) = make a loud noise to prevent a speaker from being heard:
Tom tried to make a speech defending himself but the crowd wouldn't listen to his explanation and shouted ***him*** *down (shouted* ***Tom*** *down).*
The moderate speakers were shouted down.

show

show off (tr or intr) = display (skill, knowledge etc.) purely in order to win notice or applause:
Although Jules speaks English perfectly, my cousin spoke French to him all the time just to show off (i.e. to impress us with her knowledge of French).
He is always picking up very heavy things just to show off ***his strength*** *(show* ***it*** *off).*

shut

shut down (tr or intr) = close down (see p. 305).

sit

sit back (intr) = relax, take no action, do no more work:
I have worked hard all my life and now I'm going to sit back and watch other people working.
sit out (tr or intr) = remain seated with one's partner instead of dancing:
I'm quite tired; let's sit ***this one*** *out (sit out* ***this dance****).*
sit up (intr) = stay out of bed till later than usual (usually reading, working, or waiting for someone):
I was very worried when he didn't come in and I sat up till 3 a.m. waiting for him.
She sat up all night with the sick child.

stand

stand by someone (tr) = continue to support and help him:
No matter what happens I'll stand by you, so don't be afraid.
stand for (tr) = represent:
The symbol 'x' usually stands for the unknown quantity in mathematics.

stand for Parliament = be a candidate for Parliament, offer yourself for election:
Mr Pitt stood for Parliament five years ago but he wasn't elected.
stand up for (tr) = defend verbally:
His father blamed him, but his mother stood up for him and said that he had acted sensibly.
stand up to (tr) = resist, defend oneself against (a person or force):
This type of building stands up to the gales very well.
stand out (intr) = be conspicuous, be easily seen:
She stood out from the crowd because of her height and her flaming red hair.

stay

stay up (intr) = remain out of bed till later than usual ('stay up' is practically the same as 'sit up', the only difference being that 'sit up' usually implies work, study, or waiting, while 'stay up' may be for pleasure only):
Children never want to go to bed at the proper time; they always want to stay up late.

step

step up (tr) = increase rate of, increase speed of (this usually refers to industrial production):
This new machine will step up production (step ***it*** *up).*

take

be taken aback (intr) = be surprised and disconcerted:
When she told me that she was going to ride the horse herself in the race I was completely taken aback and at first couldn't think of anything to say.
take after (tr) = resemble (one's parents/grandparents etc.):
He takes after his grandmother; she had red hair too.
My great-grandfather was terribly forgetful and I take after him; I can never remember anything.
take back (tr) = withdraw (remarks, accusations etc.):
I blamed him bitterly at first but later, when I heard the whole story, I realized that he had been right and I went to him and took back ***my remarks*** *(took* ***them*** *back).*
take down (tr) = write, usually from dictation:
He read out the names and his secretary took ***them*** *down (she took down* ***the names****/took* ***the names*** *down).*

take for (tr) = attribute wrong identity or qualities to someone:
I took him for his brother. They are extremely alike.
Do you take me for a fool?

take in (tr)
a = deceive:
At first he took us in by his stories and we tried to help him; but later we learnt that his stories were all lies.
b = receive as guests/lodgers:
When our car broke down I knocked on the door of the nearest house. The owner very kindly took ***us*** *in and gave us a bed for the night.*
People who live by the sea often take in ***paying guests*** *during the summer (take* ***paying guests*** *in/take* ***them*** *in).*
c = understand, receive into the mind:
I was thinking of something else while she was speaking and I didn't really take in ***what she was saying.***
I couldn't take in ***the lecture*** *at all. It was too difficult for me (I couldn't take* ***it*** *in).*
d = make less wide (of clothes):
I'm getting much thinner; I'll have to take in ***my clothes*** *(take* ***my clothes*** *in/take* ***them*** *in).*

take off (tr) = remove (when used of clothing 'take off' is the opposite of 'put on'):
He took off his ***coat*** *when he entered the house and put it on again when he went out. (He took* ***his coat*** *off/took* ***it*** *off.)*

take off (intr) = leave the ground (of aeroplanes):
There is often a spectators' balcony at airports, where people can watch the planes taking off and landing.

take on (tr)
a = undertake work:
She wants someone to look after her children. I shouldn't care to take on ***the job****. They are terribly spoilt. (take* ***the job*** *on/take* ***it*** *on.)*
b = accept as an opponent:
I'll take ***you*** *on at table tennis (I'll play against you).*
I took on ***Mr Pitt*** *at draughts (took* ***Mr Pitt*** *on/took* ***him*** *on).*

take out (tr) = remove, extract:
Petrol will take out ***that stain*** *(take* ***the stain*** *out/take* ***it*** *out).*
The dentist took out two of her teeth.

take somebody **out** = entertain them (usually at some public place):
Her small boy is at a boarding school quite near here. I take him out every month (and give him a meal in a restaurant).

take over (tr or intr) = assume responsibility for, or control of, in succession to somebody else:
We stop work at ten o'clock and the night shift takes over until the following morning.
Miss Smith is leaving to get married and Miss Jones will be taking over the class/Miss Jones will be taking over from Miss Smith (see **hand over**).

take to (tr)

a = begin a habit. There is usually the impression that the speaker thinks this habit bad or foolish, though this is not necessarily always the case. It is often used with the gerund:
He took to drink (began drinking too much).
He took to borrowing money from the petty cash.

b = find likeable or agreeable particularly at first meeting:
I was introduced to the new headmistress yesterday. I can't say I took to her.
He went to sea (became a sailor) *and took to the life like a duck to water.*

c = seek refuge/safety in:
When they saw that the ship was sinking the crew took to the boats.
After the failure of the coup many of the rebels took to the hills and became guerillas.

take up (tr)

a = begin a hobby, sport or kind of study (there is no feeling of criticism here):
*He took up **golf** and became very keen on it (took **it** up).*

b = occupy (a position of time or space):
He has a very small room and most of the space is taken up by a grand piano.
A lot of an MP's time is taken up with answering letters from his constituents.

talk

talk over (tr) = discuss:
*Talk **it** over with your wife and give me your answer tomorrow (talk over **my suggestion**/talk **my suggestion** over).*

think

think over (tr) = consider:
*I can't decide straight away but I'll think over **your idea** and let **you** know what I decide (I'll think **your idea** over/think **it** over).*

throw

throw away/out (tr) = jettison (rubbish etc.):
Throw away ***those old shoes.*** *Nobody could wear them now. (Throw* ***the shoes*** *away/throw* ***them*** *away.)*

throw up (tr) = abandon suddenly (some work or plan):
He suddenly got tired of the job and threw ***it*** *up (he threw up* ***the job****/threw* ***the job*** *up).*

tie

tie someone **up** = bind his hands and feet so that he cannot move:
The thieves tied up ***the night watchman*** *before opening the safe (they tied* ***the man*** *up/tied* ***him*** *up).*

try

try on (tr) = put on (an article of clothing) to see if it fits:
CUSTOMER IN DRESS SHOP: *I like this dress, could I try* ***it*** *on? (could I try* ***this dress*** *on/try on* ***this dress****?)*

try out (tr) = test:
We won't know how the plan works till we have tried ***it*** *out.*
They are trying out ***new ways of preventing noise in hospitals*** *(trying* ***them*** *out).*

turn

turn away (tr) = refuse admittance to:
The man at the door turned away ***anybody who hadn't an invitation card*** *(turned* ***them*** *away).*

turn down (tr) = refuse, reject an offer, application, applicant:
I applied for the job but they turned ***me*** *down/turned down* ***my application*** *because I didn't know German.*
He was offered £500 for the picture but he turned ***it*** *down (turned down* ***the offer****/turned* ***the offer*** *down).*

turn in (intr) = go to bed (used chiefly by sailors/campers etc.):
The campers usually turned in as soon as it got dark.
The captain turned in, not realizing that the icebergs were so close.

turn into (tr) = convert into:
I am going to turn my garage into a playroom for the children.
She turned the silver candlestick into an electric lamp.

turn on (tr) (stress on **turn**) = attack suddenly (the attacker is normally a friend or a hitherto friendly animal):
The tigress turned on the trainer and struck him to the ground.

turn on/off (tr) = switch on/off (lights, gas or electric fires, radios, taps etc.).

turn up/down (tr) = increase/decrease the pressure, force, volume (of gas or oil, lights, fires, or of radios):
Turn up the gas; it is much too low. Vegetables should be cooked quickly.
I wish the people in the next flat would turn down ***their radio.*** *You can hear every word (turn* ***the sound*** *down)turn* ***it*** *down).*
turn out (tr)
a = produce:
That creamery turns out ***two hundred tons of butter*** *a week (turns* ***it*** *out).*
b = empty, evict:
1 turn a person out = evict him from his house/flat/room:
At one time if tenants didn't pay their rent, the landlord could turn them out.
2 turn out one's pockets/handbags/drawers etc. = empty them, usually when looking for something:
'Turn out your pockets,' said the detective.
3 turn out a room usually means clean it thoroughly, first putting the furniture outside:
I try to turn out one room every month if I have time.
turn out (intr)
a = assemble, come out into the street (usually in order to welcome somebody):
The whole town turned out to welcome the winning football team when they came back with the Cup.
b = develop:
I've never made Yorkshire pudding before so I am not quite sure how it is going to turn out.
Marriages arranged by marriage bureaux frequently turn out very well.
c = be revealed. Notice the two possible constructions: *it turned out that . . .* and: *he turned out to be . . .*:
He told her that he was a bachelor but it turned out that he was married with six children (she learnt this later).
Our car broke down half way through the journey but the hiker we had picked up turned out to be an expert mechanic and was able to put things right.
Note the difference between **turn out** and **come out**. With **turn out** the fact revealed is always mentioned and there is no implication that the facts are discreditable. With **come out** we are told only that certain facts (usually discreditable) are revealed; we are not told what these facts are.

turn over (tr) = turn something so that the side previously underneath is exposed:
He turned over ***the stone****/turned* ***the stone*** *over/turned* ***it*** *over.*
The initials 'P.T.O.' at the bottom of a page mean 'Please turn over'.
'Turn over a new leaf' (begin again, meaning to do better).

turn over (intr)

a = turn upside down, upset, capsize (used of vehicles or boats):
The car struck the wall and turned over.
The canoe turned over, throwing the boys into the water.

b = (of people) change position so as to lie on the other side:
It is difficult to turn over in a hammock.
When his alarm went off he just turned over and went to sleep again.

turn up (intr) = arrive, appear (usually from the point of view of someone waiting or searching):
We arranged to meet at the station but she didn't turn up.
Don't bother to look for my umbrella; it will turn up some day.

wait

wait on (tr) = attend, serve (at home or in a restaurant):
He expected his wife to wait on him hand and foot.
The man who was waiting on us seemed very inexperienced; he got all our orders mixed up.

wash

wash up (tr or intr) = wash the plates etc., after a meal:
When we have dinner very late we don't wash up till the next morning (wash up ***the dishes****/wash* ***them*** *up).*

watch

watch out (intr) = look out.

watch out for (tr) = look out for (see p. 321).

wear

wear away (intr) = gradually reduce; make smooth or flat; hollow out (used mostly of wood or stone. The subject is usually the weather, or people who walk on, or touch the stone etc.):
It is almost impossible to read the inscription on the monument as most of the letters have been worn away (by the weather).

wear off (intr) = disappear gradually (can be used literally but is chiefly used for mental or physical feelings):
These glasses may seem uncomfortable at first but that feeling will soon wear off.
When her first feeling of shyness had worn off she started to enjoy herself.
He began to try to sit up, which showed us that the effects of the drug were wearing off.

wear out (tr or intr)
a = (tr) use till no longer serviceable; (intr) become unserviceable as a result of long use (chiefly of clothes):
Children wear out ***their shoes*** *very quickly (wear* ***their shoes*** *out/wear* ***them*** *out).*
Cheap clothes wear out quickly.
b = (tr) exhaust (used of people; very often used in the passive):
He worked all night and wanted to go on working the next day, but we saw that he was completely worn out and persuaded him to stop.

wind

wind up (tr or intr) = bring or come to an end (used of speeches or business proceedings):
The headmaster wound up ***the meeting*** *by saying that the school had had a most successful year (wound* ***the meeting*** *up/wound* ***it*** *up).*

wink

wink at (tr) = ignore purposely, pretend not to notice (an error, breach of regulations):
People are not supposed to park here at all but the police seem to wink at it provided cars don't cause an obstruction.

wipe

wipe out (tr) = destroy completely:
The epidemic wiped out ***whole families*** *(wiped* ***whole families*** *out/wiped* ***them*** *out).*

work

work out (tr) = find, by calculation or study, the solution to some problem or a method of dealing with it; study and decide on the details of a scheme:
He used his pocket calculator to work out ***the cost****/work* ***the cost*** *out.*
Tell me where you want to go and I'll work out a route.
This is the outline of the plan. We want the committee to work out ***the details*** *(work* ***them*** *out).*

320 Nouns and verbs formed by combinations listed in 319

Note that some of these compounds are hyphened and some are not; also that the verb may be the first or last part of the compound word. Definitions will normally not be given as they have been given in **319**.

break

outbreak (noun):
At the outbreak of war in 1939 the children were evacuated to the country.

breakout (noun):
There has been another prison breakout. Five men got away and are still at large.

breakdown (noun):
He had a nervous breakdown last year and spent some months in a mental hospital.
A breakdown in the middle of a desert might be fatal for the driver of the car.
A breakdown of these figures would give us a lot of useful information.

bring

upbringing (noun):
An adult's personality is said to be the combined result of inheritance, environment and upbringing.

call

call-up (noun):
In countries where there is conscription some young men go abroad at the age of 18 to avoid call-up.

come

outcome (noun):
The directors have been discussing this matter, but we don't yet know the outcome of these discussions (what they have decided).

do

overdo (verb):
It's a good thing to be polite but you needn't overdo it. I don't expect you to stand up every time I come into the room.
This steak has been overdone; it's as tough as an old boot.

fall

fall-out (noun) = radio-active dust resulting from an atomic explosion:
Countries experimenting with nuclear explosives always maintain that the fall-out will be negligible.

hold

hold-up (noun):
Hold-ups quite often take place in daylight in a crowded street, but everything is done so quickly that the thieves get away before the passers-by realize what has happened.

uphold (verb) = support or approve:
The magistrate sentenced him to a year's imprisonment. He appealed, but the court of appeal upheld the magistrate's verdict.

keep

upkeep (noun):
The upkeep of a house costs more every year, for builders and decorators keep raising their charges.

lay

layout (noun):
The new owners of the paper changed the layout completely.

outlay (noun):
The initial outlay will be heavy as we shall have to buy and equip the factory.

let

outlet (noun):
Children living in small flats in towns often haven't enough outlet for their energy.

look

look-out (noun):
He's on the look-out for a new job. If you hear of anything you might let him know.

outlook (noun):
WEATHER REPORT: *Showers and bright intervals. Further outlook – unsettled.*

overlook (verb) = fail to notice, disregard. **overlook an offence** = forgive it:
We are afraid that your order has been overlooked. We apologize for this oversight and will deal with the matter directly.

You're late, Jones. I'll overlook it this time, but see that it doesn't happen again.

overlook can also be taken literally: *His house overlooks the park.*

make

make-up (noun):

The actress said that it took her an hour to put on her make-up.

mix

mix-up (noun):

They sent Mr Jones's order to Mr Brown, and Mr Brown's to Mr Jones, a mix-up which lost them both customers.

round

round-up (noun):

Before the arrival of the visiting president the government ordered a round-up of everyone known to have connections with terrorist organizations.

run

runaway (noun, adjective):

The runaways/runaway slaves/were making for the coast.

see

oversee = supervise work/workmen.

overseer = one who does this, foreman:

In the early factories overseers used to walk up and down seeing that everyone worked as fast as possible.

sell

sell-out:

There was not a single copy left in any of the shops. The first edition had been a complete sell-out.

set

offset (verb) = balance:

The advantage of buying things cheaply in the market is sometimes offset by the terrible trouble of carrying them home.

upset (verb/noun) = knock over (usually a vessel of some kind), disarrange, distress:

That vase is top-heavy; it's very easily upset.

The canoe upset and the children had to swim to the bank.

All my plans were upset by the sudden change in weather.

She was very much upset when she heard about your accident.

outset (noun) = start:
I warned you at the outset not to trust him, but you wouldn't listen to me.

take

intake (noun) = quantity or number taken in during a given period:
This college has a yearly intake of 2,000 students.

overtake (verb) = catch up with, and usually pass:
It is dangerous to overtake at a corner.
The roadsign said: No overtaking.

take-off (noun):
The aeroplane crashed soon after take-off.

take-over (noun/adjective):
The new owners say that the take-over will not be followed by any staff changes.
A take-over bid is an offer to buy a controlling number of shares in a company.

turn

overturn (verb) = capsize, upset (especially of boats):
You can overturn a kayak and right it again if you are sufficiently skilful.

turnover (noun) = amount of money received by a shop etc. from its customers in a given period; sale and replacement of stock:
He said he had a yearly turnover of £20,000, but he didn't say how much of that was profit.
I sell cheaply, aiming at a rapid turnover of stock.

turn-out (noun):
There was a good turn-out for the football match (a lot of people came to watch it).

33 Numerals, dates, and weights and measures

Numerals

321 Cardinal numbers

1 one	11 eleven	21 twenty-one	31 thirty-one etc.
2 two	12 twelve	22 twenty-two	40 forty
3 three	13 thirteen	23 twenty-three	50 fifty
4 four	14 fourteen	24 twenty-four	60 sixty
5 five	15 fifteen	25 twenty-five	70 seventy
6 six	16 sixteen	26 twenty-six	80 eighty
7 seven	17 seventeen	27 twenty-seven	90 ninety
8 eight	18 eighteen	28 twenty-eight	100 a hundred
9 nine	19 nineteen	29 twenty-nine	1,000 a thousand
10 ten	20 twenty	30 thirty	1,000,000 a million

400 four hundred
140 a hundred and forty *or* one hundred and forty
1,006 a thousand and six *or* one thousand and six
60,127 sixty thousand, one hundred and twenty-seven
7,000 seven thousand

322 Points to notice about cardinal numbers

A When writing in words, or reading, a compound figure, **and** is placed before the last word:
3,713 three thousand, seven hundred and thirteen
5,102 five thousand, one hundred and two
365 three hundred and sixty-five

B The words **hundred, thousand,** and **million,** when used of a definitive number, are never made plural:
six hundred men *two thousand and ten pounds*

If however, these words are used loosely, merely to convey the idea of a large number, they must be made plural:
hundreds of people *thousands of birds*

Note also that in this case the preposition **of** is placed after the 'hundreds', 'thousands' etc. A definite number is never followed by **of**:
thousands of pounds but *three thousand pounds*

C **a** is more usual than **one** before **hundred, thousand** etc., when these numbers stand alone or begin an expression:

100 a hundred *1,000 a thousand*
100,000 a hundred thousand

We can also say *a hundred and one, a hundred and two* etc. and *a thousand and one* etc. up to *a thousand and ninety-nine*. Otherwise we use **one**, not **a** (see **321**):

1,140 one thousand, one hundred and forty

The expressions **dozen** (12) and **score** (20) follow the rules given in B above:

a dozen eggs, six dozen, two score (definite number)
but *dozens of eggs, scores of people* (indefinite number with **s** and **of**)

323 Ordinal numbers

first	eleventh	twenty-first	thirty-first etc.
second	twelfth	twenty-second	fortieth
third	thirteenth	twenty-third	fiftieth
fourth	fourteenth	twenty-fourth	sixtieth
fifth	fifteenth	twenty-fifth	seventieth
sixth	sixteenth	twenty-sixth	eightieth
seventh	seventeenth	twenty-seventh	ninetieth
eighth	eighteenth	twenty-eighth	hundredth
ninth	nineteenth	twenty-ninth	thousandth
tenth	twentieth	thirtieth	millionth

324 Points to notice about ordinal numbers

A Notice the irregular spelling of **fifth, eighth, ninth** and **twelfth.**

B When ordinal numbers are expressed in figures the last two letters of the written word must be added (except in dates; see **325** A):

first = 1st	*twenty-first = 21st*
second = 2nd	*forty-second = 42nd*
third = 3rd	*sixty-third = 63rd*
fourth = 4th	*eightieth = 80th*

C In compound ordinal numbers the rule about **and** is the same as for compound cardinal numbers:

101st the hundred and first

The article **the** normally precedes ordinal numbers:

the sixtieth day *the fortieth visitor*

Titles of kings etc. are written in Roman figures:

Charles V *James III* *Elizabeth II*

But in spoken English we use the ordinal numbers preceded by **the**:

Charles the Fifth *James the Third* *Elizabeth the Second*

325 Dates

A The days of the week

Sunday (Sun.)
Monday (Mon.)
Tuesday (Tues.)
Wednesday (Wed.)
Thursday (Thurs.)
Friday (Fri.)
Saturday (Sat.)

The months of the year

January (Jan.)	July
February (Feb.)	August (Aug.)
March (Mar.)	September (Sept.)
April (Apr.)	October (Oct.)
May	November (Nov.)
June	December (Dec.)

Days and months are always written with capital letters.

Dates are expressed by ordinal numbers, so, when reading or speaking, we say:
March the tenth, July the fourteenth etc. or *the tenth of March* etc.

They can, however, be written in a variety of ways; e.g. March the tenth could be written:
March 10 *March 10th* *10 March* *10th March*
10th of March *March the 10th*

B The year

When reading or speaking we use the term **hundred** but not **thousand**: The year *1987* would be read as *nineteen hundred and eighty-seven* or *nineteen eighty-seven.*

Years before the Christian era are followed by the letters B.C. (= before Christ) and years dating from the Christian era are occasionally followed or preceded by the letters A.D. (= Anno Domini, in the year of the Lord). These are read in either way: *1500 B.C.* would be read as *one thousand five hundred B.C.* or *fifteen hundred B.C.*

326 Weights, length and liquid measure

A Weights

The English weights table is as follows:

16 ounces (oz.)	=	1 pound (lb.)
14 pounds	=	1 stone (st.)
8 stone	=	1 hundredweight (cwt)
20 cwt	=	1 ton
1 pound	=	0.454 kilogram (kg)
2.2 pounds	=	1 kilogram

Plurals

ounce, pound, and **ton** can take **s** in the plural when they are used as nouns, **stone** and **hundredweight** do not take **s**: e.g. we say *six* *pound of sugar* or *six pounds of sugar*, but *ten hundredweight of coal* has no alternative.

When used in compound adjectives these terms never take **s**:
A ten-ton lorry.

The metric system of weights based on the kilo or kilogram is gradually replacing the English system. **kilo** or **kilogram** usually take **s** in the plural when used as a noun:
two kilos of apples or *two kilograms of apples*

In the metric system 1,000 kilograms = 1 metric tonne, which is the equivalent of 2,204.6 lbs in the English system.

B Length

The English table of length is as follows:

12 inches (in.)	=	1 foot (ft.)
3 feet	=	1 yard (yd.)
1,760 yards	=	1 mile (m.)
1 inch	=	2.54 centimetres (cm)
1 yard	=	0.914 metre (m)
1 mile	=	1.609 kilometres (km)

Plurals

When there is more than one inch/mile/centimetre we normally use the plural form of these words:
one inch, ten inches *one mile, four miles*
one centimetre, five centimetres

When there is more than one foot we can use either **foot** or **feet. feet** is the more usual when measuring heights. We can say:
six foot tall or *six feet tall*
two foot long or *two feet long*

When used in compound adjectives the above terms never take the plural form:
a two-mile walk *a six-inch ruler*

C Liquid measure

2 pints (pts.)	=	1 quart (qt.)
4 quarts	=	1 gallon (gal.)
1 pint	=	0.568 litre (l)
1 gallon	=	4.55 litres

Traditionally British and American measurements have been made in inches, feet, yards, miles etc. but there is now a gradual move towards the metric system.

34 Spelling rules

Introduction

Vowels are: **a e i o u**

Consonants are: **b c d f g h j k l m n p q r s t v w x y z**

A suffix is a group of letters added to the end of a word. For example: *beauty, beautiful* (*ful* is the suffix).

327 Doubling the consonant

A Words of one syllable having one vowel and ending in a single consonant double the consonant before a suffix beginning with a vowel:

run + er = runner
hit + ing = hitting
knit + ed = knitted

but *keep, keeping* (two vowels)
help, helped (two consonants)
love, loved (ending in a vowel)

B Two- or three-syllable words ending in a single consonant following a single vowel double the final consonant when the stress falls on the last syllable. (The stressed syllable is in bold type.)

*be***gin** *+ er = beginner*
*de***ter** *+ ed = deterred*
*re***cur** *+ ing = recurring*

but **mur***mur + ed = murmured*
ans*wer + er = answerer*
or*bit + ing = orbiting*

C The final consonant of **kidnap, worship, handicap** is also doubled:

kidnap, kidnapper
worship, worshipping
handicap, handicapped

D Words ending in **l** following a single vowel or two vowels pronounced separately usually double the **l**:

quarrel, quarrelling   *model, modelling*   *duel, duellist*
signal, signalled   *repel, repellent*   *refuel, refuelled*
distil, distiller   *dial, dialled*   *cruel, cruelly*
appal, appalled

Note that for the purpose of the above rules **qu** is considered as one consonant:
acquit, acquitted

328 Omission of a final e

A Words ending in **e** following a consonant drop the **e** before a suffix beginning with a vowel:
love + ing = *loving*
believe + er = *believer*
move + able = *movable*
But *likable* can also be spelt *likeable.*
Words ending in **ce** or **ge** however sometimes retain the **e**. See **329**.

B A final **e** is retained before a suffix beginning with a consonant:
engage, engagement *hope, hopeful* *fortunate, fortunately*
immediate, immediately *sincere, sincerely*
But the **e** in **able/ible** is dropped in the adverb form:
comfortable, comfortably *incredible, incredibly*
The final **e** is also dropped in the following words:
true, truly *due, duly* *whole, wholly* (notice the double **l** here)
argue, argument *judge, judgement* or *judgment*

C Words ending in **ee** do not drop an **e** before a suffix:
forsee, forseeing, forseeable *agree, agreed, agreeing, agreement*

329 Words ending in ce and ge

A Words ending in **ce** or **ge** retain the **e** before the suffix beginning with **a, o** or **u**:
courage, courageous *peace, peaceable*
manage, manageable *trace, traceable*
outrage, outrageous *replace, replaceable*
This is done to avoid changes in pronunciation, because **c** and **g** are generally pronounced soft before **e** and **i**, but hard before **a, o** or **u**.

B Words ending in **ce** change the **e** to **i** before **ous**:
vice, vicious *grace, gracious*
malice, malicious *space, spacious*

330 The suffix ful

When **full** is added to a word the second **l** is dropped:
beauty + full = *beautiful* (but note adverb form *beautifully*)
use + full = *useful* (but note adverb form *usefully*)

If the word to which the suffix is added ends in **ll** the second **l** is dropped here also:
skill + full = skilful

Note *full + fill = fulfil*

331 Words ending in **y**

Words ending in **y** following a consonant change the **y** to **i** before any suffix except **ing**:
carry + ed = *carried*
sunny + er = *sunnier*
happy + ly = *happily*
but *carry + ing* = *carrying*

y following a vowel does not change:
obey + ed = obeyed
play + er = player (see also **172** C and **9** B)

332 **ie** and **ei**

The normal rule is that **i** comes before **e** except after **c**:
believe, sieve but *deceive, receipt*

There are however the following exceptions:

beige	feint	heir	reign	their
counterfeit	foreign	inveigh	rein	veil
deign	forfeit	inveigle	seize	vein
eiderdown	freight	leisure	skein	weigh
eight	heifer	neigh	sleigh	weight
either	height	neighbour	sleight	weir
feign	heinous	neither	surfeit	weird

Index

References are to paragraph numbers. Where a higher number precedes a lower number, fuller treatment will be found under the higher number.

Some paragraphs and sections in the text are marked with a box round their serial numbers or letters, e.g. 276, E. This indicates that they deal with particularly difficult points. Students may prefer to omit these at the first reading.

after **to be about** to express the immediate future: *The President is about to make his speech* **111** C
the continuous infinitive: *She seemed to be crying* **254, 291** D
after **go** and **come** **245**
in indirect speech: statements reported by **agree/offer/promise/refuse/threaten** + infinitive **297**
after nouns and pronouns to show what is to be done with them : *I have letters to write; They have work to do* **248**
after **only** to express a disappointing or annoying sequel: *He put his hand in his pocket only to find he had lost his wallet* **246** A
as the subject of a sentence: *To save money was impossible* **252**
after **the first/the last/the only** and after superlatives: *He was the first to arrive* etc. **247**
represented by **to** alone: *Why didn't you go? I wasn't asked to* **253**
after **too, enough, so . . . as**: *too heavy to carry; small enough to fit him; Would you be so good as to explain?* **251**
use after certain verbs
verbs followed by **how/what/when/where/which/whether** + infinitive: *He showed me how to do it* **240**: verbs followed immediately by the infinitive; *I aim to finish by midnight* **239**; verbs followed immediately by the infinitive or by **that** + subject: *He promised to pay; He promised he would pay* **239** A; verbs followed by the infinitive or by **that** + subject + **should**: *He decided to send Bill; He decided that Bill should go* **239** B; verbs followed by the infinitive or object + infinitive: *I want to go; I want him to go* **241**; verbs followed by the infinitive without **to**: *You can't make a child eat* **243** E; verbs of knowing and thinking followed by the infinitive: *He is known to be in this area* **244** B; verbs followed by object + infinitive: *I encouraged him to buy his house* **242**
was/were + infinitive to express the idea of destiny: *They were never to meet again* **111** B

intention: see future with intention

INTERROGATIVE
adjectives and pronouns: *Who did you see? What did you buy?* **31**
adverbs: *why, when, where, how* **35**
an affirmative verb used when the question concerns the identity of the subject: *Who killed him? What made that noise?* **31**
how is she? compared with **what is she like?** **35**
interrogative of verbs
interrogative form used after certain adverbs and adverb phrases: see INVERSION OF SUBJECT AND VERB; interrogative form not used in indirect questions: *He asked where I lived* **100, 299** A; interrogative form not used when preceded by certain phrases such as **do you know? can you tell me? I wonder:** *Do you know why he sold the car?* **100**; interrogative and negative interrogative in question tags: *He wasn't angry, was he? You paid Paul, didn't you?* **106**; requests: *Can you help me? Will you start now?* **100** C; interrogative and negative interrogative in comment tags: *It was my fault, was it?* **107**; negative interrogative forms **101**; interrogative forms of all verbs **100** (see also each auxiliary and the various tenses)
what as adjective and pronoun: *What street is this? What is this?* **33** A
what . . . like: *What was the hotel like? What is he like?* **33** C
what is he? an enquiry about his work or profession **33** D
which compared with **who** or **what** **34**
who? and **whom?** *Who did you ask? Whom did you ask?* **32**